C-1020

CAREER EXAMINATION SERIES

THIS IS YOUR **PASSBOOK**® FOR ...

SENIOR POLICE ADMINISTRATIVE AIDE

NLC®
NATIONAL LEARNING CORPORATION®
passbooks.com

NLC®

National Learning Corporation

212 Michael Drive, Syosset, NY 11791
(516) 921-8888 • www.passbooks.com
E-mail: info@passbooks.com

PUBLISHED IN THE UNITED STATES OF AMERICA

PASSBOOK® SERIES

THE *PASSBOOK® SERIES* has been created to prepare applicants and candidates for the ultimate academic battlefield – the examination room.

At some time in our lives, each and every one of us may be required to take an examination – for validation, matriculation, admission, qualification, registration, certification, or licensure.

Based on the assumption that every applicant or candidate has met the basic formal educational standards, has taken the required number of courses, and read the necessary texts, the *PASSBOOK® SERIES* furnishes the one special preparation which may assure passing with confidence, instead of failing with insecurity. Examination questions – together with answers – are furnished as the basic vehicle for study so that the mysteries of the examination and its compounding difficulties may be eliminated or diminished by a sure method.

This book is meant to help you pass your examination provided that you qualify and are serious in your objective.

The entire field is reviewed through the huge store of content information which is succinctly presented through a provocative and challenging approach – the question-and-answer method.

A climate of success is established by furnishing the correct answers at the end of each test.

You soon learn to recognize types of questions, forms of questions, and patterns of questioning. You may even begin to anticipate expected outcomes.

You perceive that many questions are repeated or adapted so that you can gain acute insights, which may enable you to score many sure points.

You learn how to confront new questions, or types of questions, and to attack them confidently and work out the correct answers.

You note objectives and emphases, and recognize pitfalls and dangers, so that you may make positive educational adjustments.

Moreover, you are kept fully informed in relation to new concepts, methods, practices, and directions in the field.

You discover that you arre actually taking the examination all the time: you are preparing for the examination by "taking" an examination, not by reading extraneous and/or supererogatory textbooks.

In short, this PASSBOOK®, used directedly, should be an important factor in helping you to pass your test.

SENIOR POLICE ADMINISTRATIVE AIDE

DUTIES

Senior Police Administrative Aides, under general supervision, with some latitude for independent action, initiative or decision, supervise, direct, and perform difficult and responsible clerical work using both manual and computerized systems; assist in the performance of administrative work; and perform related tasks.

THE SCOPE OF THE EXAMINATION

The multiple-choice test is designed to assess the extent to which candidates have certain abilities and technical knowledge determined to be important to the performance of the tasks of a Senior Police Administrative Aide. Task categories to be tested are as follows: supervision; writing and composing documents and reports; office/clerical duties; and communicating.
The test may include questions which require mastery of technical knowledge based on such materials as departmental and administrative procedures, guidelines, and regulations; police terminology, crime definitions and classifications; departmental reference sources, forms, reports; and filing systems; standards of employee conduct; and related abilities.

HOW TO TAKE A TEST

I. YOU MUST PASS AN EXAMINATION

A. WHAT EVERY CANDIDATE SHOULD KNOW

Examination applicants often ask us for help in preparing for the written test. What can I study in advance? What kinds of questions will be asked? How will the test be given? How will the papers be graded?

As an applicant for a civil service examination, you may be wondering about some of these things. Our purpose here is to suggest effective methods of advance study and to describe civil service examinations.

Your chances for success on this examination can be increased if you know how to prepare. Those "pre-examination jitters" can be reduced if you know what to expect. You can even experience an adventure in good citizenship if you know why civil service exams are given.

B. WHY ARE CIVIL SERVICE EXAMINATIONS GIVEN?

Civil service examinations are important to you in two ways. As a citizen, you want public jobs filled by employees who know how to do their work. As a job seeker, you want a fair chance to compete for that job on an equal footing with other candidates. The best-known means of accomplishing this two-fold goal is the competitive examination.

Exams are widely publicized throughout the nation. They may be administered for jobs in federal, state, city, municipal, town or village governments or agencies.

Any citizen may apply, with some limitations, such as the age or residence of applicants. Your experience and education may be reviewed to see whether you meet the requirements for the particular examination. When these requirements exist, they are reasonable and applied consistently to all applicants. Thus, a competitive examination may cause you some uneasiness now, but it is your privilege and safeguard.

C. HOW ARE CIVIL SERVICE EXAMS DEVELOPED?

Examinations are carefully written by trained technicians who are specialists in the field known as "psychological measurement," in consultation with recognized authorities in the field of work that the test will cover. These experts recommend the subject matter areas or skills to be tested; only those knowledges or skills important to your success on the job are included. The most reliable books and source materials available are used as references. Together, the experts and technicians judge the difficulty level of the questions.

Test technicians know how to phrase questions so that the problem is clearly stated. Their ethics do not permit "trick" or "catch" questions. Questions may have been tried out on sample groups, or subjected to statistical analysis, to determine their usefulness.

Written tests are often used in combination with performance tests, ratings of training and experience, and oral interviews. All of these measures combine to form the best-known means of finding the right person for the right job.

II. HOW TO PASS THE WRITTEN TEST

A. NATURE OF THE EXAMINATION

To prepare intelligently for civil service examinations, you should know how they differ from school examinations you have taken. In school you were assigned certain definite pages to read or subjects to cover. The examination questions were quite detailed and usually emphasized memory. Civil service exams, on the other hand, try to discover your present ability to perform the duties of a position, plus your potentiality to learn these duties. In other words, a civil service exam attempts to predict how successful you will be. Questions cover such a broad area that they cannot be as minute and detailed as school exam questions.

In the public service similar kinds of work, or positions, are grouped together in one “class.” This process is known as *position-classification.* All the positions in a class are paid according to the salary range for that class. One class title covers all of these positions, and they are all tested by the same examination.

B. FOUR BASIC STEPS

1) Study the announcement

How, then, can you know what subjects to study? Our best answer is: “Learn as much as possible about the class of positions for which you’ve applied.” The exam will test the knowledge, skills and abilities needed to do the work.

Your most valuable source of information about the position you want is the official exam announcement. This announcement lists the training and experience qualifications. Check these standards and apply only if you come reasonably close to meeting them.

The brief description of the position in the examination announcement offers some clues to the subjects which will be tested. Think about the job itself. Review the duties in your mind. Can you perform them, or are there some in which you are rusty? Fill in the blank spots in your preparation.

Many jurisdictions preview the written test in the exam announcement by including a section called “Knowledge and Abilities Required,” “Scope of the Examination,” or some similar heading. Here you will find out specifically what fields will be tested.

2) Review your own background

Once you learn in general what the position is all about, and what you need to know to do the work, ask yourself which subjects you already know fairly well and which need improvement. You may wonder whether to concentrate on improving your strong areas or on building some background in your fields of weakness. When the announcement has specified “some knowledge” or “considerable knowledge,” or has used adjectives like “beginning principles of...” or “advanced … methods,” you can get a clue as to the number and difficulty of questions to be asked in any given field. More questions, and hence broader coverage, would be included for those subjects which are more important in the work. Now weigh your strengths and weaknesses against the job requirements and prepare accordingly.

3) Determine the level of the position

Another way to tell how intensively you should prepare is to understand the level of the job for which you are applying. Is it the entering level? In other words, is this the position in which beginners in a field of work are hired? Or is it an intermediate or advanced level? Sometimes this is indicated by such words as "Junior" or "Senior" in the class title. Other jurisdictions use Roman numerals to designate the level – Clerk I, Clerk II, for example. The word "Supervisor" sometimes appears in the title. If the level is not indicated by the title, check the description of duties. Will you be working under very close supervision, or will you have responsibility for independent decisions in this work?

4) Choose appropriate study materials

Now that you know the subjects to be examined and the relative amount of each subject to be covered, you can choose suitable study materials. For beginning level jobs, or even advanced ones, if you have a pronounced weakness in some aspect of your training, read a modern, standard textbook in that field. Be sure it is up to date and has general coverage. Such books are normally available at your library, and the librarian will be glad to help you locate one. For entry-level positions, questions of appropriate difficulty are chosen – neither highly advanced questions, nor those too simple. Such questions require careful thought but not advanced training.

If the position for which you are applying is technical or advanced, you will read more advanced, specialized material. If you are already familiar with the basic principles of your field, elementary textbooks would waste your time. Concentrate on advanced textbooks and technical periodicals. Think through the concepts and review difficult problems in your field.

These are all general sources. You can get more ideas on your own initiative, following these leads. For example, training manuals and publications of the government agency which employs workers in your field can be useful, particularly for technical and professional positions. A letter or visit to the government department involved may result in more specific study suggestions, and certainly will provide you with a more definite idea of the exact nature of the position you are seeking.

III. KINDS OF TESTS

Tests are used for purposes other than measuring knowledge and ability to perform specified duties. For some positions, it is equally important to test ability to make adjustments to new situations or to profit from training. In others, basic mental abilities not dependent on information are essential. Questions which test these things may not appear as pertinent to the duties of the position as those which test for knowledge and information. Yet they are often highly important parts of a fair examination. For very general questions, it is almost impossible to help you direct your study efforts. What we can do is to point out some of the more common of these general abilities needed in public service positions and describe some typical questions.

1) General information

Broad, general information has been found useful for predicting job success in some kinds of work. This is tested in a variety of ways, from vocabulary lists to questions about current events. Basic background in some field of work, such as sociology or economics, may be sampled in a group of questions. Often these are principles which have become familiar to most persons through exposure rather than through formal training. It is difficult to advise you how to study for these questions; being alert to the world around you is our best suggestion.

2) Verbal ability

An example of an ability needed in many positions is verbal or language ability. Verbal ability is, in brief, the ability to use and understand words. Vocabulary and grammar tests are typical measures of this ability. Reading comprehension or paragraph interpretation questions are common in many kinds of civil service tests. You are given a paragraph of written material and asked to find its central meaning.

3) Numerical ability

Number skills can be tested by the familiar arithmetic problem, by checking paired lists of numbers to see which are alike and which are different, or by interpreting charts and graphs. In the latter test, a graph may be printed in the test booklet which you are asked to use as the basis for answering questions.

4) Observation

A popular test for law-enforcement positions is the observation test. A picture is shown to you for several minutes, then taken away. Questions about the picture test your ability to observe both details and larger elements.

5) Following directions

In many positions in the public service, the employee must be able to carry out written instructions dependably and accurately. You may be given a chart with several columns, each column listing a variety of information. The questions require you to carry out directions involving the information given in the chart.

6) Skills and aptitudes

Performance tests effectively measure some manual skills and aptitudes. When the skill is one in which you are trained, such as typing or shorthand, you can practice. These tests are often very much like those given in business school or high school courses. For many of the other skills and aptitudes, however, no short-time preparation can be made. Skills and abilities natural to you or that you have developed throughout your lifetime are being tested.

Many of the general questions just described provide all the data needed to answer the questions and ask you to use your reasoning ability to find the answers. Your best preparation for these tests, as well as for tests of facts and ideas, is to be at your physical and mental best. You, no doubt, have your own methods of getting into an exam-taking mood and keeping "in shape." The next section lists some ideas on this subject.

IV. KINDS OF QUESTIONS

Only rarely is the "essay" question, which you answer in narrative form, used in civil service tests. Civil service tests are usually of the short-answer type. Full instructions for answering these questions will be given to you at the examination. But in case this is your first experience with short-answer questions and separate answer sheets, here is what you need to know:

1) Multiple-choice Questions

Most popular of the short-answer questions is the "multiple choice" or "best answer" question. It can be used, for example, to test for factual knowledge, ability to solve problems or judgment in meeting situations found at work.

A multiple-choice question is normally one of three types—

- It can begin with an incomplete statement followed by several possible endings. You are to find the one ending which *best* completes the statement, although some of the others may not be entirely wrong.
- It can also be a complete statement in the form of a question which is answered by choosing one of the statements listed.
- It can be in the form of a problem – again you select the best answer.

Here is an example of a multiple-choice question with a discussion which should give you some clues as to the method for choosing the right answer:

When an employee has a complaint about his assignment, the action which will *best* help him overcome his difficulty is to

A. discuss his difficulty with his coworkers
B. take the problem to the head of the organization
C. take the problem to the person who gave him the assignment
D. say nothing to anyone about his complaint

In answering this question, you should study each of the choices to find which is best. Consider choice "A" – Certainly an employee may discuss his complaint with fellow employees, but no change or improvement can result, and the complaint remains unresolved. Choice "B" is a poor choice since the head of the organization probably does not know what assignment you have been given, and taking your problem to him is known as "going over the head" of the supervisor. The supervisor, or person who made the assignment, is the person who can clarify it or correct any injustice. Choice "C" is, therefore, correct. To say nothing, as in choice "D," is unwise. Supervisors have and interest in knowing the problems employees are facing, and the employee is seeking a solution to his problem.

2) True/False Questions

The "true/false" or "right/wrong" form of question is sometimes used. Here a complete statement is given. Your job is to decide whether the statement is right or wrong.

SAMPLE: A roaming cell-phone call to a nearby city costs less than a non-roaming call to a distant city.

This statement is wrong, or false, since roaming calls are more expensive.

This is not a complete list of all possible question forms, although most of the others are variations of these common types. You will always get complete directions for answering questions. Be sure you understand *how* to mark your answers – ask questions until you do.

V. RECORDING YOUR ANSWERS

Computer terminals are used more and more today for many different kinds of exams.

For an examination with very few applicants, you may be told to record your answers in the test booklet itself. Separate answer sheets are much more common. If this separate answer sheet is to be scored by machine – and this is often the case – it is highly important that you mark your answers correctly in order to get credit.

An electronic scoring machine is often used in civil service offices because of the speed with which papers can be scored. Machine-scored answer sheets must be marked with a pencil, which will be given to you. This pencil has a high graphite content which responds to the electronic scoring machine. As a matter of fact, stray dots may register as answers, so do not let your pencil rest on the answer sheet while you are pondering the correct answer. Also, if your pencil lead breaks or is otherwise defective, ask for another.

Since the answer sheet will be dropped in a slot in the scoring machine, be careful not to bend the corners or get the paper crumpled.

The answer sheet normally has five vertical columns of numbers, with 30 numbers to a column. These numbers correspond to the question numbers in your test booklet. After each number, going across the page are four or five pairs of dotted lines. These short dotted lines have small letters or numbers above them. The first two pairs may also have a "T" or "F" above the letters. This indicates that the first two pairs only are to be used if the questions are of the true-false type. If the questions are multiple choice, disregard the "T" and "F" and pay attention only to the small letters or numbers.

Answer your questions in the manner of the sample that follows:

32. The largest city in the United States is
    - A. Washington, D.C.
    - B. New York City
    - C. Chicago
    - D. Detroit
    - E. San Francisco

1) Choose the answer you think is best. (New York City is the largest, so "B" is correct.)
2) Find the row of dotted lines numbered the same as the question you are answering. (Find row number 32)
3) Find the pair of dotted lines corresponding to the answer. (Find the pair of lines under the mark "B.")
4) Make a solid black mark between the dotted lines.

VI. BEFORE THE TEST

Common sense will help you find procedures to follow to get ready for an examination. Too many of us, however, overlook these sensible measures. Indeed, nervousness and fatigue have been found to be the most serious reasons why applicants fail to do their best on civil service tests. Here is a list of reminders:

- Begin your preparation early – Don't wait until the last minute to go scurrying around for books and materials or to find out what the position is all about.
- Prepare continuously – An hour a night for a week is better than an all-night cram session. This has been definitely established. What is more, a night a week for a month will return better dividends than crowding your study into a shorter period of time.
- Locate the place of the exam – You have been sent a notice telling you when and where to report for the examination. If the location is in a different town or otherwise unfamiliar to you, it would be well to inquire the best route and learn something about the building.
- Relax the night before the test – Allow your mind to rest. Do not study at all that night. Plan some mild recreation or diversion; then go to bed early and get a good night's sleep.
- Get up early enough to make a leisurely trip to the place for the test – This way unforeseen events, traffic snarls, unfamiliar buildings, etc. will not upset you.
- Dress comfortably – A written test is not a fashion show. You will be known by number and not by name, so wear something comfortable.
- Leave excess paraphernalia at home – Shopping bags and odd bundles will get in your way. You need bring only the items mentioned in the official notice you received; usually everything you need is provided. Do not bring reference books to the exam. They will only confuse those last minutes and be taken away from you when in the test room.
- Arrive somewhat ahead of time – If because of transportation schedules you must get there very early, bring a newspaper or magazine to take your mind off yourself while waiting.
- Locate the examination room – When you have found the proper room, you will be directed to the seat or part of the room where you will sit. Sometimes you are given a sheet of instructions to read while you are waiting. Do not fill out any forms until you are told to do so; just read them and be prepared.
- Relax and prepare to listen to the instructions
- If you have any physical problem that may keep you from doing your best, be sure to tell the test administrator. If you are sick or in poor health, you really cannot do your best on the exam. You can come back and take the test some other time.

VII. AT THE TEST

The day of the test is here and you have the test booklet in your hand. The temptation to get going is very strong. Caution! There is more to success than knowing the right answers. You must know how to identify your papers and understand variations in the type of short-answer question used in this particular examination. Follow these suggestions for maximum results from your efforts:

1) Cooperate with the monitor

The test administrator has a duty to create a situation in which you can be as much at ease as possible. He will give instructions, tell you when to begin, check to see that you are marking your answer sheet correctly, and so on. He is not there to guard you, although he will see that your competitors do not take unfair advantage. He wants to help you do your best.

2) Listen to all instructions

Don't jump the gun! Wait until you understand all directions. In most civil service tests you get more time than you need to answer the questions. So don't be in a hurry. Read each word of instructions until you clearly understand the meaning. Study the examples, listen to all announcements and follow directions. Ask questions if you do not understand what to do.

3) Identify your papers

Civil service exams are usually identified by number only. You will be assigned a number; you must not put your name on your test papers. Be sure to copy your number correctly. Since more than one exam may be given, copy your exact examination title.

4) Plan your time

Unless you are told that a test is a "speed" or "rate of work" test, speed itself is usually not important. Time enough to answer all the questions will be provided, but this does not mean that you have all day. An overall time limit has been set. Divide the total time (in minutes) by the number of questions to determine the approximate time you have for each question.

5) Do not linger over difficult questions

If you come across a difficult question, mark it with a paper clip (useful to have along) and come back to it when you have been through the booklet. One caution if you do this – be sure to skip a number on your answer sheet as well. Check often to be sure that you have not lost your place and that you are marking in the row numbered the same as the question you are answering.

6) Read the questions

Be sure you know what the question asks! Many capable people are unsuccessful because they failed to *read* the questions correctly.

7) Answer all questions

Unless you have been instructed that a penalty will be deducted for incorrect answers, it is better to guess than to omit a question.

8) Speed tests

It is often better NOT to guess on speed tests. It has been found that on timed tests people are tempted to spend the last few seconds before time is called in marking answers at random – without even reading them – in the hope of picking up a few extra points. To discourage this practice, the instructions may warn you that your score will be "corrected" for guessing. That is, a penalty will be applied. The incorrect answers will be deducted from the correct ones, or some other penalty formula will be used.

9) Review your answers

If you finish before time is called, go back to the questions you guessed or omitted to give them further thought. Review other answers if you have time.

10) Return your test materials

If you are ready to leave before others have finished or time is called, take ALL your materials to the monitor and leave quietly. Never take any test material with you. The monitor can discover whose papers are not complete, and taking a test booklet may be grounds for disqualification.

VIII. EXAMINATION TECHNIQUES

1) Read the general instructions carefully. These are usually printed on the first page of the exam booklet. As a rule, these instructions refer to the timing of the examination; the fact that you should not start work until the signal and must stop work at a signal, etc. If there are any *special* instructions, such as a choice of questions to be answered, make sure that you note this instruction carefully.

2) When you are ready to start work on the examination, that is as soon as the signal has been given, read the instructions to each question booklet, underline any key words or phrases, such as *least, best, outline, describe* and the like. In this way you will tend to answer as requested rather than discover on reviewing your paper that you *listed without describing*, that you selected the *worst* choice rather than the *best* choice, etc.

3) If the examination is of the objective or multiple-choice type – that is, each question will also give a series of possible answers: A, B, C or D, and you are called upon to select the best answer and write the letter next to that answer on your answer paper – it is advisable to start answering each question in turn. There may be anywhere from 50 to 100 such questions in the three or four hours allotted and you can see how much time would be taken if you read through all the questions before beginning to answer any. Furthermore, if you come across a question or group of questions which you know would be difficult to answer, it would undoubtedly affect your handling of all the other questions.

4) If the examination is of the essay type and contains but a few questions, it is a moot point as to whether you should read all the questions before starting to answer any one. Of course, if you are given a choice – say five out of seven and the like – then it is essential to read all the questions so you can eliminate the two that are most difficult. If, however, you are asked to answer all the questions, there may be danger in trying to answer the easiest one first because you may find that you will spend too much time on it. The best technique is to answer the first question, then proceed to the second, etc.

5) Time your answers. Before the exam begins, write down the time it started, then add the time allowed for the examination and write down the time it must be completed, then divide the time available somewhat as follows:

- If 3-1/2 hours are allowed, that would be 210 minutes. If you have 80 objective-type questions, that would be an average of 2-1/2 minutes per question. Allow yourself no more than 2 minutes per question, or a total of 160 minutes, which will permit about 50 minutes to review.
- If for the time allotment of 210 minutes there are 7 essay questions to answer, that would average about 30 minutes a question. Give yourself only 25 minutes per question so that you have about 35 minutes to review.

6) The most important instruction is to *read each question* and make sure you know what is wanted. The second most important instruction is to *time yourself properly* so that you answer every question. The third most important instruction is to *answer every question.* Guess if you have to but include something for each question. Remember that you will receive no credit for a blank and will probably receive some credit if you write something in answer to an essay question. If you guess a letter – say "B" for a multiple-choice question – you may have guessed right. If you leave a blank as an answer to a multiple-choice question, the examiners may respect your feelings but it will not add a point to your score. Some exams may penalize you for wrong answers, so in such cases *only*, you may not want to guess unless you have some basis for your answer.

7) Suggestions
   a. Objective-type questions
      1. Examine the question booklet for proper sequence of pages and questions
      2. Read all instructions carefully
      3. Skip any question which seems too difficult; return to it after all other questions have been answered
      4. Apportion your time properly; do not spend too much time on any single question or group of questions
      5. Note and underline key words – *all, most, fewest, least, best, worst, same, opposite,* etc.
      6. Pay particular attention to negatives
      7. Note unusual option, e.g., unduly long, short, complex, different or similar in content to the body of the question
      8. Observe the use of "hedging" words – *probably, may, most likely,* etc.
      9. Make sure that your answer is put next to the same number as the question
      10. Do not second-guess unless you have good reason to believe the second answer is definitely more correct
      11. Cross out original answer if you decide another answer is more accurate; do not erase until you are ready to hand your paper in
      12. Answer all questions; guess unless instructed otherwise
      13. Leave time for review

   b. Essay questions
      1. Read each question carefully
      2. Determine exactly what is wanted. Underline key words or phrases.
      3. Decide on outline or paragraph answer

4. Include many different points and elements unless asked to develop any one or two points or elements
5. Show impartiality by giving pros and cons unless directed to select one side only
6. Make and write down any assumptions you find necessary to answer the questions
7. Watch your English, grammar, punctuation and choice of words
8. Time your answers; don't crowd material

8) Answering the essay question

Most essay questions can be answered by framing the specific response around several key words or ideas. Here are a few such key words or ideas:

M's: manpower, materials, methods, money, management
P's: purpose, program, policy, plan, procedure, practice, problems, pitfalls, personnel, public relations

a. Six basic steps in handling problems:
   1. Preliminary plan and background development
   2. Collect information, data and facts
   3. Analyze and interpret information, data and facts
   4. Analyze and develop solutions as well as make recommendations
   5. Prepare report and sell recommendations
   6. Install recommendations and follow up effectiveness

b. Pitfalls to avoid
   1. *Taking things for granted* – A statement of the situation does not necessarily imply that each of the elements is necessarily true; for example, a complaint may be invalid and biased so that all that can be taken for granted is that a complaint has been registered
   2. *Considering only one side of a situation* – Wherever possible, indicate several alternatives and then point out the reasons you selected the best one
   3. *Failing to indicate follow up* – Whenever your answer indicates action on your part, make certain that you will take proper follow-up action to see how successful your recommendations, procedures or actions turn out to be
   4. *Taking too long in answering any single question* – Remember to time your answers properly

IX. AFTER THE TEST

Scoring procedures differ in detail among civil service jurisdictions although the general principles are the same. Whether the papers are hand-scored or graded by machine we have described, they are nearly always graded by number. That is, the person who marks the paper knows only the number – never the name – of the applicant. Not until all the papers have been graded will they be matched with names. If other tests, such as training and experience or oral interview ratings have been given, scores will be combined. Different parts of the examination usually have different weights. For example, the written test might count 60 percent of the final grade, and a rating of training and experience 40 percent. In many jurisdictions, veterans will have a certain number of points added to their grades.

After the final grade has been determined, the names are placed in grade order and an eligible list is established. There are various methods for resolving ties between those who get the same final grade – probably the most common is to place first the name of the person whose application was received first. Job offers are made from the eligible list in the order the names appear on it. You will be notified of your grade and your rank as soon as all these computations have been made. This will be done as rapidly as possible.

People who are found to meet the requirements in the announcement are called "eligibles." Their names are put on a list of eligible candidates. An eligible's chances of getting a job depend on how high he stands on this list and how fast agencies are filling jobs from the list.

When a job is to be filled from a list of eligibles, the agency asks for the names of people on the list of eligibles for that job. When the civil service commission receives this request, it sends to the agency the names of the three people highest on this list. Or, if the job to be filled has specialized requirements, the office sends the agency the names of the top three persons who meet these requirements from the general list.

The appointing officer makes a choice from among the three people whose names were sent to him. If the selected person accepts the appointment, the names of the others are put back on the list to be considered for future openings.

That is the rule in hiring from all kinds of eligible lists, whether they are for typist, carpenter, chemist, or something else. For every vacancy, the appointing officer has his choice of any one of the top three eligibles on the list. This explains why the person whose name is on top of the list sometimes does not get an appointment when some of the persons lower on the list do. If the appointing officer chooses the second or third eligible, the No. 1 eligible does not get a job at once, but stays on the list until he is appointed or the list is terminated.

X. HOW TO PASS THE INTERVIEW TEST

The examination for which you applied requires an oral interview test. You have already taken the written test and you are now being called for the interview test – the final part of the formal examination.

You may think that it is not possible to prepare for an interview test and that there are no procedures to follow during an interview. Our purpose is to point out some things you can do in advance that will help you and some good rules to follow and pitfalls to avoid while you are being interviewed.

What is an interview supposed to test?

The written examination is designed to test the technical knowledge and competence of the candidate; the oral is designed to evaluate intangible qualities, not readily measured otherwise, and to establish a list showing the relative fitness of each candidate – as measured against his competitors – for the position sought. Scoring is not on the basis of "right" and "wrong," but on a sliding scale of values ranging from "not passable" to "outstanding." As a matter of fact, it is possible to achieve a relatively low score without a single "incorrect" answer because of evident weakness in the qualities being measured.

Occasionally, an examination may consist entirely of an oral test – either an individual or a group oral. In such cases, information is sought concerning the technical knowledges and abilities of the candidate, since there has been no written examination for this purpose. More commonly, however, an oral test is used to supplement a written examination.

Who conducts interviews?

The composition of oral boards varies among different jurisdictions. In nearly all, a representative of the personnel department serves as chairman. One of the members of the board may be a representative of the department in which the candidate would work. In some cases, "outside experts" are used, and, frequently, a businessman or some other representative of the general public is asked to serve. Labor and management or other special groups may be represented. The aim is to secure the services of experts in the appropriate field.

However the board is composed, it is a good idea (and not at all improper or unethical) to ascertain in advance of the interview who the members are and what groups they represent. When you are introduced to them, you will have some idea of their backgrounds and interests, and at least you will not stutter and stammer over their names.

What should be done before the interview?

While knowledge about the board members is useful and takes some of the surprise element out of the interview, there is other preparation which is more substantive. It *is* possible to prepare for an oral interview – in several ways:

1) Keep a copy of your application and review it carefully before the interview

This may be the only document before the oral board, and the starting point of the interview. Know what education and experience you have listed there, and the sequence and dates of all of it. Sometimes the board will ask you to review the highlights of your experience for them; you should not have to hem and haw doing it.

2) Study the class specification and the examination announcement

Usually, the oral board has one or both of these to guide them. The qualities, characteristics or knowledges required by the position sought are stated in these documents. They offer valuable clues as to the nature of the oral interview. For example, if the job involves supervisory responsibilities, the announcement will usually indicate that knowledge of modern supervisory methods and the qualifications of the candidate as a supervisor will be tested. If so, you can expect such questions, frequently in the form of a hypothetical situation which you are expected to solve. NEVER go into an oral without knowledge of the duties and responsibilities of the job you seek.

3) Think through each qualification required

Try to visualize the kind of questions you would ask if you were a board member. How well could you answer them? Try especially to appraise your own knowledge and background in each area, *measured against the job sought*, and identify any areas in which you are weak. Be critical and realistic – do not flatter yourself.

4) Do some general reading in areas in which you feel you may be weak

For example, if the job involves supervision and your past experience has NOT, some general reading in supervisory methods and practices, particularly in the field of human relations, might be useful. Do NOT study agency procedures or detailed manuals. The oral board will be testing your understanding and capacity, not your memory.

5) Get a good night's sleep and watch your general health and mental attitude

You will want a clear head at the interview. Take care of a cold or any other minor ailment, and of course, no hangovers.

What should be done on the day of the interview?

Now comes the day of the interview itself. Give yourself plenty of time to get there. Plan to arrive somewhat ahead of the scheduled time, particularly if your appointment is in the fore part of the day. If a previous candidate fails to appear, the board might be ready for you a bit early. By early afternoon an oral board is almost invariably behind schedule if there are many candidates, and you may have to wait. Take along a book or magazine to read, or your application to review, but leave any extraneous material in the waiting room when you go in for your interview. In any event, relax and compose yourself.

The matter of dress is important. The board is forming impressions about you – from your experience, your manners, your attitude, and your appearance. Give your personal appearance careful attention. Dress your best, but not your flashiest. Choose conservative, appropriate clothing, and be sure it is immaculate. This is a business interview, and your appearance should indicate that you regard it as such. Besides, being well groomed and properly dressed will help boost your confidence.

Sooner or later, someone will call your name and escort you into the interview room. *This is it.* From here on you are on your own. It is too late for any more preparation. But remember, you asked for this opportunity to prove your fitness, and you are here because your request was granted.

What happens when you go in?

The usual sequence of events will be as follows: The clerk (who is often the board stenographer) will introduce you to the chairman of the oral board, who will introduce you to the other members of the board. Acknowledge the introductions before you sit down. Do not be surprised if you find a microphone facing you or a stenotypist sitting by. Oral interviews are usually recorded in the event of an appeal or other review.

Usually the chairman of the board will open the interview by reviewing the highlights of your education and work experience from your application – primarily for the benefit of the other members of the board, as well as to get the material into the record. Do not interrupt or comment unless there is an error or significant misinterpretation; if that is the case, do not hesitate. But do not quibble about insignificant matters. Also, he will usually ask you some question about your education, experience or your present job – partly to get you to start talking and to establish the interviewing "rapport." He may start the actual questioning, or turn it over to one of the other members. Frequently, each member undertakes the questioning on a particular area, one in which he is perhaps most competent, so you can expect each member to participate in the examination. Because time is limited, you may also expect some rather abrupt switches in the direction the questioning takes, so do not be upset by it. Normally, a board member will not pursue a single line of questioning unless he discovers a particular strength or weakness.

After each member has participated, the chairman will usually ask whether any member has any further questions, then will ask you if you have anything you wish to add. Unless you are expecting this question, it may floor you. Worse, it may start you off on an extended, extemporaneous speech. The board is not usually seeking more information. The question is principally to offer you a last opportunity to present further qualifications or to indicate that you have nothing to add. So, if you feel that a significant qualification or characteristic has been overlooked, it is proper to point it out in a sentence or so. Do not compliment the board on the thoroughness of their examination – they have been sketchy, and you know it. If you wish, merely say, "No thank you, I have nothing further to add." This is a point where you can "talk yourself out" of a good impression or fail to present an important bit of information. Remember, *you close the interview yourself.*

The chairman will then say, "That is all, Mr. _______, thank you." Do not be startled; the interview is over, and quicker than you think. Thank him, gather your belongings and take your leave. Save your sigh of relief for the other side of the door.

How to put your best foot forward

Throughout this entire process, you may feel that the board individually and collectively is trying to pierce your defenses, seek out your hidden weaknesses and embarrass and confuse you. Actually, this is not true. They are obliged to make an appraisal of your qualifications for the job you are seeking, and they want to see you in your best light. Remember, they must interview all candidates and a non-cooperative candidate may become a failure in spite of their best efforts to bring out his qualifications. Here are 15 suggestions that will help you:

1) Be natural – Keep your attitude confident, not cocky

If you are not confident that you can do the job, do not expect the board to be. Do not apologize for your weaknesses, try to bring out your strong points. The board is interested in a positive, not negative, presentation. Cockiness will antagonize any board member and make him wonder if you are covering up a weakness by a false show of strength.

2) Get comfortable, but don't lounge or sprawl

Sit erectly but not stiffly. A careless posture may lead the board to conclude that you are careless in other things, or at least that you are not impressed by the importance of the occasion. Either conclusion is natural, even if incorrect. Do not fuss with your clothing, a pencil or an ashtray. Your hands may occasionally be useful to emphasize a point; do not let them become a point of distraction.

3) Do not wisecrack or make small talk

This is a serious situation, and your attitude should show that you consider it as such. Further, the time of the board is limited – they do not want to waste it, and neither should you.

4) Do not exaggerate your experience or abilities

In the first place, from information in the application or other interviews and sources, the board may know more about you than you think. Secondly, you probably will not get away with it. An experienced board is rather adept at spotting such a situation, so do not take the chance.

5) If you know a board member, do not make a point of it, yet do not hide it

Certainly you are not fooling him, and probably not the other members of the board. Do not try to take advantage of your acquaintanceship – it will probably do you little good.

6) Do not dominate the interview

Let the board do that. They will give you the clues – do not assume that you have to do all the talking. Realize that the board has a number of questions to ask you, and do not try to take up all the interview time by showing off your extensive knowledge of the answer to the first one.

7) Be attentive

You only have 20 minutes or so, and you should keep your attention at its sharpest throughout. When a member is addressing a problem or question to you, give him your undivided attention. Address your reply principally to him, but do not exclude the other board members.

8) Do not interrupt

A board member may be stating a problem for you to analyze. He will ask you a question when the time comes. Let him state the problem, and wait for the question.

9) Make sure you understand the question

Do not try to answer until you are sure what the question is. If it is not clear, restate it in your own words or ask the board member to clarify it for you. However, do not haggle about minor elements.

10) Reply promptly but not hastily

A common entry on oral board rating sheets is "candidate responded readily," or "candidate hesitated in replies." Respond as promptly and quickly as you can, but do not jump to a hasty, ill-considered answer.

11) Do not be peremptory in your answers

A brief answer is proper – but do not fire your answer back. That is a losing game from your point of view. The board member can probably ask questions much faster than you can answer them.

12) Do not try to create the answer you think the board member wants

He is interested in what kind of mind you have and how it works – not in playing games. Furthermore, he can usually spot this practice and will actually grade you down on it.

13) Do not switch sides in your reply merely to agree with a board member

Frequently, a member will take a contrary position merely to draw you out and to see if you are willing and able to defend your point of view. Do not start a debate, yet do not surrender a good position. If a position is worth taking, it is worth defending.

14) Do not be afraid to admit an error in judgment if you are shown to be wrong

The board knows that you are forced to reply without any opportunity for careful consideration. Your answer may be demonstrably wrong. If so, admit it and get on with the interview.

15) Do not dwell at length on your present job

The opening question may relate to your present assignment. Answer the question but do not go into an extended discussion. You are being examined for a *new* job, not your present one. As a matter of fact, try to phrase ALL your answers in terms of the job for which you are being examined.

Basis of Rating

Probably you will forget most of these "do's" and "don'ts" when you walk into the oral interview room. Even remembering them all will not ensure you a passing grade. Perhaps you did not have the qualifications in the first place. But remembering them will help you to put your best foot forward, without treading on the toes of the board members.

Rumor and popular opinion to the contrary notwithstanding, an oral board wants you to make the best appearance possible. They know you are under pressure – but they also want to see how you respond to it as a guide to what your reaction would be under the pressures of the job you seek. They will be influenced by the degree of poise you display, the personal traits you show and the manner in which you respond.

ABOUT THIS BOOK

This book contains tests divided into Examination Sections. Go through each test, answering every question in the margin. At the end of each test look at the answer key and check your answers. On the ones you got wrong, look at the right answer choice and learn. Do not fill in the answers first. Do not memorize the questions and answers, but understand the answer and principles involved. On your test, the questions will likely be different from the samples. Questions are changed and new ones added. If you understand these past questions you should have success with any changes that arise. Tests may consist of several types of questions. We have additional books on each subject should more study be advisable or necessary for you. Finally, the more you study, the better prepared you will be. This book is intended to be the last thing you study before you walk into the examination room. Prior study of relevant texts is also recommended. NLC publishes some of these in our Fundamental Series. Knowledge and good sense are important factors in passing your exam. Good luck also helps. So now study this Passbook, absorb the material contained within and take that knowledge into the examination. Then do your best to pass that exam.

EXAMINATION SECTION

EXAMINATION SECTION
TEST 1

DIRECTIONS: Each question or incomplete statement is followed by several suggested answers or completions. Select the one that BEST answers the question or completes the statement. *PRINT THE LETTER OF THE CORRECT ANSWER IN THE SPACE AT THE RIGHT.*

1. You answer a phone complaint from a person concerning an improper labeling practice in a shop in his neighborhood. Upon listening to the complaint, you get the impression that the person is exaggerating and may be too excited to view the matter clearly. Of the following, your BEST course would be to 1.____

   A. tell the man that you can understand his anger but think it is not a really serious problem
   B. suggest to the man that he file a complaint with the Department of Consumer Affairs
   C. tell the man to stay away from the shop and have his friends do the same
   D. take down the information that the man offers so that he will see that the Police Department is concerned

2. Suppose that late at night you receive a call on 911. The caller turns out to be an elderly man who is not able to get out much, and who is calling you not because he needs help but because he wants to talk with someone. The BEST way to handle such a situation is to 2.____

   A. explain to him that the number is for emergencies and his call may prevent others from getting the help they need
   B. talk to him if not many calls are coming in but excuse yourself and cut him off if you are busy
   C. cut him off immediately when you find out he does not need help because this will be the most effective way of discouraging him
   D. suggest that he call train or bus information as the clerks there are often not busy at night

3. While you are on duty, you receive a call from a person whose name you recognize to be that of a person who calls frequently about matters of no importance. The caller requests your name and your supervisor's name so that she can report you for being impolite to her. You should 3.____

   A. ask her when and how you were impolite to her
   B. tell her that she should not call about such minor matters
   C. make a report about her complaint for your superior
   D. give her the information that she requests

4. Of the following, the MOST important reason for requiring each employee of the Police Department to be responsible for good public relations is that 4.____

   A. the Police Department has better morale when employees join in an effort to improve public relations
   B. the public judges the Department according to impressions received at every level in the Department

C. most employees will not behave well toward the public unless required to do so
D. employees who improve public relations will receive commendations from superiors

5. Assume that you are in the Bureau of Public Relations. You receive a telephone call from a citizen who asks if a study has been made of the advisability of combining the city's police and fire departments. Assume that you have no information on the subject. 5.____
Of the following, your BEST course would be to

A. tell the caller that undoubtedly the subject has been studied, but that you do not have the information available
B. suggest to the caller that he telephone the Fire Department's Community Relations section for further information
C. explain to the caller that the functions of the two departments are distinct and that combining them would be inefficient
D. take the caller's number in order to call back, and then find information or referrals to give him

6. Suppose that Police Department officials have discouraged representatives of the press from contacting police administrative aides (except aides in the Public Relations Bureau) for information. 6.____
Of the following, the BEST reason for such a policy would be to

A. assure proper control over information released to the press by the Department
B. increase the value of official press releases of the Department
C. make press representatives realize that the Department is not seeking publicity
D. reduce the chance of crimes being committed in imitation of those reported in the press

7. People who phone the Police Department often use excited, emotional, and sometimes angry speech. 7.____
The BEST policy for you to take when speaking to this type of caller is to

A. tell the person directly that he must speak in a more civil way
B. tell the caller to call back when he is in a better mood
C. give the person time to settle down, by doing most of the talking yourself
D. speak calmly yourself to help the caller to gradually become more relaxed

8. On a particularly busy evening, the police administrative aide assigned to the telephones had answered a tremendous number of inquiries and complaints by irate citizens. 8.____
His patience was exhausted when he received a call from a citizen who reported, *Officer, a bird just flew into my bedroom. What should I do?* In a release of tension, the aide responded, *Keep it for seven days; and if no one claims it, it is yours.*
This response by the aide would usually be considered

A. *advisable,* because the person should see how unusual his question was
B. *advisable,* because he avoided offering police services that were unavailable
C. *not advisable,* because such a remark might be regarded as insulting rather than humorous
D. *not advisable,* because the person might not want a bird for a pet

9. While temporarily assigned to switchboard duty, you receive a call from a man who says his uncle in Pittsburgh has just called him and threatened to commit suicide. The man is convinced his uncle intends to carry out his threat. 9.____
Of the following, you should

A. advise the man to have neighbors of the uncle check to see if the uncle is all right
B. politely inform the man that such out-of-town incidents are beyond the authority of the local precinct
C. take the uncle's name, address, and telephone number and immediately contact police authorities in Pittsburgh
D. get the man's name, address, and telephone number so that you can determine whether the call is a hoax

10. Assume that in the course of your assigned duties, you have just taken a necessary action which you feel has angered a citizen. After he has gone, you suddenly realize that the incident might result in an unjustified complaint. The MOST advisable action for you to take now would be to 10.____

A. contact the person and apologize to him
B. make complete notes on the incident and on any witnesses who might be helpful
C. ask your superior what you might expect in case of such a complaint, without giving any hint of the actual occurrence
D. accept the situation as one of the hazards of your job

11. Your job may bring you in contact with people from the community who are confronted with emergencies, and are experiencing feelings of tension, anxiety, or even hostility. It is good to keep in mind what attitude is most helpful to people who, in such situations, need information and help. Suppose a person approaches you under circumstances like these. 11.____
Which of the following would be BEST to do?

A. Present similar examples of your own problems to make the person feel that his problems are not unusual.
B. Recognize the person's feelings, present information on available services, and make suggestions as to proper procedures.
C. Expect that some of the information is exaggerated and encourage the person to let some time pass before seeking further help.
D. Have the person wait while you try to make arrangements for his problem to be solved.

12. Suppose that while on duty you receive a call from the owner of a gas station which is located within the precinct. The owner is annoyed with a certain rule made by the Police Department which concerns the operation of such stations. You agree with him. 12.____
Of the following, the BEST action for you to take is to

A. make a report on the call and suggest to the owner that he write a letter to the Department about the rule
B. tell the owner that there is little that can be done since such rules are departmental policy
C. tell the owner that you agree with his complaint and that you will write a memo of his call
D. establish good relations with the owner by suggesting how to word a letter that will get action from the Department

13. Suppose that you are working at the switchboard when a call comes in late at night from a woman who reports that her neighbors are having a very noisy party. She gives you her first name, surname, and address, and you ask whether her title is *Miss* or *Mrs.* She replies that her title is irrelevant to her complaint, and wants to know why you ask. Of the following possible ways of handling this, which is BEST? 13.____

A. Insist that the title is necessary for identification purposes.
B. Tell her that it is merely to find out what her marital status is.
C. Agree that the information is not necessary and ask her how she wants to be referred to.
D. Find out why she shows such a peculiar reaction to a request for harmless information.

14. While covering an assignment on the switchboard, you receive a call from a young girl who tells you of rumored plans for a gang fight in her neighborhood. You should 14.____

A. take down the information so that a patrol squad can investigate the area and possibly keep the fight from starting
B. discourage the girl from becoming alarmed by reminding her that it is only a rumor
C. realize that this is a teenager looking for attention, humor her, and dismiss the matter
D. take down the information but tell the girl that you need concrete information, and not just rumors, to take any action on her call

15. The one of the following which would MOST likely lead to friction among police administrative aides in a unit would be for the supervisor in charge of the unit to 15.____

A. defend the actions of the aides he supervises when discussing them with his own supervisor
B. get his men to work together as a team in completing the work of the unit
C. praise each of the aides he supervises *in confidence* as the best aide in the unit
D. consider the point of view of the aides he supervises when assigning unpleasant tasks

16. Suppose that a police administrative aide who had been transferred to your office from another unit in your Department because of difficulties with his supervisor has been placed under your supervision. The BEST course of action for you to take FIRST is to 16.____

A. analyze the aide's past grievance to determine if the transfer was the best settlement of the problem
B. advise him of the difficulties his former supervisor had with other employees and encourage him not to feel bad about the transfer
C. warn him that you will not tolerate any nonsense and that he will be watched carefully while assigned to your unit
D. instruct him in the duties he will be performing in your unit and make him feel *wanted* in his new position

17. In which of the following circumstances would it be MOST appropriate for you to use an impersonal style of writing rather than a personal style, which relies on the use of personal pronouns and other personal references? 17.____
When writing a memorandum to

A. give your opinion to an associate on the advisability of holding a weekly staff meeting
B. furnish your superior with data justifying a proposed outlay of funds for new equipment
C. give your version of an incident which resulted in a complaint by a citizen about your behavior
D. support your request for a transfer to another division

18. A newly appointed supervisor should learn as much as possible about the backgrounds of his subordinates. The statement is generally CORRECT because 18.____

A. effective handling of subordinates is based upon knowledge of their individual differences
B. knowing their backgrounds assures they will be treated objectively, equally, and without favor
C. some subordinates perform more efficiently under one supervisor than under another
D. subordinates have confidence in a supervisor who knows all about them

19. You have found it necessary, for valid reasons, to criticize the work of one of the female police administrative aides. She later comes to your desk and accuses you of criticizing her work because she is a woman. 19.____
The BEST way for you to deal with this employee is to

A. ask her to apologize, since you would never allow yourself to be guilty of his kind of discrimination
B. discuss her complaint with her, explaining again and at greater length the reason for your criticism
C. assure her you wish to be fair, and ask her to submit a written report to you on her complaint
D. apologize for hurting her feelings and promise that she will be left alone in the future

20. The following steps are recognized steps in teaching an employee a new skill: 20.____
I. Demonstrate how to do the work
II. Let the learner do the work himself
III. Explain the nature and purpose of the work
IV. Correct poor procedures by suggestion and demonstration

The CORRECT order for these steps is:

A. III, II, IV, I
B. II, I, III, IV
C. III, I, II, IV
D. I, III, II, IV

21. Suppose you have arranged an interview with a subordinate to try to help him overcome a serious shortcoming in his technical work. While you do not intend to talk to him about his attitude, you have noticed that he seems to be suspicious and resentful of people in authority. You need a record of the points covered in the discussion since further interviews are likely to be necessary.
Your BEST course would be to 21.____

A. write a checklist of points you wish to discuss and carefully check the points off as the interview progresses
B. know exactly how you wish to proceed, and then make written notes during the interview of your subordinate's comments
C. frankly tell your subordinate that you are recording the talk on tape but place the recorder where it will not hinder discussion
D. keep in mind what you wish to accomplish and make notes on the interview immediately after it is over

22. A police administrative aide has explained a complicated procedure to several subordinates. He has been talking clearly, allowing time for information to sink in. He has also encouraged questions. Yet, he still questions his subordinates after his explanation, with the obvious objective of finding out whether they completely understand the procedure.
Under these circumstances, the action of the police administrative aide, in asking questions about the procedure, is 22.____

A. *not advisable,* because subordinates who do not now know the procedure which has been explained so carefully can read and study it
B. *not advisable,* because he endangers his relationship with his subordinates by insulting their intelligence
C. *advisable,* because subordinates basically resent instructions and seldom give their full attention in a group situation
D. *advisable,* because the answers to his questions help him to determine whether he has gained his objective

23. The most competent of the police administrative aides is a pleasant, intelligent young woman who breaks the rules of the Department by occasionally making long personal telephone calls during working hours. You have not talked to her up until now about this fault. However, the calls are beginning to increase, and you decide to deal directly with the problem.
The BEST way to approach the subject with her would be to 23.____

A. review with her the history of her infractions of the rules
B. point out that her conduct is not fair to the other workers
C. tell her that her personal calls are excessive and discuss it with her
D. warn her quietly that you intend to apply penalties if necessary

24. Assume that you are supervising eight male police administrative aides who do similar clerical work. A group of four of them work on each side of a row of files which can be moved without much trouble. You notice that in each group there is a clique of three aides, leaving one member isolated. The two isolated members are relative newcomers to the unit though they have been there a few months.
Your BEST course in such a case would be to 24.____

A. ignore the situation because to concern yourself with informal social arrangements of your subordinates would distract you from more important matters
B. ask each of the cliques to invite the isolated member in their working group to lunch with them from time to time
C. tell each group that you cannot allow cliques to form as it is bad for the morale of the unit
D. find an excuse to move the file cabinets to the side of the room and then move the desks of the two isolated members close together

25. Suppose that your supervisor, who has recently been promoted and transferred to your division, asks you to review a certain procedure with a view to its possible revision. You know that several years ago a sergeant made a lengthy and intensive report based on a similar review. 25.____
Which of the following would it be BEST for you to do FIRST?

A. Ask your supervisor if he is aware of the previous report.
B. Read the sergeant's report before you begin work to see what bearing it has on your assignment.
C. Begin work on the review without reading his report so that you will have a fresh point of view.
D. Ask the sergeant to assist you in your review.

26. Using form letters in business correspondence is LEAST effective when 26.____

A. answering letters on a frequently recurring subject
B. giving the same information to many addressees
C. the recipient is only interested in the routing information contained in the form letter
D. a reply must be keyed to the individual requirements of the intended reader

27. From the viewpoint of an office administrator, the BEST of the following reasons for distributing the incoming mail before the beginning of the regular work day is that 27.____

A. distribution can be handled quickly and most efficiently at that time
B. distribution later in the day may be distracting to or interfere with other employees
C. the employees who distribute the mail can then perform other tasks during the rest of the day
D. office activities for the day based on the mall may then be started promptly

28. Suppose you have had difficulty locating a document in the files because you could not decide where it should have been filed. You learn that other people in the office have had the same problem. You know that the document will be needed from time to time in the future. 28.____
Your BEST course, when refiling the document, would be to

A. make a written note of where you found it so that you will find it more easily the next time
B. reclassify it and file it in the file where you first looked for it
C. file it where you found it and put cross-reference sheets in the other likely files
D. make a mental association to help you find it the next time and put it back where you found it

29. Suppose that your supervisor is attending a series of meetings of police captains in Philadelphia and will not be back until next Wednesday. He has left no instructions with you as to how you should handle telephone calls for him. 29.____
In most instances, your BEST course would be to say,

A. He isn't here just now
B. He is out of town and won't be back until next Wednesday
C. He won't be in today
D. He is in Philadelphia attending a meeting of police captains

30. The one of the following which is USUALLY an important *by-product* of the preparation of a procedure manual is that 30.____

A. information uncovered in the process of preparation may lead to improvement of procedures
B. workers refer to the manual instead of bothering their supervisors for information
C. supervisors use the manual for training stenographers
D. employees have equal access to information needed to do their jobs

31. You have been asked to organize a clerical job and supervise police administrative aides who will do the actual work. The job consists of removing, from several boxes of data processing cards which are arranged in alphabetical order, the cards of those whose names appear on certain lists. The person removing the card then notes a date on the card. Assume that the work will be done accurately whatever system is used. 31.____
Which of the following statements describes both the MOST efficient method and the BEST reasons for using that method?
Have

A. two aides work together, one calling names and the other extracting cards, and dating them, because the average production of any two aides working together should be higher, under these circumstances, than that of any two aides working alone
B. each aide work alone, because it is easier to check spelling when reading the names than when listening to them
C. two aides work together, one calling names and the other extracting cards and dating them, because social interaction tends to make work go faster
D. each aide work alone, because the average production of any two aides, each working alone, should be higher, under these circumstances, than that of any two aides working together

32. The term *work flow,* when used in connection with office management or the activities in an office, generally means the 32.____

A. rate of speed at which work flows through a single section of an office
B. use of charts in the analysis of various office functions
C. number of individual work units which can be produced by the average employee
D. step-by-step physical routing of work through its various procedures

Questions 33-40.

DIRECTIONS:

Name of Offense	V	A	N	D	S	B	R	U	G	H
Code Letter	c	o	m	p	l	e	x	i	t	y
File Number	1	2	3	4	5	6	7	8	9	0

Assume that each of the above capital letters is the first letter of the name of an offense, that the small letter directly beneath each capital letter is the code letter for the offense, and that the number directly beneath each code letter is the file number for the offense.

In each of Questions 33 through 40, the code letters and file numbers should correspond to the capital letters.

If there is an error only in Column 2, mark your answer A.
If there is an error only in Column 3, mark your answer B.
If there is an error in both Column 2 and Column 3, mark your answer C.
If both Columns 2 and 3 are correct, mark your answer D.

Sample Questions:

COLUMN 1	COLUMN 2	COLUMN 3
BNARGHSVVU	emoxtylcci	6357905118

The code letters in Column 2 are correct, but the first 5 in Column 3 should be 2. Therefore, the answer is B.

	COLUMN 1	COLUMN 2	COLUMN 3	
				32.____
33.	HGDSBNBSVR	ytplxmelcx	0945736517	33.____
34.	SDGUUNHVAH	lptiimycoy	5498830120	34.____
35.	BRSNAAVUDU	exlmooctpi	6753221848	35.____
36.	VSRUDNADUS	cleipmopil	1568432485	36.____
37.	NDSHVRBUAG	mplycxeiot	3450175829	37.____
38.	GHUSNVBRDA	tyilmcexpo	9085316742	38.____
39.	DBSHVURANG	pesycixomt	4650187239	39.____
40.	RHNNASBDGU	xymnolepti	7033256398	40.____

KEY (CORRECT ANSWERS)

1. B	11. B	21. D	31. D
2. A	12. A	22. D	32. D
3. D	13. C	23. C	33. C
4. B	14. A	24. D	34. D
5. D	15. C	25. A	35. A
6. A	16. D	26. D	36. C
7. D	17. B	27. D	37. B
8. C	18. A	28. C	38. D
9. C	19. B	29. B	39. A
10. B	20. C	30. A	40. C

EXAMINATION SECTION
TEST 1

DIRECTIONS: Each question or incomplete statement is followed by several suggested answers or completions. Select the one that BEST answers the question or completes the statement. *PRINT THE LETTER OF THE CORRECT ANSWER IN THE SPACE AT THE RIGHT.*

Questions 1-8.

DIRECTIONS: Each of Questions 1 through 8 consists of a statement which contains a word (one of those underlined) that is either incorrectly used because it is not in keeping with the meaning the quotation is evidently intended to convey or is misspelled. There is only one INCORRECT word in each quotation. Of the four underlined words, determine if the first one should be replaced by the word lettered A, the second replaced by the word lettered B, the third replaced by the word lettered C, or the fourth replaced by the word lettered D. Print the letter of the replacement word you have selected in the space at the right.

1. Whether one depends on fluorescent or artificial light or both, adequate standards should be maintained by means of systematic tests. 1.____

   A. natural B. safeguards
   C. established D. routine

2. A policeman has to be prepared to assume his knowledge as a social scientist in the community. 2.____

   A. forced B. role
   C. philosopher D. street

3. It is practically impossible to indicate whether a sentence is too long simply by measuring its length. 3.____

   A. almost B. tell C. very D. guessing

4. Strong leaders are required to organize a community for delinquency prevention and for dissemination of organized crime and drug addiction. 4.____

   A. tactics B. important C. control D. meetings

5. The demonstrators, who were taken to the Criminal Courts building in Manhattan (because it was large enough to accommodate them), contended that the arrests were unwarrented. 5.____

   A. exhibitors B. legirons
   C. adjudicate D. unwarranted

6. They were guaranteed a calm atmosphere, free from harrassment, which would be conducive to quiet consideration of the indictments. 6.____

   A. guarenteed B. atmospher
   C. harassment D. inditements

7. The alleged killer was occasionally permitted to excercise in the corridor. 7.____

A. alledged
B. ocasionally
C. permited
D. exercise

8. Defense counsel stated, in affect, that their conduct was permissible under the First Amendment. 8.____

A. council
B. effect
C. there
D. permissable

Questions 9-12.

DIRECTIONS: Each of the two sentences in Questions 9 through 12 may be correct or may contain errors in punctuation, capitalization, or grammar. If there is an error only in sentence I, mark your answer A. If there is an error only in sentence II, mark your answer B. If there is an error in both sentence I and sentence II, mark your answer C. If both sentence I and sentence II are correct, mark your answer D.

9. 9.____
   I. It is very annoying to have a pencil sharpener, which is not in working order.
   II. Patrolman Blake checked the door of Joe's Restaurant and found that the lock has been jammed.

10. 10.____
   I. When you are studying a good textbook is important.
   II. He said he would divide the money equally between you and me.

11. 11.____
   I. Since he went on the city council a year ago, one of his primary concerns has been safety in the streets.
   II. After waiting in the doorway for about 15 minutes, a black sedan appeared.

12. 12.____
   I. The question is, "What is the difference between a lawful and an unlawful demonstration?"
   II. The captain assigned two detectives, John and I, to the investigation.

Questions 13-14.

DIRECTIONS: In each of Questions 13 and 14, the four sentences are from a paragraph in a report. They are not in the right order. Which of the following arrangements is the BEST one?

13. 13.____
   I. Most organizations favor one of the types but always include the others to a lesser degree.
   II. However, we can detect a definite trend toward greater use of symbolic control.
   III. We suggest that our local police agencies are today primarily utilizing material control.
   IV. Control can be classified into three types: physical, material, and symbolic

   The CORRECT answer is:

   A. IV, II, III, I
   B. II, I, IV, III
   C. III, IV, II, I
   D. IV, I, III, II

14. I. They can and do take advantage of ancient political and geographical boundaries, which often give them sanctuary from effective police activity. 14.____
II. This country is essentially a country of small police forces, each operating independently within the limits of its jurisdiction.
III. The boundaries that define and limit police operations do not hinder the movement of criminals, of course.
IV. The machinery of law enforcement in America is fragmented, complicated, and frequently overlapping.
The CORRECT answer is:

A. III, I, II, IV
B. II, IV, I, III
C. IV, II, III, I
D. IV, III, II, I

15. Generally, the frequency with which reports are to be submitted or the length of the interval which they cover should depend MAINLY on the 15.____

A. amount of time needed to prepare the reports
B. degree of comprehensiveness required in the reports
C. availability of the data to be included in the reports
D. extent of the variations in the data with the passage of time

16. Suppose you have to write a report on a serious infraction of rules by one of the Police Administrative Aides you supervise. The circumstances in which the infraction occurred are quite complicated. The BEST way to organize this report would be to 16.____

A. give all points equal emphasis throughout the report
B. include more than one point in a paragraph only if necessary to equalize the size of paragraphs
C. place the least important points before the most important points
D. present each significant point in a separate paragraph t

17. Suppose that police expenses in the city in a certain year amounted to 7.5% of total expenses. 17.____
In indicating this percentage on a *pie* or circular chart, which is 360, the size of the angle between the two radiuses would be MOST NEARLY

A. 3.7
B. 7.5
C. 27
D. 54

18. Suppose that in police precinct A, where there are 4180 children, 627 children entered a contest sponsored by the Police Community Relations Bureau. In precinct B, where there were 7840 children, 1960 children entered the contest. The total percentage of all children in both precincts who entered the contest amounted to MOST NEARLY 18.____

A. 19.5%
B. 20%
C. 21.5%
D. 22.5%

19. If Circle A represents Police Administrative Aides (PAA's) who scored above 85 on a PAA test and Circle B represents PAA's who scored above 85 on a Senior PAA test, then the diagram at the right means that 19.____

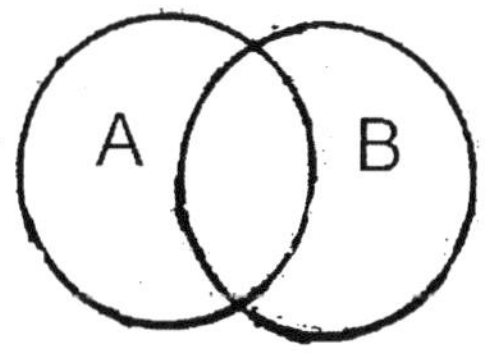

A. no PAA who scored above 85 on a PAA test scored above 85 on the Senior PAA test
B. the majority of PAA's who scored above 85 on a PAA test scored above 85 on the Senior PAA test
C. there were some PAA's who did not take the Senior PAA test
D. some PAA's who scored above 85 on a PAA test scored above 85 on the Senior PAA test

20. Suppose that in 1844 the city had a population of 550,000 and a police force of 200, and that in 1982 the city had a population of 8,000,000 and a police force of 32,000. If the ratio of police to population in 1982 is compared with the same ratio in 1844, what is the resulting relationship of the 1982 ratio to the 1844 ratio? 20.____

A. 160:11 B. 160:1 C. 16:1 D. 11:1

Questions 21-24.

DIRECTIONS: Questions 21 through 24 are to be answered SOLELY on the basis of the information contained in the following passage.

Of those arrested in the city in 1983 for felonies or misdemeanors, only 32% were found guilty of any charge. Fifty-six percent of such arrestees were acquitted or had their cases dismissed, 11% failed to appear for trial, and 1% received other dispositions. Of those found guilty, only 7.4% received any sentences of over one year in jail. Only 50% of those found guilty were sentenced to any further time in jail. When considered with the low probability of arrests for most crimes, these figures make it clear that the crime control system in the city poses little threat to the average criminal. Delay compounds the problem. The average case took four appearances for disposition after arraignment. Twenty percent of all cases took eight or more appearances to reach a disposition. Forty-four percent of all cases took more than one year to disposition.

21. According to the above passage, crime statistics for 1983 indicate that 21.____

A. there is a low probability of arrests for all crimes in the city
B. the average criminal has much to fear from the law in the city
C. over 10% of arrestees in the city charged with felonies or misdemeanors did not show up for trial
D. criminals in the city are less likely to be caught than criminals in the rest of the country t

22. The percentage of those arrested in 1983 who received sentences of over one year in jail amounted MOST NEARLY to 22.____

A. .237 B. 2.4 C. 23.7 D. 24.0

23. According to the above passage, the percentage of arrestees in 1983 who were found guilty was 23.____

A. 20% of those arrested for misdemeanors
B. 11% of those arrested for felonies
C. 50% of those sentenced to further time in jail
D. 32% of those arrested for felonies or misdemeanors

24. According to the above paragraph, the number of appearances after arraignment and before disposition amounted to 24.____

A. an average of four
B. eight or more in 44% of the cases
C. over four for cases which took more than a year
D. between four and eight for most cases

Questions 25-27.

DIRECTIONS: Questions 25 through 27 are to be answered SOLELY on the basis of the information contained in the following paragraph.

The traditional characteristics of a police organization, which do not foster group-centered leadership, are being changed daily by progressive police administrators. These characteristics are authoritarian and result in a leader-centered style with all determination of policy and procedure made by the leader. In the group-centered style, policies and procedures are a matter for group discussion and decision. The supposedly modern view is that the group-centered style is the most conducive to improving organizational effectiveness. By contrast, the traditional view regards the group-centered style as an idealistic notion of psychologists. It is questionable, however, that the situation determines the appropriate leadership style. In some circumstances, it will be leader-centered; in others, group-centered. Nevertheless, police supervisors will see more situations calling for a leadership style that, while flexible, is primarily group-centered. Thus, the supervisor in a police department must have a capacity not just to issue orders but to engage in behavior involving organizational leadership which primarily emphasizes goals and work facilitation.

25. According to the above passage, there is reason to believe that with regard to the effectiveness of different types of leadership, the 25.____

A. leader-centered type is better than the individual-centered type or the group-centered type
B. leader-centered type is best in some situations and the group-centered type best in other situations
C. group-centered type is better than the leader-centered type in all situations
D. authoritarian type is least effective in democratic countries

26. According to the above passage, police administrators today are 26.____

A. more likely than in the past to favor making decisions on the basis of discussions with subordinates
B. likely in general to favor traditional patterns of leadership in their organizations
C. more likely to be progressive than conservative
D. practical and individualistic rather than idealistic in their approach to police problems

27. According to the above passage, the role of the police department is changing in such a way that its supervisors must 27.____

A. give greater consideration to the needs of individual subordinates
B. be more flexible in dealing with infractions of department rules

C. provide leadership which stresses the goals of the department and helps the staff to reach them
D. refrain from issuing orders and allow subordinates to decide how to carry out their assignments

Questions 28-31.

DIRECTIONS: Questions 28 through 31 are to be answered SOLELY on the basis of the information contained in the following paragraph.

Under the provisions of the Bank Protection Act of 1968, enacted July 8, 1968, each Federal banking supervisory agency, as of January 7, 1969, had to issue rules establishing minimum standards with which financial institutions under their control must comply with respect to the installation, maintenance, and operation of security devices and procedures, reasonable in cost, to discourage robberies, burglaries, and larcenies, and to assist in the identification and apprehension of persons who commit such acts. The rules set the time limits within which the affected banks and savings and loan associations must comply with the standards, and the rules require the submission of periodic reports on the steps taken. A violator of a rule under this Act is subject to a civil penalty not to exceed $100 for each day of the violation. The enforcement of these regulations rests with the responsible banking supervisory agencies.

28. The Bank Protection Act of 1968 was designed to 28.____

A. provide Federal police protection for banks covered by the Act
B. have organizations covered by the Act take precautions against criminals
C. set up a system for reporting all bank robberies to the FBI
D. insure institutions covered by the Act from financial loss due to robberies, burglaries, and larcenies

29. Under the provisions of the Bank Protection Act of 1968, each Federal banking supervisory agency was required to set up rules for financial institutions covered by the Act governing the 29.____

A. hiring of personnel
B. punishment of burglars
C. taking of protective measures
D. penalties for violations

30. Financial institutions covered by the Bank Protection Act of 1968 were required to 30.____

A. file reports at regular intervals on what they had done to prevent theft
B. identify and apprehend persons who commit robberies, burglaries, and larcenies
C. draw up a code of ethics for their employees
D. have fingerprints of their employees filed with the FBI

31. Under the provisions of the Bank Protection Act of 1968, a bank which is subject to the rules established under the Act and which violates a rule is liable to a penalty of NOT ______ than $100 for each ______. 31.____

A. more; violation
B. less; day of violation
C. less; violation
D. more; day of violation

Questions 32-36.

DIRECTIONS: Questions 32 through 36 are to be answered SOLELY on the basis of the information contained in the following paragraph.

A statement which is offered in an attempt to prove the truth of the matters therein stated, but which is not made by the author as a witness before the court at the particular trial in which it is so offered, is hearsay. This is so whether the statement consists of words (oral or written), of symbols used as a substitute for words, or of signs or other conduct offered as the equivalent of a statement. Subject to some well-established exceptions, hearsay is not generally acceptable as evidence, and it does not become competent evidence just because it is received by the court without objection. One basis for this rule is simply that a fact cannot be proved by showing that somebody stated it was a fact. Another basis for the rule is the fundamental principle that in a criminal prosecution the testimony of the witness shall be taken before the court, so that at the time he gives the testimony offered in evidence he will be sworn and subject to cross-examination, the scrutiny of the court, and confrontation by the accused.

32. Which of the following is hearsay? A(n) 32.____

A. written statement by a person not present at the court hearing where the statement is submitted as proof of an occurrence
B. oral statement in court by a witness of what he saw
C. written statement of what he saw by a witness present in court
D. re-enactment by a witness in court of what he saw

33. In a criminal case, a statement by a person not present in court is 33.____

A. *acceptable* evidence if not objected to by the prosecutor
B. *acceptable* evidence if not objected to by the defense lawyer
C. *not acceptable* evidence except in certain well-settled circumstances
D. *not acceptable* evidence under any circumstances

34. The rule on hearsay is founded on the belief that 34.____

A. proving someone said an act occurred is not proof that the act did occur
B. a person who has knowledge about a case should be willing to appear in court
C. persons not present in court are likely to be unreliable witnesses
D. permitting persons to testify without appearing in court will lead to a disrespect for law

35. One reason for the general rule that a witness in a criminal case must give his testimony in court is that 35.____

A. a witness may be influenced by threats to make untrue statements
B. the opposite side is then permitted to question him
C. the court provides protection for a witness against unfair questioning
D. the adversary system is designed to prevent a miscarriage of justice

36. Of the following, the MOST appropriate title for the above passage would be 36.____

A. WHAT IS HEARSAY?
B. RIGHTS OF DEFENDANTS
C. TRIAL PROCEDURES
D. TESTIMONY OF WITNESSES

Questions 37-40.

DIRECTIONS: Questions 37 through 40 are to be answered SOLELY on the basis *of* the following graphs.

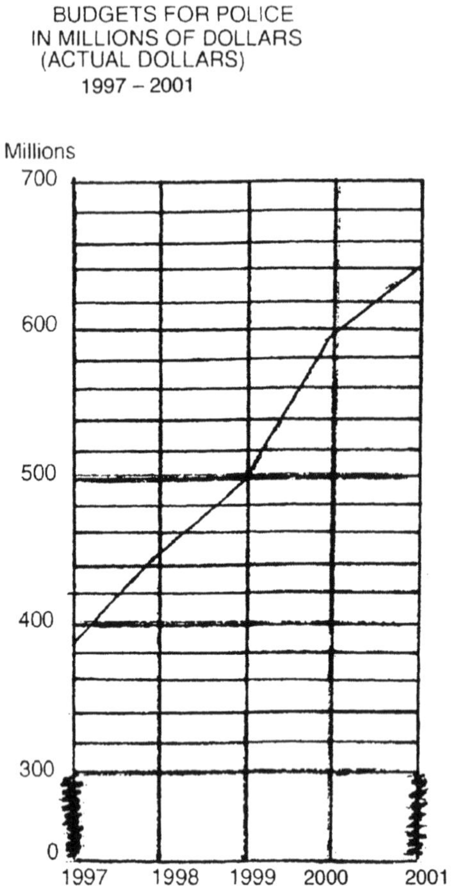

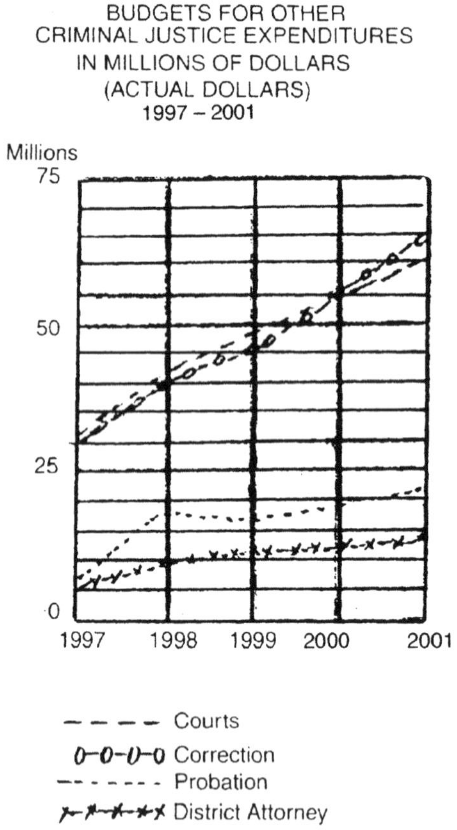

37. In 2001, the amount of money budgeted for courts amounted to APPROXIMATELY what percentage of the amount of money budgeted for police? 37.____

A. 10% B. 20% C. 30% D. 40%

38. In 2000, the police budget exceeded the sum of amounts budgeted for the four other criminal justice expenditures MOST NEARLY by 38.____

A. $410,000,000
B. $459,000,000
C. $475,000,000
D. $487,000,000

39. Between which of the following years did the amount of money budgeted for one category of criminal justice decrease by about one million dollars? 39.____

A. 1997-1998
B. 1998-1999
C. 1999-2000
D. 2000-2001

40. If the 1998 dollar was worth 96% of the 1997 dollar and the 1999 dollar was worth 90% of the 1997 dollar, the increase in the budget for Correction from 1998 to 1999, in terms of the 1997 dollar, amounted to 40.____

A. $2,100,000 B. $4,200,000
C. $4,320,000 D. $4,700,000

KEY (CORRECT ANSWERS)

1. A	11. C	21. C	31. D
2. B	12. B	22. B	32. A
3. B	13. D	23. D	33. C
4. C	14. C	24. A	34. A
5. D	15. D	25. B	35. B
6. C	16. D	26. A	36. A
7. D	17. C	27. C	37. A
8. B	18. C	28. B	38. B
9. C	19. D	29. C	39. B
10. A	20. D	30. A	40. A

EXAMINATION SECTION
TEST 1

DIRECTIONS: Each question or incomplete statement is followed by several suggested answers or completions. Select the one that BEST answers the question or completes the statement. *PRINT THE LETTER OF THE CORRECT ANSWER IN THE SPACE AT THE RIGHT.*

1. You are operating the switchboard and you receive an outside call for an extension line which is busy. 1.____
The one of the following which you should do FIRST is to

   A. ask the caller to try again later
   B. ask the caller to wait and inform him every thirty seconds about the status of the extension line
   C. tell the caller the line is busy and ask him if he wishes to wait
   D. tell the caller the line is busy and that you will connect him as soon as possible

2. A person comes to your work area. He makes comments which make no sense, gives foolish opinions, and tells you that he has enemies who are after him. He appears to be mentally ill. 2.____
Of the following, the FIRST action to take is to

   A. humor him by agreeing and sympathizing with him
   B. try to reason with him and point out that his fears or opinions are unfounded
   C. have him arrested immediately
   D. tell him to leave at once

3. You are speaking with someone on the telephone who asks you a question which you cannot answer. You estimate that you can probably obtain the requested information in about five minutes. 3.____
Of the following, the MOST appropriate course of action would be to tell the caller that

   A. the information will take a short while to obtain, and then ask her for her name and number so that you can call her back when you have the information
   B. the information is available now, but she should call back later
   C. you do not know the answer and refer her to another division you think might be of service
   D. she is being placed on *hold* and that you will be with her in about five minutes

4. A person with a very heavy foreign accent comes to your work area and starts talking to you. He is very excited and is speaking too rapidly for you to understand what he is saying. 4.____
Of the following, the FIRST action for you to take is to

   A. refer the person to your supervisor
   B. continue your work and ignore the person in the hope that he will be discouraged and leave the building
   C. ask or motion to the person to speak more slowly and have him repeat what he is trying to communicate
   D. assume that the person is making a complaint, tell him that his problem will be taken care of, and then go back to your work

5. Assume that you are responsible for handling supplies. You notice that you are running low on a particular type of manila file folder exceptionally fast. You believe that someone in the precinct is taking the folders for other than official use. 5.____
In this situation, the one of the following that you should do FIRST is to

A. put up a notice stating that supplies have been disappearing and ask for the staff's cooperation in eliminating the problem
B. speak to your supervisor about the matter and let him decide on a course of action
C. watch the supply cabinet to determine who is taking the folders
D. ignore the situation and put in a requisition for additional folders

6. One afternoon, several of the officers ask you to perform different tasks. Each task requires a half day of work. Each officer tells you that his assignment must be finished by 4 P.M. the next day. 6.____
Of the following, the BEST way to handle this situation is to

A. do the assignments as quickly as you can, in the order in which the officers handed them to you
B. do some work on each assignment in the order of the ranks of the assigning officers and hand in as much as you are able to finish
C. speak to your immediate supervisor in order to determine the priority of assignments
D. accept all four assignments but explain to the last officer that you may not be able to finish his job

7. Every morning, several officers congregate around your work station during their breaks. You find their conversations very distracting. 7.____
The one of the following which you should do FIRST is to

A. ask them to cooperate with you by taking their breaks somewhere else
B. concentrate as best you can because their breaks do not last very long
C. reschedule your break to coincide with theirs
D. tell your supervisor that the officers are very uncooperative

8. One evening when you are very busy, you answer the phone and find that you are speaking with one of the neighborhood cranks, an elderly man who constantly complains that his neighbors are noisy. 8.____
In this situation, the MOST appropriate action for you to take is to

A. hang up and go on with your work
B. note the complaint and process it in the usual way
C. tell the man that his complaint will be investigated and then forget about it
D. tell the man that you are very busy and ask him to call back later

9. One morning you answer a telephone call for Lieutenant Jones, who is busy on another line. You inform the caller that Lieutenant Jones is on another line and this party says he will hold. After two minutes, Lieutenant Jones is still speaking on the first call. 9.____
Of the following, the FIRST thing for you to do is to

A. ask the second caller whether it is an emergency
B. signal Lieutenant Jones to let him know there is another call waiting for him
C. request that the second caller try again later
D. inform the second caller that Lieutenant Jones' line is still busy

10. The files in your office have been overcrowded and difficult to work with since you started working there. One day your supervisor is transferred and another aide in your office decides to discard three drawers of the oldest materials. 10.____
For him to take this action is

A. *desirable;* it will facilitate handling the more active materials
B. *undesirable;* no file should be removed from its point of origin
C. *desirable;* there is no need to burden a new supervisor with unnecessary information
D. *undesirable;* no file should be discarded without first noting what material has been discarded

11. You have been criticized by the lieutenant-in-charge because of spelling errors in some of your typing. You have only copied the reports as written, and you realize that the errors occurred in work given to you by Sergeant X. 11.____
Of the following, the BEST way for you to handle this situation is to

A. tell the lieutenant that the spelling errors are Sergeant X's, not yours, because they occur only when you type his reports
B. tell the lieutenant that you only type the reports as given to you, without implicating anyone
C. inform Sergeant X that you have been unjustly criticized because of his spelling errors and politely request that he be more careful in the future
D. use a dictionary whenever you have doubt regarding spelling

12. You have recently found several items misfiled. You believe that this occurred because a new administrative aide in your section has been making mistakes. 12.____
The BEST course of action for you to take is to

A. refile the material and say nothing about it
B. send your supervisor an anonymous note of complaint about the filing errors
C. show the errors to the new administrative aide and tell him why they are errors in filing
D. tell your supervisor that the new administrative aide makes a lot of errors in filing

13. One of your duties is to record information on a standard printed form regarding missing cars. One call you receive concerns a custom-built auto which has apparently been stolen. There seems to be no place on the form for many of the details which the owner gives you. 13.____
Of the following, the BEST way for you to obtain an adequate description of this car would be to

A. complete the form as best you can and attach another sheet containing the additional information the owner gives you
B. complete the form as best you can and request that the owner submit a photograph of the missing car
C. scrap the form since it is inadequate in this case and make out a report based on the information the owner gives you
D. complete the form as best you can and ignore extraneous information that the form does not call for

14. One weekend, you develop a painful infection in one hand. You know that your typing speed will be much slower than normal, and the likelihood of your making mistakes will be increased. 14.____
Of the following, the BEST course of action for you to take in this situation is to

A. report to work as scheduled and do your typing assignments as best you can without complaining
B. report to work as scheduled and ask your co-workers to divide your typing assignments until your hand heals
C. report to work as scheduled and ask your supervisor for non-typing assignments until your hand heals
D. call in sick and remain on medical leave until your hand is completely healed so that you can perform your normal duties

15. When filling out a departmental form during an interview concerning a citizen complaint, an administrative aide should know the purpose of each question that he asks the citizen. 15.____
For such information to be supplied by the department is

A. *advisable,* because the aide may lose interest in the job if he is not fully informed about the questions he has to ask
B. *inadvisable,* because the aide may reveal the true purpose of the questions to the citizens
C. *advisable,* because the aide might otherwise record superficial or inadequate answers if he does not fully understand the questions
D. *inadvisable,* because the information obtained through the form may be of little importance to the aide

16. Which one of the following is NOT a generally accepted rule of telephone etiquette for an administrative aide? 16.____

A. Answer the telephone as soon as possible after the first ring
B. Speak in a louder than normal tone of voice, on the assumption that the caller is hard-of-hearing
C. Have a pencil and paper ready at all times with which to make notes and take messages
D. Use the tone of your voice to give the caller the impression of cooperativeness and willingness to be of service

17. The one of the following which is the BEST reason for placing the date and time of receipt of incoming mail is that this procedure 17.____

A. aids the filing of correspondence in alphabetical order
B. fixes responsibility for promptness in answering correspondence
C. indicates that the mail has been checked for the presence of a return address
D. makes it easier to distribute the mail in sequence

18. Which one of the following is the FIRST step that you should take when filing a document by subject? 18.____

A. Arrange related documents by date with the latest date in front
B. Check whether the document has been released for filing
C. Cross-reference the document if necessary
D. Determine the category under which the document will be filed

19. The one of the following which is NOT generally employed to keep track of frequently used material requiring future attention is a 19.____

A. card tickler file
B. dated follow-up folder
C. periodic transferral of records
D. signal folder

20. Assume that a newly appointed administrative aide arrives 15 minutes late for the start of his tour of duty. One of his co-workers tells him not to worry because he has signed him in on time. The co-worker assures him that he would be willing to cover for him anytime he is late and hopes the aide will do the same for him. The aide agrees to do so.
This arrangement is 20.____

A. *desirable;* it prevents both men from getting a record for tardiness
B. *undesirable;* signing in for each other is dishonest
C. *desirable;* cooperation among co-workers is an important factor in morale
D. *undesirable;* they will get caught if one is held up in a lengthy delay

21. An administrative aide takes great pains to help a citizen who approaches him with a problem. The citizen thanks the aide curtly and without enthusiasm.
Under these circumstances, it would be MOST courteous for the aide to 21.____

A. tell the citizen he was glad to be of service
B. ask the citizen to put the compliment into writing and send it to his supervisor
C. tell the citizen just what pains he took to render this service so that the citizen will be fully aware of his efforts
D. make no reply and ignore the citizen's remarks

22. Assume that your supervisor spends a week training you, a newly appointed administrative aide, to sort fingerprints for filing purposes. After doing this type of filing for several days, you get an idea which you believe would improve upon the method in use.
Of the following, the BEST action for you to take in this situation is to 22.____

A. wait to see whether your idea still looks good after you have had more experience
B. try your idea out before bringing it up with your supervisor
C. discuss your idea with your supervisor
D. forget about this idea since the fingerprint sorting system was devised by experts

23. Which one of the following is NOT a useful filing practice? 23.____

A. Filing active records in the most accessible parts of the file cabinet
B. Filling a file drawer to capacity in order to save space
C. Gluing small documents to standard-size paper before filing
D. Using different colored labels for various filing categories

24. A citizen comes in to make a complaint to an administrative aide. 24.____
The one of the following actions which would be the MOST serious example of discourtesy would be for the aide to

A. refuse to look up from his desk even though he knows someone is waiting to speak to him
B. not use the citizen's name when addressing him once his identity has been ascertained
C. interrupt the citizen's story to ask questions
D. listen to the complaint and refer the citizen to a special office

25. Suppose that one of your neighbors walks into the precinct where you are an administrative aide and asks you to make 100 copies of a letter on the office duplicating machine for his personal use. 25.____
Of the following, what action should you take FIRST in this situation?

A. Pretend that you do not know the person and order him to leave the building
B. Call a police officer and report the person for attempting to make illegal use of police equipment
C. Tell the person that you will copy the letter but only when you are off duty
D. Explain to the person that you cannot use police equipment for non-police work

---

KEY (CORRECT ANSWERS)

1.	C	11.	D
2.	A	12.	C
3.	A	13.	A
4.	C	14.	C
5.	B	15.	C
6.	C	16.	B
7.	A	17.	B
8.	B	18.	B
9.	D	19.	C
10.	D	20.	B

21. A
22. C
23. B
24. A
25. D

TEST 2

DIRECTIONS: Each question or incomplete statement is followed by several suggested answers or completions. Select the one that BEST answers the question or completes the statement. *PRINT THE LETTER OF THE CORRECT ANSWER IN THE SPACE AT THE RIGHT.*

Questions 1-6.

DIRECTIONS: Questions 1 through 6 are to be answered on the basis *of* the information supplied in the chart below.

LAW ENFORCEMENT OFFICERS KILLED
(By Type of Activity)

2006-2015

LAW ENFORCEMENT OFFICERS KILLED
(By Type of Activity)

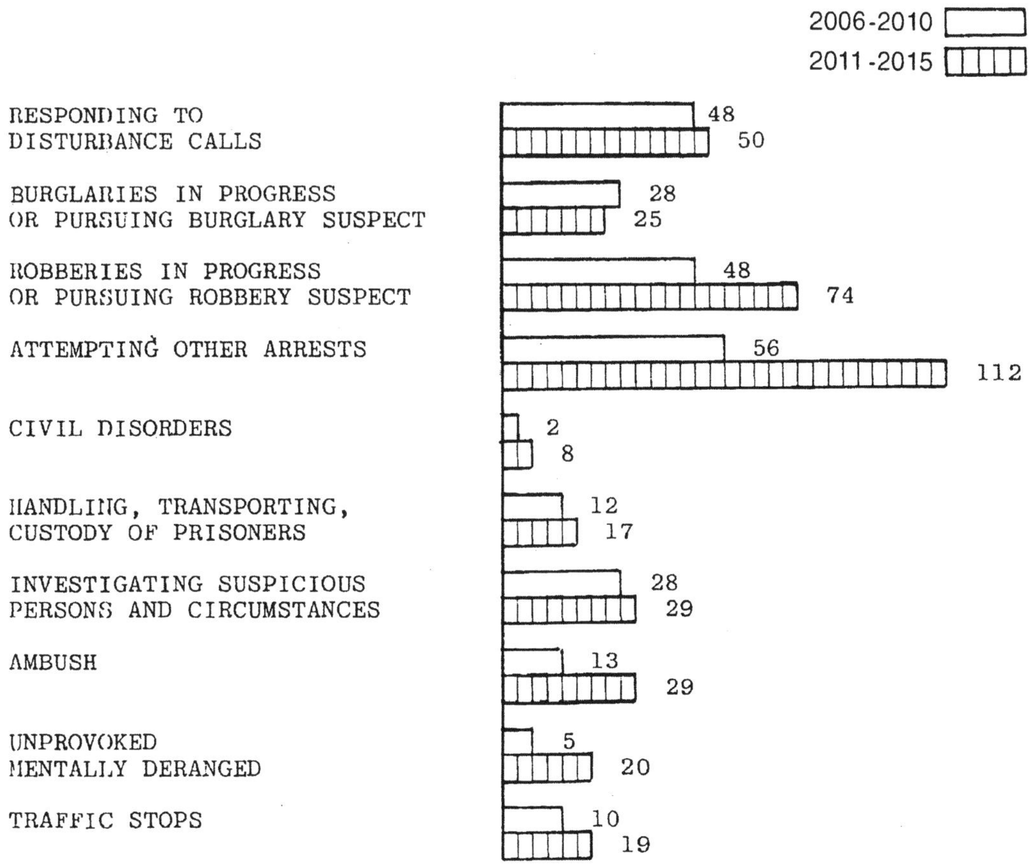

1. According to the above chart, the percent of the total number of law enforcement officers killed from 2006-2015 in activities related to burglaries and robberies is MOST NEARLY _______ percent. 1.____

   A. 8.4 B. 19.3 C. 27.6 D. 36.2

2. According to the above chart, the two of the following categories which increased from 2006-10 to 2011-15 by the same percent are 2.____

   A. ambush and traffic stops
   B. attempting other arrests and ambush
   C. civil disorders and unprovoked mentally deranged
   D. response to disturbance calls and investigating suspicious persons and circumstances

3. According to the above chart, the percentage increase in law enforcement officers killed from the 2006-10 period to the 2011-15 period is MOST NEARLY _______ percent. 3.____

   A. 34 B. 53 C. 65 D. 100

4. According to the above chart, in which one of the following activities did the number of law enforcement officers killed increase by 100 percent? 4.____

   A. Ambush
   B. Attempting other arrests
   C. Robberies in progress or pursuing robbery suspect
   D. Traffic stops

5. According to the above chart, the two of the following activities during which the total number of law enforcement officers killed from 2006 to 2015 was the same are 5.____

   A. burglaries in progress or pursuing burglary suspect and investigating suspicious persons and circumstances
   B. handling, transporting, custody of prisoners and traffic stops
   C. investigating suspicious persons and circumstances and ambush
   D. responding to disturbance calls and robberies in progress or pursuing robbery suspect

6. According to the categories in the above chart, the one of the following statements which can be made about law enforcement officers killed from 2006 to 2010 is that 6.____

   A. the number of law enforcement officers killed during civil disorders equals one-sixth of the number killed responding to disturbance calls
   B. the number of law enforcement officers killed during robberies in progress or pursuing robbery suspect equals 25 percent of the number killed while handling or transporting prisoners
   C. the number of law enforcement officers killed during traffic stops equals one-half the number killed for unprovoked reasons or by the mentally deranged
   D. twice as many law enforcement officers were killed attempting other arrests as were killed during burglaries in progress or pursuing burglary suspect

Questions 7-10.

DIRECTIONS: Assume that all arrests fall into two mutually exclusive categories, felonies and misdemeanors. Last week 620 arrests were made in Precinct A, of which 403 were for felonies. Questions 7 through 10 are to be answered on the basis of this information.

7. The percent of all arrests made in Precinct A last week which were for felonies was ______ percent. 7.____

A. 55 B. 60 C. 65 D. 70

8. If 3/5 of all persons arrested for felonies and 1/4 of all persons arrested for misdemeanors were carrying weapons, then the number of arrests involving persons carrying weapons in Precinct A last week was MOST NEARLY 8.____

A. 135 B. 295 C. 415 D. 525

9. If five times as many men as women were arrested for felonies, and half as many women as men were arrested for misdemeanors, then the number of women arrested in Precinct A last week was APPROXIMATELY 9.____

A. 90 B. 120 C. 175 D. 210

10. If the ratio of arrests made on weekends (Friday through Sunday) to arrests made on weekdays (Monday through Thursday) is 2:1, then the number of arrests made in . Precinct A last weekend was 10.____

A. 308 B. 340 C. 372 D. 413

11. The police precincts covering the county receive calls at the average rate of two per minute during the 8 A.M. to 4 P.M. tour, but this rate increases by 50 percent during the 4 P.M. to 12 A.M. tour. However, the initial rate decreases by 50 percent during the 12 A.M. to 8 A.M. tour. 11.____
The number of calls received by the precincts covering the county on this basis in one 24-hour day is

A. 960 B. 1440 C. 2880 D. 3360

12. If an administrative aide is expected to handle 15 calls per hour and Precinct C averages 840 calls during the 4 P.M. to 12 A.M. tour, then the number of aides needed in Precinct C to handle calls during this tour is 12.____

A. 4 B. 5 C. 6 D. 7

13. If in a group of ten administrative aides, four type 40 words per minute, one types 45, two type 50, two type 60, and one types 65, then the average speed in the group is ______ words per minute. 13.____

A. 49 B. 50 C. 51 D. 52

14. An administrative aide works from midnight to 8 A.M. on a certain day and then is off for 64 hours. 14.____
He is due back at work at

A. 8 A.M.
B. 12 noon
C. 4 P.M.
D. 12 midnight

15. If a certain aide takes one hour to type 2 accident reports or 6 missing person reports, then the length of time he will require to finish 7 accident reports and 15 missing persons reports is _______ hours _______ minutes. 15._____

A. 6; 0 B. 6; 30 C. 8; 0 D. 8; 40

16. If one administrative aide can alphabetize 320 reports per hour and another can do 280 per hour, then the number of reports that both could alphabetize during an 8-hour tour is 16._____

A. 4800 B. 5200 C. 5400 D. 5700

17. If 1000 candidates applied for administrative aide, and out of those applying 7/8 appear for the written test, and out of those who take the written test 66 2/3 percent pass it, and out of those who pass the written test 85 percent pass the medical exam, then the number of candidates still eligible to become administrative aides will be about 17._____

A. 245 B. 495 C. 585 D. 745

18. If the number of murders in the city in 1980 was 415, and the number of murders has increased by 8 percent each year since that year, then in 1983 we would expect the number of murders to be about 18._____

A. 484 B. 523 C. 548 D. 565

19. If a person reported missing on April 15 was found murdered on July 4, how many days was he missing? (Include April 15 but NOT July 4 in the total.) 19._____

A. 76 B. 80 C. 82 D. 84

20. Suppose that a pile of 96 file cards measures one inch in height and that it takes you 1/2 hour to file these cards away.
If you are given three piles of cards which measure 2 1/2 inches high, 1 3/4 inches high, and 3 3/8 inches high, respectively, the time it would take to file the cards is MOST NEARLY _______ hours and _______ minutes. 20._____

A. 2; 30 B. 3; 50 C. 6; 45 D. 8; 15

Questions 21-30.

DIRECTIONS: Questions 21 through 30 test how good you are at catching mistakes in typing or printing. In each question, the name and addresses in Column I should be an exact copy of the name and address in Column I.
Mark your answer
A. if there is no mistake in either name or address
B. if there is a mistake in both name and address
C. if there is a mistake only in the name
D. if there is a mistake only in the address

	COLUMN I	COLUMN II	
21.	Milos Yanocek 33-60 14 Street Long Island City, NY 11011	Milos Yanocek 33-60 14 Street Long Island City, NY 11001	21._____

22.	Alphonse Sabattelo 24 Minnetta Lane New York, NY 10006	Alphonse Sabbattelo 24 Minetta Lane New York, NY 10006	22.____
23.	Helen Stearn 5 Metropolitan Oval Bronx, NY 10462	Helene Stearn 5 Metropolitan Oval Bronx, NY 10462	23.____
24.	Jacob Weisman 231 Francis Lewis Boulevard Forest Hills, NY 11325	Jacob Weisman 231 Francis Lewis Boulevard Forest Hill, NY 11325	24.____
25.	Riccardo Fuente 135 West 83 Street New York, NY 10024	Riccardo Fuentes 134 West 88 Street New York, NY 10024	25.____
26.	Dennis Lauber 52 Avenue D Brooklyn, NY 11216	Dennis Lauder 52 Avenue D Brooklyn, NY 11216	26.____
27.	Paul Cutter 195 Galloway Avenue Staten Island, NY 10356	Paul Cutter 175 Galloway Avenue Staten Island, NY 10365	27.____
28.	Sean Donnelly 45-58 41 Avenue Woodside, NY 11168	Sean Donnelly 45-58 41 Avenue Woodside, NY 11168	28.____
29.	Clyde Willot 1483 Rockaway Avenue Brooklyn, NY 11238	Clyde Willat 1483 Rockway Avenue Brooklyn, NY 11238	29.____
30.	Michael Stanakis 419 Sheriden Avenue Staten Island, NY 10363	Michael Stanakis 419 Sheraden Avenue Staten Island, NY 10363	30.____

Questions 31-40.

DIRECTIONS: Questions 31 through 40 are to be answered only on the basis of the following information.

Column I consists of serial numbers of dollar bills. Column II shows different ways of arranging the corresponding serial numbers.

The serial numbers of dollar bills in Column I begin and end with a capital letter and have an eight-digit number in between. The serial numbers in Column I are to be arranged according to the following rules:

First: In alphabetical order according to the first letter
Second: When two or more serial numbers have the same first letter, in alphabetical order according to the last letter

Third: When two or more serial numbers have the same first and last letters, in numerical order, beginning with the lowest number.

The serial numbers in Column I are numbered (1) through (5) in the order in which they are listed. In Column II, the numbers (1) through (5) are arranged in four different ways to show different arrangements of the corresponding serial numbers. Choose the answer in Column II in which the serial numbers are arranged according to the above rules.

SAMPLE QUESTION:

	COLUMN I		COLUMN II
(1)	E75044127B	(A)	4, 1, 3, 2, 5
(2)	B96399104A	(B)	4, 1, 2, 3,5
(3)	B93939086A	(C)	4,3, 2, 5,1
(4)	B47064465H	(D)	3, 2, 5, 4,1
(5)	B99040922A		

In the sample question, the four serial numbers starting with B should be put before the serial numbers starting with E. The serial numbers starting with B and ending with A should be put before the serial number starting with B and ending with H. The three serial numbers starting with B and ending with A should be listed in numerical order, beginning with the lowest number. The correct way to arrange the serial numbers, therefore, is

(3) B93939086A
(2) B96399104A
(5) B99040922A
(4) B47064465H
(1) E75044127B

Since the order of arrangement is 3, 2, 5, 4, 1, the answer to the sample question is (D).

		COLUMN I	COLUMN II	
31.	(1)	P44343314Y	A. 2, 3, 1, 4, 5	31.____
	(2)	P44141341S	B. 1, 5, 3, 2, 4	
	(3)	P44141431L	C. 4, 2, 3, 5, 1	
	(4)	P41143413W	D. 5, 3, 2, 4, 1	
	(5)	P44313433H		
32.	(1)	D89077275M	A. 3, 2, 5, 3, 1	32.____
	(2)	D98073724N	B. 1, 4, 3, 2, 5	
	(3)	D90877274N	C. 4, 1, 5, 2, 3	
	(4)	D98877275M	D. 1, 3, 2, 5, 3	
	(5)	D98873725N		
33.	(1)	H32548137E	A. 2, 4, 5, 1, 3	33.____
	(2)	H35243178A	B. 1, 5, 2, 3, 4	
	(3)	H35284378F	C. 1, 5, 2, 4, 3,	
	(4)	H35288337A	D. 2, 1, 5, 3, 4	
	(5)	H32883173B		

34. (1) K24165039H
(2) F24106599A
(3) L21406639G
(4) C24156093A
(5) K24165593D

A. 4, 2, 5, 3, 1
B. 2, 3, 4, 1, 5
C. 4, 2, 5, 1, 3
D. 1, 3, 4, 5, 2

34.____

35. (1) H79110642E
(2) H79101928E
(3) A79111567F
(4) H79111796E
(5) A79111618F

A. 2, 1, 3, 5, 4
B. 2, 1, 4, 5, 3
C. 3, 5, 2, 1, 4
D. 4, 3, 5, 1, 2

35.____

36. (1) P16388385W
(2) R16388335V
(3) P16383835W
(4) R18386865V
(5) P18686865W

A. 3, 4, 5, 2, 1
B. 2, 3, 4, 5, 1
C. 2, 4, 3, 1, 5
D. 3, 1, 5, 2, 4

36.____

37. (1) B42271749G
(2) B42271779G
(3) E43217779G
(4) B42874119C
(5) E42817749G

A. 4, 1, 5, 2, 3
B. 4, 1, 2, 5, 3
C. 1, 2, 4, 5, 3
D. 5, 3, 1, 2, 4

37.____

38. (1) M57906455S
(2) N87077758S
(3) N87707757B
(4) M57877759B
(5) M57906555S

A. 4, 1, 5, 3, 2
B. 3, 4, 1, 5, 2
C. 4, 1, 5, 2, 3
D. 1, 5, 3, 2, 4

38.____

39. (1) C69336894Y
(2) C69336684V
(3) C69366887W
(4) C69366994Y
(5) C69336865V

A. 2, 5, 3, 1, 4
B. 3, 2, 5, 1, 4
C. 3, 1, 4, 5, 2
D. 2, 5, 1, 3, 4

39.____

40. (1) A56247181D
(2) A56272128P
(3) H56247128D
(4) H56272288P
(5) A56247188D

A. 1, 5, 3, 2, 4
B. 3, 1, 5, 2, 4
C. 3, 2, 1, 5, 4
D. 1, 5, 2, 3, 4

40.____

Questions 41-48.

DIRECTIONS: Questions 41 through 48 are to be answered only on the basis of the following passage.

Auto theft is prevalent and costly. In 2015, 486,000 autos valued at over $500 million were stolen. About 28 percent of the inhabitants of Federal prisons are there as a result of conviction of interstate auto theft under the Dyer Act. In California alone, auto thefts cost the criminal justice system approximately $60 million yearly.

The great majority of auto theft is for temporary use rather than resale, as evidenced by the fact that 88 percent of autos stolen in 2015 were recovered. In Los Angeles, 64 percent of stolen autos that were recovered were found within two days and about 80 percent within a week. Chicago reports that 71 percent of the recovered autos were found within four miles of the point of theft. The FBI estimates that 8 percent of stolen cars are taken for the purpose of stripping them for parts, 12 percent for resale, and 5 percent for use in another crime. Auto thefts are primarily juvenile acts. Although only 21 percent of all arrests for nontraffic offenses in 2015 were of individuals under 18 years of age, 63 percent of auto theft arrests were of persons under 18. Auto theft represents the start of many criminal careers; in an FBI sample of juvenile auto theft offenders, 41 percent had no prior arrest record.

41. In the passage above, the discussion of the reasons for auto theft does NOT include the percent of 41.____

    A. autos stolen by prior offenders
    B. recovered stolen autos found close to the point of theft
    C. stolen autos recovered within a week
    D. stolen autos which were recovered

42. Assuming the figures in the above passage remain constant, you may logically estimate the cost of auto thefts to the California criminal justice system over a five-year period beginning in 2015 to have been about ______ million. 42.____

    A. $200 B. $300 C. $440 D. $500

43. According to the above passage, the percent of stolen autos in Los Angeles which were not recovered within a week was ______ percent. 43.____

    A. 12 B. 20 C. 29 D. 36

44. According to the above passage, MOST auto thefts are committed by 44.____

    A. former inmates of Federal prisons
    B. juveniles
    C. persons with a prior arrest record
    D. residents of large cities

45. According to the above passage, MOST autos are stolen for 45.____

    A. resale
    B. stripping of parts
    C. temporary use
    D. use in another crime

46. According to the above passage, the percent of persons arrested for auto theft who were under 18 46.____

    A. equals nearly the same percent of stolen autos which were recovered
    B. equals nearly two-thirds of the total number of persons arrested for nontraffic offenses
    C. is the same as the percent of persons arrested for nontraffic offenses who were under 18
    D. is three times the percent of persons arrested for nontraffic offenses who were under 18

47. An APPROPRIATE title for the above passage is 47.____

A. How Criminal Careers Begin
B. Recovery of Stolen Cars
C. Some Statistics on Auto Theft
D. The Costs of Auto Theft

48. Based on the above passage, the number of cars taken for use in another crime in 1995 was 48.____

A. 24,300 B. 38,880 C. 48,600 D. 58,320

Questions 49-55.

DIRECTIONS: Questions 49 through 55 are to be answered only on the basis of the following passage.

Burglar alarms are designed to detect intrusion automatically. Robbery alarms enable a victim of a robbery or an attack to signal for help. Such devices can be located in elevators, hallways, homes and apartments, businesses and factories, and subways, as well as on the street in high-crime areas. Alarms could deter some potential criminals from attacking targets so protected. If alarms were prevalent and not visible, then they might serve to suppress crime generally. In addition, of course, the alarms can summon the police when they are needed.

All alarms must perform three functions: sensing or initiation of the signal, transmission of the signal, and annunciation of the alarm. A burglar alarm needs a sensor to detect human presence or activity in an unoccupied enclosed area like a building or a room. A robbery victim would initiate the alarm by closing a foot or wall switch, or by triggering a portable transmitter which would send the alarm signal to a remote receiver. The signal can sound locally as a loud noise to frighten away a criminal, or it can be sent silently by wire to a central agency. A centralized annunciator requires either private lines from each alarmed point, or the transmission of some information on the location of the signal.

49. A conclusion which follows LOGICALLY from the above passage is that 49.____

A. burglar alarms employ sensor devices; robbery alarms make use of initiation devices
B. robbery alarms signal intrusion without the help of the victim; burglar alarms require the victim to trigger a switch
C. robbery alarms sound locally; burglar alarms are transmitted to a central agency
D. the mechanisms for a burglar alarm and a robbery alarm are alike

50. According to the above passage, alarms can be located 50.____

A. in a wide variety of settings
B. only in enclosed areas
C. at low cost in high-crime areas
D. only in places where potential criminals will be deterred

51. According to the above passage, which of the following is ESSENTIAL if a signal is to be received in a central office? 51.____

A. A foot or wall switch
B. A noise producing mechanism
C. A portable reception device
D. Information regarding the location of the source

52. According to the above passage, an alarm system can function WITHOUT a 52.____

A. centralized annunciating device
B. device to stop the alarm
C. sensing or initiating device
D. transmission device

53. According to the above passage, the purpose of robbery alarms is to 53.____

A. find out automatically whether a robbery has taken place
B. lower the crime rate in high-crime areas
C. make a loud noise to frighten away the criminal
D. provide a victim with the means to signal for help

54. According to the above passage, alarms might aid in lessening crime if they were 54.____

A. answered promptly by police
B. completely automatic
C. easily accessible to victims
D. hidden and widespread

55. Of the following, the BEST title for the above passage is 55.____

A. Detection of Crime by Alarms
B. Lowering the Crime Rate
C. Suppression of Crime
D. The Prevention of Robbery

KEY (CORRECT ANSWERS)

1. C	11. C	21. D	31. D	41. A	51. D
2. C	12. D	22. B	32. B	42. B	52. A
3. B	13. A	23. C	33. A	43. B	53. D
4. B	14. D	24. A	34. C	44. B	54. D
5. B	15. A	25. B	35. C	45. C	55. A
6. D	16. A	26. C	36. D	46. D	
7. C	17. B	27. D	37. B	47. C	
8. B	18. B	28. A	38. A	48. A	
9. C	19. B	29. B	39. A	49. A	
10. D	20. B	30. D	40. D	50. A	

EXAMINATION SECTION
TEST 1

DIRECTIONS: Each question or incomplete statement is followed by several suggested answers or completions. Select the one that BEST answers the question or completes the statement. *PRINT THE LETTER OF THE CORRECT ANSWER IN THE SPACE AT THE RIGHT.*

1. As an administrative aide, it is your job to type reports prepared by several patrolmen. These reports are then returned to them for review and signature. Patrolman X consistently submits reports to you which contain misspellings and incorrect punctuation. Of the following, the BEST action for you to take is to 1.____

   A. tell your supervisor that something must be done about Patrolman X's poor English
   B. ask Patrolman X for permission to correct any mistakes
   C. assemble all of the patrolmen and tell them that you refuse to correct their mistakes
   D. tell Patrolman X to be more careful

2. On a chart used in your precinct, there appear small figures of men, women, and children to denote population trends. Your supervisor assigns you to suggest possible symbols for a chart which will be used to indicate daily vehicular traffic flow in the area covered by this precinct. In this situation, your BEST course of action would be to 2.____

   A. tell your supervisor an artist should be hired to draw these symbols
   B. make up a list of possible symbols, such as cars and trucks
   C. say that any decision as to the symbols to be used should be made at a higher level
   D. find out how many vehicles use the area

3. As an administrative aide, you are assigned to the telephone switchboard. An extremely irate citizen calls complaining in bigoted terms about a group of Black teenagers who congregate in front of his house. The caller insists on speaking to whoever is in charge. At the moment, Sergeant X, a black man, is in charge. The BEST course of action for you to take is to 3.____

   A. inform the caller that the teenagers may meet wherever they wish
   B. tell the caller that Sergeant X, a black man, is in charge, and ask him to call back later when a white man will be there
   C. tell the caller that you resent his bigotry and insist that he call back when he has calmed down
   D. acquaint Sergeant X with the circumstances and connect the caller with him

4. Assume that you have access to restricted materials such as conviction records. A friend asks you, unofficially, if a man he has recently met has a record of conviction. The BEST thing for you to do is to 4.____

   A. give your friend the information he wants and inform your supervisor of your actions
   B. tell your friend that you are not allowed to give out such information
   C. tell your friend you will try to get the information for him but do not take any action
   D. give him the information because it is a matter of public record

5. Assume that you are an administrative aide assigned to a busy telephone information center. 5.____
Of the following, which is the MOST important technique to use when answering the telephone?

A. Using many technical police terms
B. Speaking slowly, in a monotone, for clarity
C. Using formal English grammar
D. Speaking clearly and distinctly

6. As an administrative aide, you are asked by an officer working in an adjacent office to type a very important letter without mistakes or corrections exactly as he has prepared it. 6.____
As you are typing, you notice a word which, according to the dictionary, is misspelled.
Under the circumstances, you should

A. ignore the error and type it exactly as prepared
B. change the spelling without telling the officer
C. ask the officer if you should change the spelling
D. change the spelling and tell the officer

7. As an administrative aide, you are in charge of a large complex of files. In an effort to be helpful, some officers who frequently use the file have begun to refile material they had been using. Unfortunately, they often make errors. 7.____
Of the following, your BEST course of action is to

A. ask them to leave the files for you to put away
B. ask your supervisor to reprimand them
C. frequently check the whole filing system for errors
D. tell them they are making mistakes and insist they leave the files alone

8. One afternoon several of the police officers ask you to do different tasks. Each task will take about half a day to complete, but each officer insists that his work must be completed immediately. 8.____
Your BEST course of action is to

A. do a little of each assignment given to you
B. ask your fellow workers to help you with the assignment
C. speak to your supervisor in order to determine the priority of the assignments
D. do the work in the order of the rank of the officers giving the assignments

Questions 9-12.

DIRECTIONS: Questions 9 through 12 are to be answered on the basis of the following passage.

It should be emphasized that one goal of law enforcement is the reduction of stress between one population group and another. When no stress exists between populations, law enforcement can deal with other tensions or simply perform traditional police functions. However, when stress between populations does exist, law enforcement, in its efforts to prevent disruptive behavior, becomes committed to reducing that stress (if for no other reason than its responsibility to maintain an orderly environment). The type of stress to be reduced, unlike the tension stemming from social change, is stress generated through intergroup and interracial friction. Of course, all sources of tension are inextricably interrelated, but friction between different populations in the community is of immediate concern to law enforcement.

9. The above passage emphasizes that, during times of stress between groups in the community, it is necessary for the police to attempt to 9.____

A. continue their traditional duties
B. eliminate tension resulting from social change
C. reduce intergroup stress
D. punish disruptive behavior.

10. Based on the above passage, police concern with tension among groups in a community is MOST likely to stem prinarily from their desire to 10.____

A. establish racial justice
B. prevent violence
C. protect property
D. unite the diverse groups

11. According to the above passage, enforcers of the law are responsible for 11.____

A. analyzing consequences of population-group hostility
B. assisting social work activities
C. creating order in the environment
D. explaining group behavior

12. The factor which produces the tension accompanying social change is 12.____

A. a disorderly environment
B. disruptive behavior
C. inter-community hostility
D. not discussed in the above passage

Questions 13-19.

DIRECTIONS: Questions 13 through 19 are to be answered on the basis of the information given in the passage below.

From a nationwide point of view, the need for new housing units during the years immediately ahead will be determined by four major factors. The most important factor is the net change in household formations -- that is, the difference between the number of new households that are formed and the number of existing households that are dissolved, whether by death or other circumstances. During the 1990's, as the children born during the decades of the 60's and 70's come of age and marry, the total number of households is expected to increase at a rate of more than 1,000,000 annually. The second factor affecting the need for new housing units is *removals* -- that is, existing units that are demolished, damaged beyond repair, or otherwise removed from the housing supply. A third factor is the number of existing vacancies. To some extent, vacancies can satisfy the housing demand caused by increases in total number of households or by removals, although population shifts that are already under way mean that some areas will have a surfeit of vacancies and other areas will be faced with serious shortages of housing. A final factor, and one that has only recently assumed major importance, is the increasing demand for second homes. These may take any form from a shack in the woods for the city dweller to a *pied-a-terre* in the city for a suburbanite. Whatever the form, however, it is certain that increasing leisure time, rising amounts of discretionary income, and improvements in transportation are leading more and more Americans to look on a second home not as a rich man's luxury but as the common man's right.

13. The above passage uses the term *housing units* to refer to 13.____

A. residences of all kinds
B. apartment buildings only
C. one-family houses only
D. the total number of families in the United States

14. The passage uses the word *removals* to mean 14.____

A. the shift of population from one area to another
B. vacancies that occur when families move
C. financial losses suffered when a building is damaged or destroyed
D. former dwellings that are demolished or can no longer be used for housing

15. The expression *pied-a-terre* appears in the next-to-last sentence in the passage. A person who is not familiar with the expression should be able to tell from the way it is used here that it *probably* means 15.____

A. a suburban home owned by a commuter
B. a shack in the woods
C. a second home that is used from time to time
D. overnight lodging for a traveler in a strange city

16. Of the factors described in the passage as having an important influence on the demand for housing, which factor-- taken alone -- is LEAST likely to encourage the construction of new housing? 16.____
The

A. net change in household formations
B. destruction of existing housing
C. existence of vacancies
D. use of second homes

17. Based on the above passage, the TOTAL increase in the number of households during the 1990's is expected to be MOST NEARLY 17.____

A. 1,000,000
B. 10,000,000
C. 100,000,000
D. 1,000,000,000

18. Which one of the following conclusions could MOST logically be drawn from the information given in the passage? 18.____

A. The population of the United States is increasing at the rate of about 1,000,000 people annually.
B. There is already a severe housing shortage in all parts of the country.
C. The need for additional housing units is greater in some parts of the country than in others.
D. It is still true that only wealthy people can afford to keep up more than one home.

19. Which one of the following conclusions could NOT logically be drawn from the information given in the passage? 19.____

    A. The need for new housing will be even greater in the 2000's than in the 1990's.
    B. Demolition of existing housing must be taken into account in calculating the need for new housing construction.
    C. Having a second home is more common today than it was in the 1960's.
    D. Part of the housing needs of the 1990's can be met by vacancies.

20. You are making a report on the number of incoming calls handled by two different switchboards. Over a five-day period, the total count of incoming calls per day for both switchboards together was 2,773. The average number of incoming calls per day for Switchboard A was 301. 20.____
You cannot find one day's tally for Switchboard B, but the total for the other four days for Switchboard B comes to 1,032.
Determine from this how many incoming calls must have been reported on the *missing* tally for Switchboard B.

    A. 236 B. 258 C. 408 D. 1,440

21. Assume that one-page notices for distribution may be reproduced by photocopy or by a designer. The cost for photocopying is 5 1/2 cents per copy. It can also be reproduced by a designer for an initial preparation cost of $1.38 plus a per-copy cost of one cent. 21.____
Strictly according to cost, which of the following is the LOWEST number of copies at which it would be more economical to choose the designer instead of photocopying?

    A. 15 B. 30 C. 45 D. 138

22. An employee completed 75% of a clerical assignment in four days. How much of it did he complete in the last two days if he finished 3/8 of it in the first two days? 22.____

    A. 1/4 B. 3/8 C. 5/8 D. 3/4

23. Seven hundred people are to be scheduled for interviews. If 58% of these 700 people have already been scheduled, how many more must be scheduled? 23.____

    A. 138 B. 294 C. 406 D. 410

24. In recent years, an average of 35% of the violations reported in any given month have been corrected by the time of a follow-up inspection one month later. Last month, 240 violations were reported, and this month's follow-up inspections show that 93 of them have been corrected. 24.____
How many more violations have been corrected than would have been expected, based on the average rate?

    A. 5 B. 9 C. 33 D. 58

25. Suppose that, on a scaled drawing of an office floor plan, 1/2 inch equals 2 feet. An office that is actually 12 feet wide and 17 feet long has which of the following dimensions on this scaled drawing? 25.____
______ wide and ______ long.

    A. 3"; 4.25" B. 6"; 8.5" C. 12"; 17" D. 24"; 34"

KEY (CORRECT ANSWERS)

1. B
2. B
3. D
4. B
5. D
6. C
7. A
8. C
9. C
10. B
11. C
12. D
13. A
14. D
15. C
16. C
17. B
18. C
19. A
20. A
21. C
22. B
23. B
24. B
25. A

TEST 2

DIRECTIONS: Each question or incomplete statement is followed by several suggested answers or completions. Select the one that BEST answers the question or completes the statement. *PRINT THE LETTER OF THE CORRECT ANSWER IN THE SPACE AT THE RIGHT.*

1. Suppose that employees in a certain division put in a total of 1,250 hours of overtime in 2014. In 2015, total overtime hours for the same division were 2% less than in 2014, but in 2016 overtime hours increased by 8% over the 2015 total. How many overtime hours were worked by the staff of this division in 2016? 1.____

   A. 1,323 B. 1,331 C. 1,350 D. 1,375

2. A particular operation currently involves 75 employees, 80% of whom work in the field and the rest of whom are office staff. A management study has shown that in order to be truly efficient, the operation should have a ratio of at least 1 office employee to every 3 field employees, and the study recommends that the number of field employees remain the same as at present. What is the MINIMUM number of employees needed to carry out the operation efficiently, according to this recommendation? 2.____

   A. 65 B. 75 C. 80 D. 100

Questions 3-6.

DIRECTIONS: Questions 3 through 6 are to be answered on the basis of the information given in the passage below.

Data processing is by no means a new invention. In one form or another, it has been carried on throughout the entire history of civilization. In its most general sense, data processing means organizing data so that it can be used for a specific purpose a procedure commonly known simply as *record-keeping* or *paperwork.* With the development of modern office equipment, and particularly with the recent introduction of computers, the techniques of data processing have become highly elaborate and sophisticated, but the basic purpose remains the same: turning raw data into useful information.

The key concept here is usefulness. The data, or input, that is to be processed can be compared to the raw material that is to go into a manufacturing process. The information, or output, that results from data processing -- like the finished product of a manufacturer -- should be clearly usable. A collection of data has little value unless it is converted into information that serves a specific function.

3. The expression *paperwork,* as it is used in this passage, 3.____

   A. shows that the author regards such operations as a waste of time
   B. has the same general meaning as *data processing*
   C. refers to methods of record-keeping that are no longer in use
   D. indicates that the public does not understand the purpose of data processing

4. The passage indicates that the use of computers has 4.____

   A. greatly simplified the clerical work in an office
   B. led to more complicated systems for the handling of data
   C. had no effect whatsoever on data processing
   D. made other modern office machines obsolete

5. Which of the following BEST expresses the basic principle of data processing as it is described in the passage? 5.____

   A. Input - processing - output
   B. Historical record-keeping - modern techniques - specific functions
   C. Office equipment - computer - accurate data
   D. Raw material - manufacturer - retailer

6. According to the above passage, data processing may be described as 6.____

   A. a new management technique
   B. computer technology
   C. information output
   D. record-keeping

Questions 7-10.

DIRECTIONS: Questions 7 through 10 are to be answered on the basis of the following passage.

Analysis of current data reveals that motor vehicle transportation actually requires less space than was used for other types of transportation in the pre-automobile era, even including the substantial area taken by freeways. The reason is that when the fast-moving through traffic is put on built-for-the-purpose arterial roads, then the amount of ordinary space needed for strictly local movement and for access to property drops sharply. Even the amount of land taken for urban expressways turns out to be surprisingly small in terms either of total urban acreage or of the volume of traffic they carry. No existing or contemplated urban expressway system requires as much as 3 percent of the land in the areas it serves, and this would be exceptionally high. The Los Angeles freeway system, when complete, will occupy only 2 percent of the available land; the same is true of the District of Columbia, where only 0.75 percent will be pavement, with the remaining 1.25 percent as open space. California studies estimate that, in a typical California urban community, 1.6 to 2 percent of the area should be devoted to freeways, which will handle 50 to 60 percent of all traffic needs, and about ten times as much land to the ordinary roads and streets that carry the rest of the traffic. By comparison, when John A. Sutter laid out Sacramento in 1850, he provided 38 percent of the area for streets and sidewalks. The French architect, Pierre L'Enfant, proposed 59 percent of the area of the District of Columbia for roads and streets; urban renewal in Southwest Washington, incorporating a modern street network, reduced the acreage of space for pedestrian and vehicular traffic in the renewal area from 48.2 to 41.5 percent of the total. If we are to have a reasonable consideration of the impact of highway transportation on contemporary urban development, it would be well to understand these relationships.

7. The author of this passage says that 7.____

   A. modern transportation uses less space than was used for transportation before the auto age
   B. expressways require more space than streets in terms of urban acreage
   C. typical urban communities were poorly designed in terms of relationship between space used for traffic and that used for other purposes
   D. the need for local and access roads would increase if the number of expressways were increased

8. According to the above passage, it was originally planned that the percent of the area to be used for roads and streets in the District of Columbia should be MOST NEARLY 8.____

   A. 40% B. *45%* C. 50% D. 60%

9. The above passage states that the amount of space needed for local traffic 9.____

   A. *increases* when arterial highways are constructed
   B. *decreases* when arterial highways are constructed
   C. *decreases* when there is more land available
   D. *increases* when there is more land available

10. According to the above passage, studies estimate that, in a typical California urban community, the amount of land devoted to ordinary roads and streets as compared with that devoted to freeways should be MOST NEARLY ______ as much. 10.____

    A. one-half B. one-tenth C. twice D. ten times

Questions 11-13.

DIRECTIONS: Questions 11 through 13 are to be answered on the basis of the following passage.

A glaring exception to the usual practice of the judicial trial as a means of conflict resolution is the utilization of administrative hearings. The growing tendency to create administrative bodies with rule-making and quasi-judicial powers has shattered many standard concepts. A comprehensive examination of the legal process cannot neglect these newer patterns.

In the administrative process, the legislative, executive, and judicial functions are mixed together, and many functions, such as investigating, advocating, negotiating, testifying, rule-making, and adjudicating, are carried out by the same agency. The reason for the breakdown of the separation-of-powers formula is not hard to find. It was felt by Congress, and state and municipal legislatures, that certain regulatory tasks could not be performed efficiently, rapidly, expertly, and with due concern for the public interest by the traditional branches of government. Accordingly, regulatory agencies were delegated powers to consider disputes from the earliest stage of investigation to the final stages of adjudication entirely within each agency itself, subject only to limited review in the regular courts.

11. The above passage states that the usual means for conflict resolution is through the use of 11.____

    A. judicial trial B. administrative hearing
    C. legislation D. regulatory agencies

12. The above passage *implies* that the use of administrative hearing in resolving conflict is a(n) ______ approach. 12.____

A. traditional
B. new
C. dangerous
D. experimental

13. The above passage states that the reason for the breakdown of the separation-of-powers formula in the administrative process is that 13.____

A. Congress believed that certain regulatory tasks could be better performed by separate agencies
B. legislative and executive functions are incompatible in the same agency
C. investigative and regulatory functions are not normally reviewed by the courts
D. state and municipal legislatures are more concerned with efficiency than with legality

14. An employee examining the summonses of individuals appearing for hearings noticed that the address one one summons was the same as that of an individual who had appeared earlier that day. He asked the second respondent if he knew the first respondent. 14.____
The MOST appropriate evaluation of the employee's behavior is that he should

A. not have mentioned any other respondent to the second respondent
B. not waste time inspecting summonses in such detail
C. be commended for inspecting summonses so carefully
D. be commended for his investigation of the respondents

15. An employee is assigned to maintain all types of frequently used reference materials such as booklets and technical papers. He keeps these in a pile on a shelf in order of arrival. When new material arrives, he puts it on top of the pile. Which of the following BEST evaluates the employee's handling of this reference material? His system is MOST likely to result in ______ filing and ______ retrieval. 15.____

A. fast; slow
B. slow; slow
C. fast; fast
D. slow; fast

16. An employee computes statistics relating to proceedings. The method he devised consists of organizing his source . and summary documents in such a manner that at any time another employee can assume the work. This method takes a little more time than other possible methods. 16.____
Which of the following statements BEST evaluates the judgment of the employee in devising such a method?
The employee has used

A. *good* judgment because it is important to provide for continuity
B. *poor* judgment because he is not using the fastest method
C. *good* judgment because, if a job is done as fast as possible, it becomes tiring
D. *poor* judgment because it is not an employee's responsibility to prepare for a replacement

17. Assume that it is your job to receive incoming telephone calls. Those calls which you cannot handle yourself have to be transferred to the appropriate office. 17.____
If you receive an outside call for an extension line which is busy, the one of the following which you should do FIRST is to

A. interrupt the person speaking on the extension and tell him a call is waiting
B. tell the caller the line is busy and let him know every thirty seconds whether or not it is free
C. leave the caller on *hold* until the extension is free
D. tell the caller the line is busy and ask him if he wishes to wait

18. On one occasion in a certain office, an elderly employee collapsed, apparently the victim of a heart attack. Chaos broke out in the office as several people tried to help him and several others tried to get assistance.
Of the following, the MOST certain way of avoiding such chaos in the future is to 18.____

A. keep a copy of heart attack procedures on file so that it can be referred to by any member of the staff when an emergency occurs
B. provide each member of the staff with a first aid book which is to be kept in an accessible location
C. train all members of the staff in the proper procedure for handling such emergencies, assigning specific responsibilities
D. post, in several places around the office, a list of specific procedures to follow in each of several different emergencies

19. Your superior has subscribed to several publications directly related to your division's work, and he has asked you to see to it that the publications are circulated among the supervisory personnel in the division. There are eight supervisors involved.
The BEST method of insuring that all eight see these publications is to 19.____

A. place the publication in the division's general reference library as soon as it arrives
B. inform each supervisor whenever a publication arrives and remind all of them that they are responsible for reading it
C. prepare a standard slip that can be stapled to each publication, listing the eight supervisors and saying, *Please read, initial your name, and pass along*
D. send a memo to the eight supervisors saying that they may wish to purchase individual subscriptions in their own names if they are interested in seeing each issue

20. Assume that you have been asked to prepare a narrative summary of the monthly reports submitted by employees in your division.
In preparing your summary of this month's reports, the FIRST step to take is to 20.____

A. read through the reports, noting their general content and any unusual features
B. decide how many typewritten pages your summary should contain
C. make a written summary of each separate report, so that you will not have to go back to the original reports again
D. ask each employee which points he would prefer to see emphasized in your summary

21. Your superior has telephoned a number of key officials in your agency to ask whether they can meet at a certain time next month. He has found that they can all make it, and he has asked you to confirm the meeting.
Which of the following is the BEST way to confirm such a meeting? 21.____

A. Note the meeting on your superior's calendar
B. Post a notice of the meeting on the agency bulletin board
C. Call the officials on the day of the meeting to remind them of the meeting
D. Write a memo to each official involved repeating the time and place of the meeting

22. Of the following, the worker who is MOST likely to create a problem in maintaining safety is one who 22.____

A. disregards hazards
B. feels tired
C. resents authority
D. gets bored

23. Assume that a new regulation requires that certain kinds of private organizations file information forms with your department. You have been asked to write the short explanatory message that will be printed on the front cover of the pamphlet containing the forms and instructions. Which of the following would be the MOST appropriate way of beginning this message? 23.____

A. Get the readers' attention by emphasizing immediately that there are legal penalties for organizations that fail to file before a certain date
B. Briefly state the nature of the enclosed forms and the types of organizations that must file
C. Say that your department is very sorry to have to put organizations to such an inconvenience
D. Quote the entire regulation adopted by the city, even if it is quite long and is expressed in complicated legal language

24. Suppose that you have been told to make up the vacation schedule for the 15 employees in a particular unit. In order for the unit to operate effectively, only a few employees can be on vacation at the same time.
Which of the following is the MOST advisable approach in making up the schedule? 24.____

A. Draw up a schedule assigning vacations in alphabetical order
B. Find out when the supervisors want to take their vacations, and randomly assign whatever periods are left to the non-supervisory personnel
C. Assign the most desirable times to employees of longest standing, and the least desirable times to the newest employees
D. Have all employees state their own preferences, and then work out any conflicts in consultation with the people involved

25. Assume that you have been asked to prepare job descriptions for various positions in your department.
Which of the following are the BASIC points that should be covered in a job description? 25.____

A. General duties and responsibilities of the position, with examples of day-to-day tasks
B. Comments on the performances of present employees
C. Estimates of the number of openings that may be available in each category during the coming year
D. Instructions for carrying out the specific tasks assigned to your department

KEY (CORRECT ANSWERS)

1. A
2. C
3. B
4. B
5. A

6. D
7. A
8. D
9. B
10. D

11. A
12. B
13. A
14. A
15. A

16. A
17. D
18. C
19. C
20. A

21. D
22. A
23. B
24. D
25. A

TEST 3

DIRECTIONS: Each question or incomplete statement is followed by several suggested answers or completions. Select the one that BEST answers the question or completes the statement. *PRINT THE LETTER OF THE CORRECT ANSWER IN THE SPACE AT THE RIGHT.*

Questions 1-6.

DIRECTIONS: Questions 1 through 6 consist of sets of names and addresses. In each question, the name and address in Column II should be an exact copy of the name and address in Column I. If there is:
a mistake only in the name, mark your answer A,
a mistake only in the address, mark your answer B,
a mistake in both name and address, mark your answer C,
NO mistake in either name or address, mark your answer D.

SAMPLE QUESTION

COLUMN I	COLUMN II
Christina Magnusson 288 Greene Street New York, NY 10003	Christina Magnusson 288 Greene Street New York, NY 10013

Since there is a mistake only in the address (the zone number should be 10003 instead of 10013), the answer to the sample question is B.

	COLUMN I	COLUMN II	
1.	Ms. Joan Kelly 313 Franklin Ave. Brooklyn, NY 11202	Ms. Joan Kielly 318 Franklin Ave. Brooklyn, NY 11202	1.____
2.	Mrs. Eileen Engel 47-24 86 Road Queens, NY 11122	Mrs. Ellen Engel 47-24 86 Road Queens, NY 11122	2.____
3.	Marcia Michaels 213 E. 81 St. New York, NY 10012	Marcia Michaels 213 E. 81 St. New York, NY 10012	3.____
4.	Rev. Edward J. Smyth 1401 Brandeis Street San Francisco, CA 96201	Rev. Edward J. Smyth 1401 Brandies Street San Francisco, CA 96201	4.____
5.	Alicia Rodriguez 24-68 81 St. Elmhurst, NY 11122	Alicia Rodriguez 2468 81 St. Elmhurst, NY 11122	5.____
6.	Ernest Eisemann 21 Columbia St. New York, NY 10007	Ernest Eisermann 21 Columbia St. New York, NY 10007	6.____

Questions 7-11.

DIRECTIONS: Questions 7 through 11 each consist of five serial numbers which must be arranged according to the directions given below.

The serial numbers of dollar bills in Column I begin and end with a capital letter and have an eight-digit number in between. They are to be arranged as follows:

First: In alphabetical order according to the first letter
Second: When two or more serial numbers have the same first letter, in alphabetical order according to the last letter
Third: When two or more serial numbers have the same first and last letters, in numerical order, beginning with the lowest number

The serial numbers in Column I are numbered 1 through 5 in the order in which they are listed. In Column II, the numbers 1 through 5 are arranged in four different ways to show different arrangements of the corresponding serial numbers. Choose the answer in Column II in which the serial numbers are arranged according to the above rules.

SAMPLE QUESTION

COLUMN I	COLUMN II
1. E75044127B	A. 4, 1, 3, 2, 5
2. B96399104A	B. 4, 1, 2, 3, 5
3. B93939086A	C. 4, 3, 2, 5, 1
4. B47064465H	D. 3, 2, 5, 4, 1
5. B99040922A	

In the sample question, the four serial numbers starting with B should be put before the serial number starting with E. The serial numbers starting with B and ending with A should be put before the serial number starting with B and ending with H. The three serial numbers starting with B and ending with A should be listed in numerical order, beginning with the lowest number. The correct way to arrange the serial numbers, therefore, is:

3. B93939086A
2. B96399104A
5. B99040922A
4. B47064465H
1. E75044127B

Since the order of arrangement is 3, 2, 5, 4, 1, the answer to the sample question is D.

7. COLUMN I | COLUMN II | 7.____

1. S55126179E	A. 1, 5, 2, 3, 4	
2. R55136177Q	B. 3, 4, 1, 5, 2	
3. P55126177R	C. 3, 5, 2, 1, 4	
4. S55126178R	D. 4, 3, 1, 5, 2	
5. R55126180P		

8.
1. T64217813Q — A. 4, 1, 3, 2, 5 — 8.____
2. I64217817O — B. 2, 4, 3, 1, 5
3. T64217818O — C. 4, 1, 5, 2, 3
4. I64217811Q — D. 2, 3, 4, 1, 5
5. T64217816Q

9.
1. C83261824G — A. 2, 4, 1, 5,3 — 9.____
2. C78361833C — B. 4, 2, 1, 3, 5
3. G83261732G — C. 3, 1, 5, 2, 4
4. C88261823C — D. 2, 3, 5, 1, 4
5. G83261743C

10.
1. A11710107H — A. 2, 1, 4, 3, 5 — 10.____
2. H17110017A — B. 3, 1, 5, 2, 4
3. A11170707A — C. 3, 4, 1, 5, 2
4. Il17170171H — D. 3, 5, 1, 2, 4
5. A11710177A

11.
1. R26794821S — A. 3, 2,4, 1, 5 — 11.____
2. O26794821T — B. 3, 4, 2, 1, 5
3. M26794827Z — C. 4, 2, 1, 3, 5
4. Q26794821R — D. 5, 4, 1, 2, 3
5. S26794821P

Questions 12-16.

DIRECTIONS: Questions 12 through 16 each consist of three lines of code letters and numbers. The numbers on each line should correspond with the code letters on the same line in accordance with the table below.

Code Letters	Q	S	L	Y	M	0	U	N	W	Z
Corresponding Numbers	1	2	3	4	5	6	7	8	9	0

On some of the lines, an error exists in the coding. Compare the letters and numbers in each question carefully. If you find an error on:

only ONE of the lines in the question, mark your answer A,
any TWO lines in the question, mark your answer B,
all THREE lines in the question, mark your answer C,
NONE of the lines in the question, mark your answer D.

SAMPLE:

M O Q N W Z Q S - 56189012
Q W N M O L Y U - 19865347
L O N L M Y W N - 36835489

In the above sample, the first line is correct since each code letter, as listed, has the correct corresponding number. On the second line, an error exists because code letter M should have the nuriber 5 instead of the number 6. On the third line, an error exists - because the code letter W should have the number 9 instead of the nuriber 8. Since there are errors on two of the three lines, the correct answer is B.

12.	S M U W O L Q N	25796318	12.____
	U L S Q N M Z L	73218503	
	N M Y Q Z U S L	85410723	
13.	Y U W W M Y Q Z	47995410	13.____
	S O S O S Q S O	26262126	
	Z U N L W M Y W	07839549	
14.	Q U L S W Z Y N	17329045	14.____
	Z Y L Q W O Y W	04319639	
	QL U Y W Z S O	13749026	
15.	N L Q Z O Y U M	83106475	15.____
	S Q M U W Z O M	21579065	
	M M Y W M Z S Q	55498021	
16.	N Q L O W Z Z U	81319007	16.____
	S M Y L U N Z O	25347806	
	U W M S N Z O L	79528013	

Questions 17-24.

DIRECTIONS: Each of Questions 17 through 24 represents five cards to be filed, numbered 1 through 5 in Column I. Each card is made up of the employee's name, the date of a work assignment, and the work assignment code number shown in parentheses. The cards are to be filed according to the following rules:

First: File in alphabetical order
Second: When two or more cards have the same employee's name, file according to the assignment date beginning with the earliest date
Third: When two or more cards have the same employee's name and the same date, file according to the work assignment number beginning with the lowest number.

Column II shows the cards arranged in four different orders. Pick the answer (A, B, C, or D) in Column II which shows the cards arranged correctly according to the above filing rules.

SAMPLE QUESTION

COLUMN I				COLUMN II
1.	Cluney	4/8/72	(486503)	A. 2, 3, 4, 1, 5
2.	Roster	5/10/71	(246611)	B. 2, 5, 1, 3, 4
3.	Altool	10/15/72	(711433)	C. 3, 2, 1, 4, 5
4.	Cluney	2/18/72	(527610)	D. 3, 5, 1, 4, 2
5.	Cluney	4/8/72	(486500)	

The correct way to file the cards is:

3.	Altool	10/15/72	(711433)
5.	Cluney	4/8/72	(486500)
1.	Cluney	4/8/72	(486503)
4.	Cluney	12/18/72	(527610)
2.	Roster	5/10/71	(246611)

The correct filing order is shown by the numbers in front of each name (3, 5, 1, 4, 2). The answer to the sample question is the letter in Column II in front of the numbers 3, 5, 1, 4, 2. This answer is D.

Now answer Questions 17 through 24 according to these rules.

17. COLUMN I / COLUMN II — 17.____

				COLUMN II
1.	Kohls	4/2/72	(125677)	A. 1, 2, 3, 4, 5
2.	Keller	3/21/72	(129698)	B. 3, 2, 1, 4, 5
3.	Jackson	4/10/72	(213541)	C. 3, 1, 2, 4, 5
4.	Richards	1/9/73	(347236)	D. 5, 2, 1, 3, 4
5.	Richmond	12/11/71	(379321)	

18. 18.____

1.	Burroughs	5/27/72	(237896)	A. 1, 4, 3, 2, 5
2.	Charlson	1/16/72	(114537)	B. 4, 1, 5, 3, 2
3.	Carlsen	12/2/72	(114377)	C. 1, 4, 3, 5, 2
4.	Burton	5/1/72	(227096)	D. 4, 1, 3, 5, 2
5.	Charlson	12/2/72	(114357)	

19. 19.____

1.	Ungerer	11/11/72	(537924)	A. 1, 5, 3, 2, 4
2.	Winters	11/10/72	(657834)	B. 5, 1, 3, 4, 2
3.	Ventura	12/1/72	(698694)	C. 3, 5, 1, 2, 4
4.	winters	10/11/72	(675654)	D. 1, 5, 3, 4, 2
5.	Ungaro	11/10/72	(684325)	

20. 20.____

1.	Norton	3/12/73	(071605)	A. 1, 4, 2, 4, 5
2.	Morris	2/26/73	(068931)	B. 3, 5, 2, 4, 1
3.	Morse	5/12/73	(142358)	C. 2, 4, 3, 5, 1
4.	Morris	2/26/73	(068391)	D. 4, 2, 5, 3, 1
5.	Morse	2/26/73	(068391)	

21. 21.____

1.	Eger	4/19/72	(874129)	A. 3, 4, 1, 2, 5
2.	Eihler	5/19/73	(875329)	B. 1, 4, 5, 2, 3
3.	Ehrlich	11/19/72	(874839)	C. 4, 1, 3, 2, 5
4.	Eger	4/19/72	(876129)	D. 1, 4, 3, 5, 2
5.	Eihler	5/19/72	(874239)	

	COLUMN I			COLUMN II	
22.	1. Johnson	12/21/72	(786814)	A. 2, 4, 3, 5, 1	22.____
	2. Johns	12/21/73	(801024)	B. 4, 2, 5, 3, 1	
	3. Johnson	12/12/73	(762814)	C. 4, 5, 3, 1, 2	
	4. Jackson	12/12/73	(862934)	D. 5, 3, 1, 2, 4	
	5. Johnson	12/12/73	(762184)		
23.	1. Fuller	7/12/72	(598310)	A. 2, 1, 5, 4, 3	23.____
	2. Fuller	7/2/72	(598301)	B. 1, 2, 4, 5, 3	
	3. Fuller	7/22/72	(598410)	C. 1, 4, 5, 2, 3	
	4. Fuller	7/17/73	(598710)	D. 2, 1, 3, 5, 4	
	5. Fuller	7/17/73	(598701)		
24.	1. Perrine	10/27/69	(637096)	A. 3, 4, 5, 1, 2	24.____
	2. Perrone	11/14/72	(767609)	B. 3, 2, 5, 4, 1	
	3. Perrault	10/15/68	(629706)	C. 5, 3, 1, 4, 2	
	4. Perrine	10/17/72	(373656)	D. 4, 5, 1, 2, 3	
	5. Perine	10/17/71	(376356)		

Questions 25-30.

DIRECTIONS: Questions 25 through 30 are to be answered on the basis of the information given in the passage below.

It is often said that no system will work if the people who carry it out do not want it to work. In too many cases, a departmental reorganization that seemed technically sound and economically practical has proved to be a failure because the planners neglected to take the human factor into account. The truth is that employees are likely to feel threatened when they learn that a major change is in the wind. It does not matter whether or not the change actually poses a threat to an employee; the fact that he believes it does or fears it might is enough to make him feel insecure. Among the dangers he fears, the foremost is the possibility that his job may cease to exist and that he may be laid off or shunted into a less skilled position at lower pay. Even if he knows that his own job category is secure, however, he is likely to fear losing some of the important intangible advantages of his present position for instance, he may fear that he will be separated from his present companions and thrust in with a group of strangers, or that he will find himself in a lower position on the organizational ladder if a new position is created above his.

It is important that management recognize these natural fears and take them into account in planning any kind of major change. While there is no cut-and-dried formula for preventing employee resistance, there are several steps that can be taken to reduce employees' fears and gain their cooperation. First, unwarranted fears can be dispelled if employees are kept informed of the planning from the start and if they know exactly what to expect. Next, assurance on matters such as retraining, transfers, and placement help should be given as soon as it is clear what direction the reorganization will take. Finally, employees' participation in the planning should be actively sought. There is a great psychological difference between feeling that a change is being forced upon one from the outside, and feeling that one is an insider who is helping to bring about a change.

25. According to the above passage, employees who are not in real danger of losing their jobs because of a proposed reorganization 25.____

A. will be eager to assist in the reorganization
B. will pay little attention to the reorganization
C. should not be taken into account in planning the reorganization
D. are nonetheless likely to feel threatened by the reorganization

26. The passage mentions the *intangible advantages* of a position. Which of the following BEST describes the kind of advantages alluded to in the passage? 26.____

A. Benefits such as paid holidays and vacations
B. Satisfaction of human needs for things like friendship and status
C. Qualities such as leadership and responsibility
D. A work environment that meets satisfactory standards of health and safety

27. According to the passage, an employee's fear that a reorganization may separate him from his present companions is a(n) 27.____

A. childish and immature reaction to change
B. unrealistic feeling, since this is not going to happen
C. possible reaction that the planners should be aware of
D. incentive to employees to participate in the planning

28. On the basis of the above passage, it would be *desirable,* when planning a departmental reorganization, to 28.____

A. be governed by employee feelings and attitudes
B. give some employees lower positions
C. keep employees informed
D. lay off those who are less skilled

29. What does the passage say can be done to help gain employees' cooperation in a reorganization? 29.____

A. Making sure that the change is technically sound, that it is economically practical, and that the human factor is taken into account
B. Keeping employees fully informed, offering help in fitting them into new positions, and seeking their participation in the planning
C. Assuring employees that they will not be laid off, that they will not be reassigned to a group of strangers, and that no new positions will be created on the organization ladder
D. Reducing employees' fears, arranging a retraining program, and providing for transfers

30. Which of the following suggested titles would be MOST appropriate for this passage? 30.____

A. PLANNING A DEPARTMENTAL REORGANIZATION
B. WHY EMPLOYEES ARE AFRAID
C. LOOKING AHEAD TO THE FUTURE
D. PLANNING FOR CHANGE: THE HUMAN FACTOR

KEY (CORRECT ANSWERS)

1. C
2. A
3. D
4. B
5. C

6. A
7. C
8. B
9. A
10. D

11. A
12. D
13. D
14. B
15. A

16. C
17. B
18. A
19. B
20. D

21. D
22. B
23. D
24. C
25. D

26. B
27. C
28. C
29. B
30. D

EXAMINATION SECTION
TEST 1

DIRECTIONS: Each question or incomplete statement is followed by several suggested answers or completions. Select the one that BEST answers the question or completes the statement. *PRINT THE LETTER OF THE CORRECT ANSWER IN THE SPACE AT THE RIGHT.*

1. In almost every organization, there is a nucleus of highly important functions commonly designated as *management*. Which of the following statements BEST characterizes *management?* 1.____

   A. Getting things done through others
   B. The highest level of intelligence in any organization
   C. The process whereby democratic and participative activities are maximized
   D. The *first among equals*

2. Strategies in problem-solving are important to anyone aspiring to advancement in the field of administration. Which of the following is BEST classified as the first step in the process of problem-solving? 2.____

   A. Collection and organization of data
   B. The formulation of a plan
   C. The definition of the problem
   D. The development of a method and methodology

3. One of the objectives of preparing a budget is to 3.____

   A. create optimistic goals which each department can attempt to meet
   B. create an overall company goal by combining the budgets of the various departments
   C. be able to compare planned expenditures against actual expenditures
   D. be able to identify accounting errors

4. The rise in demand for *systems* personnel in industrial and governmental organizations over the past five years has been extraordinary. 4.____
   In which of the following areas would a *systems* specialist assigned to an agency be LEAST likely to be of assistance?

   A. Developing, recommending, and establishing an effective cost and inventory system
   B. Development and maintenance of training manuals
   C. Reviewing existing work procedures and recommending improvements
   D. Development of aptitude tests for new employees

5. Management experts have come to the conclusion that the traditional forms of motivation used in industry and government, which emphasize authority over and economic rewards for the employee, are no longer appropriate. 5.____
   To which of the following factors do such experts attribute the GREATEST importance in producing this change?

   A. The desire of employees to satisfy material needs has become greater and more complex.

B. The desire for social satisfaction has become the most important aspect of the job for the average worker.
C. With greater standardization of work processes, there has been an increase in the willingness of workers to accept discipline.
D. In general, employee organizations have made it more difficult for management to fire an employee.

6. In preparing a budget, it is usually considered advisable to start the initial phases of preparation at the operational level of management. 6.____
Of the following, the justification that management experts usually advance as MOST reasonable for this practice is that operating managers, as a consequence of their involvement, will

A. develop a background in finance or accounting
B. have an understanding of the organizational structure
C. tend to feel responsible for carrying out budget objectives
D. have the ability to see the overall financial picture

7. An administrative officer has been asked by his superior to write a concise, factual report with objective conclusions and recommendations based on facts assembled by other researchers. 7.____
Of the following factors, the administrative officer should give LEAST consideration to

A. the educational level of the person or persons for whom the report is being prepared
B. the use to be made of the report
C. the complexity of the problem
D. his own feelings about the importance of the problem

8. In an agency, upon which of the following is a supervisor's effectiveness MOST likely to depend? 8.____
The

A. degree to which a supervisor allows subordinates to participate in the decision-making process and the setting of objectives
B. degree to which a supervisor's style meets management's objectives and subordinates' needs
C. strength and forcefulness of the supervisor in pursuing his objectives
D. expertise and knowledge the supervisor has about the specific work to be done

9. For authority to be effective, which of the following is the MOST basic requirement? 9.____
Authority must be

A. absolute B. formalized C. accepted D. delegated

10. Management no longer abhors the idea of employees taking daily work breaks, but prefers to schedule such breaks rather than to allot to each employee a standard amount of free time to be taken off during the day as he wishes. Which of the following BEST expresses the reason management theorists give for the practice of scheduling such breaks? 10.____

A. Many jobs fall into natural work units which are scheduled, and the natural time to take a break is at the end of the unit.

B. Taking a scheduled break permits socialization and a feeling of accomplishment.
C. Managers have concluded that scheduling rest periods seems to reduce the incidence of unscheduled ones.
D. Many office workers who really need such breaks are hesitant about taking them unless they are scheduled.

11. The computer represents one of the major developments of modern technology. It is widely used in both scientific and managerial activities because of its many advantages. Which of the following is NOT an advantage gained by management in the use of the computer? 11.____
A computer

A. provides the manager with a greatly enlarged memory so that he can easily be provided with data for decision making
B. relieves the manager of basic decision-making responsibility, thereby giving him more time for directing and controlling
C. performs routine, repetitive calculations with greater precision and reliability than employees
D. provides a capacity for rapid simulations of alternative solutions to problem solving

12. A supervisor of a unit in a division is usually responsible for all of the following EXCEPT 12.____

A. the conduct of subordinates in the achievement of division objectives
B. maintaining quality standards in the unit
C. the protection and care of materials and equipment in the unit
D. performing the most detailed tasks in the unit himself

13. You have been assigned to teach a new employee the functions and procedures of your office. 13.____
In your introductory talk, which of the following approaches is PREFERABLE?

A. Advise the new employee of the employee benefits and services available to him, over and above his salary.
B. Discuss honestly the negative aspects of departmental procedures and indicate methods available to overcome them.
C. Give the new employee an understanding of the general purpose of office procedures and functions and of their relevance to departmental objectives.
D. Give a basic and detailed explanation of the operations of your office, covering all functions and procedures.

14. It is your responsibility to assign work to several clerks under your supervision. One of the clerks indignantly refuses to accept an assignment and asks to be given something else. He has not yet indicated why he does not want the assignment, but is sitting there glaring at you, awaiting your reaction. 14.____
Of the following, which is the FIRST action you should take?

A. Ask the employee into your office in order to reprimand him and tell him emphatically that he must accept the assignment.
B. Talk to the employee privately in an effort to find the reason for his indignation and refusal, and then base your action upon your findings.

C. Let the matter drop for a day or two to allow the employee to cool off before you insist that he accept the assignment.
D. Inform the employee quietly and calmly that as his supervisor you have selected him for this assignment and that you fully expect him to accept it.

15. Administrative officers are expected to be able to handle duties delegated to them by their supervisors and to be able, as they advance in status, to delegate tasks to assistants. 15.____
When considering whether to delegate tasks to a subordinate, which of the following questions should be LEAST important to an administrative officer?
In the delegated tasks,

A. how significant are the decisions to be made, and how much consultation will be involved?
B. to what extent is uniformity and close coordination of activity required?
C. to what extent must speedy-on-the-spot decisions be made?
D. to what extent will delegation relieve the administrative officer of his burden of responsibility?

16. A functional forms file is a collection of forms which are grouped by 16.____

A. purpose B. department C. title D. subject

17. All of the following are reasons to consult a records retention schedule except one. 17.____
Which one is that?
To determine

A. whether something should be filed
B. how long something should stay in file
C. who should be assigned to filing
D. when something on file should be destroyed

18. Listed below are four of the steps in the process of preparing correspondence for filing. 18.____
If they were to be put in logical sequence, the SECOND step would be

A. preparing cross-reference sheets or cards
B. coding the correspondence using a classification system
C. sorting the correspondence in the order to be filed
D. checking for follow-up action required and preparing a follow-up slip

19. New material added to a file folder should USUALLY be inserted 19.____

A. in the order of importance (the most important in front)
B. in the order of importance (the most important in back)
C. chronologically (most recent in front)
D. chronologically (most recent in back)

20. An individual is looking for a name in the white pages of a telephone directory. 20.____
Which of the following BEST describes the system of filing found there?
A(n)______ file

A. alphabetic B. sequential
C. locator D. index

21. The MAIN purpose of a tickler file is to 21.____

A. help prevent overlooking matters that require future attention
B. check on adequacy of past performance
C. pinpoint responsibility for recurring daily tasks
D. reduce the volume of material kept in general files

22. Which of the following BEST describes the process of reconciling a bank statement? 22.____

A. Analyzing the nature of the expenditures made by the office during the preceding month
B. Comparing the statement of the bank with the banking records maintained in the office
C. Determining the liquidity position by reading the bank statement carefully
D. Checking the service charges noted on the bank statement

23. From the viewpoint of preserving agency or institutional funds, which of the following is the LEAST acceptable method for making a payment? 23.____
A check made out to

A. cash
B. a company
C. an individual
D. a partnership

24. In general, the CHIEF economy of using multicopy forms is in 24.____

A. the paper on which the form is printed
B. printing the form
C. employee time
D. carbon paper

25. Suppose your supervisor has asked you to develop a form to record certain information needed. 25.____
The FIRST thing you should do is to

A. determine the type of data that will be recorded repeatedly so that it can be pre-printed
B. study the relationship of the form to the job to be accomplished so that the form can be planned
C. determine the information that will be recorded in the same place on each copy of the form so that it can be used as a check
D. find out who will be responsible for supplying the information so that space can be provided for their signatures

26. An administrative officer in charge of a small fund for buying office supplies has just written a check to Charles Laird, a supplier, and has sent the check by messenger to him. A half-hour later, the messenger telephones the administrative officer. He has lost the check. 26.____
Which of the following is the MOST important action for the administrative officer to take under these circumstances?

A. Ask the messenger to return and write a report describing the loss of the check.
B. Make a note on the performance record of the messenger who lost the check.
C. Take the necessary steps to have payment stopped on the check.
D. Refrain from doing anyting since the check may be found shortly.

27. A petty cash fund is set up PRIMARILY to 27.____

A. take care of small investments that must be made from time to time
B. take care of small expenses that arise from time to time
C. provide a fund to be used as the office wants to use it with little need to maintain records
D. take care of expenses that develop during emergencies, such as machine breakdowns and fires

28. Of the following, which is usually the MOST important guideline in writing business letters? 28.____
A letter should be

A. neat
B. written in a formalized style
C. written in clear language intelligible to the reader
D. written in the past tense

29. Suppose you are asked to edit a policy statement. You note that personal pronouns like *you, we,* and *I* are used freely. 29.____
Which of the following statements BEST applies to this use of personal pronouns?
It

A. is proper usage because written business language should not be different from carefully spoken business language
B. requires correction because it is ungrammatical
C. is proper because it is clearer and has a warmer tone
D. requires correction because policies should be expressed in an impersonal manner

30. Good business letters are coherent. 30.____
To be coherent means to

A. keep only one unifying idea in the message
B. present the total message
C. use simple, direct words for the message
D. tie together the various ideas in the message

31. Proper division of a letter into paragraphs requires that the writer of business letters should, as much as possible, be sure that 31.____

A. each paragraph is short
B. each paragraph develops discussion of just one topic
C. each paragraph repeats the theme of the total message
D. there are at least two paragraphs for every message

32. An editor is given a letter with this initial paragraph: 32.____
We have received your letter, which we read with interest, and we are happy to respond to your question. In fact, we talked with several people in our office to get ideas to send to you.
Which of the following is it MOST reasonable for the editor to conclude?
The paragraph is

A. concise
B. communicating something of value
C. unnecessary
D. coherent

33. As soon as you pick up the phone, a very angry caller begins immediately to complain about city agencies and *red tape*. He says that he has been shifted to two or three different offices. It turns out that he is seeking information which is not immediately available to you. You believe you know, however, where it can be found. Which of the following actions is the BEST one for you to take? 33.____

A. To eliminate all confusion, suggest that the caller write the mayor stating explicitly what he wants.
B. Apologize by telling the caller how busy city agencies now are, but also tell him directly that you do not have the information he needs.
C. Ask for the caller's telephone number and assure him you will call back after you have checked further.
D. Give the caller the name and telephone number of the person who might be able to help, but explain that you are not positive he will get results.

34. Suppose that one of your duties is to dictate responses to routine requests from the public for information. A letter writer asks for information which, as expressed in a one-sentence, explicit agency rule, cannot be given out to the public.
Of the following ways of answering the letter, which is the MOST efficient? 34.____

A. Quote verbatim that section of the agency rules which prohibits giving this information to the public.
B. Without quoting the rule, explain why you cannot accede to the request and suggest alternative sources.
C. Describe how carefully the request was considered before classifying it as subject to the rule forbidding the issuance of such information.
D. Acknowledge receipt of the letter and advise that the requested information is not released to the public.

35. Suppose you assist in supervising a staff which has rather high morale, and your own supervisor asks you to poll the staff to find out who will be able to work overtime this particular evening to help complete emergency work.
Which of the following approaches would be MOST likely to win their cooperation while maintaining their morale? 35.____

A. Tell them that the better assignments will be given only to those who work overtime.
B. Tell them that occasional overtime is a job requirement .
C. Assure them they'll be doing you a personal favor.
D. Let them know clearly why the overtime is needed.

36. Suppose that you have been asked to write and to prepare for reproduction new departmental vacation leave regulations.
After you have written the new regulations, all of which fit on one page, which one of the following would be the BEST method of reproducing 1000 copies? 36.____

A. An outside private printer, because you can best maintain confidentiality using this technique
B. Xeroxing, because the copies will have the best possible appearance

C. Typing copies, because you will be certain that there are the fewest possible errors
D. Including it in the next company newsletter

37. Administration is the center, but not necessarily the source, of all ideas for procedural improvement. 37.____
The MOST significant implication that this principle bears for the administrative officer is that

A. before procedural improvements are introduced, they should be approved by a majority of the staff
B. it is the unique function of the administrative officer to derive and introduce procedural improvements
C. the administrative officer should derive ideas and suggestions for procedural improvement from all possible sources, introducing any that promise to be effective
D. the administrative officer should view employee grievances as the chief source of procedural improvements

38. Your bureau is assigned an important task. 38.____
Of the following, the function that you, as an administrative officer, can LEAST reasonably be expected to perform under these circumstances is

A. division of the large job into individual tasks
B. establishment of *production lines* within the bureau
C. performance personally of a substantial share of all the work
D. check-up to see that the work has been well done

39. Suppose that you have broken a complex job into its smaller components before making assignments to the employees under your jurisdiction. 39.____
Of the following, the LEAST advisable procedure to follow from that point is to

A. give each employee a picture of the importance of his work for the success of the total job
B. establish a definite line of work flow and responsibility
C. post a written memorandum of the best method for performing each job
D. teach a number of alternative methods for doing each job

40. As an administrative officer, you are requested to draw up an organization chart of the whole department. 40.____
Of the following, the MOST important characteristic of such a chart is that it will

A. include all peculiarities and details of the organization which distinguish it from any other
B. be a schematic representation of purely administrative functions within the department
C. present a modification of the actual departmental organization in the light of principles of scientific management
D. present an accurate picture of the lines of authority and responsibility

KEY (CORRECT ANSWERS)

1.	A	11.	B	21.	A	31.	B
2.	C	12.	D	22.	B	32.	C
3.	C	13.	C	23.	A	33.	C
4.	D	14.	B	24.	C	34.	A
5.	D	15.	D	25.	B	35.	D
6.	C	16.	A	26.	C	36.	B
7.	D	17.	C	27.	B	37.	C
8.	B	18.	A	28.	C	38.	C
9.	C	19.	C	29.	D	39.	D
10.	C	20.	A	30.	D	40.	D

TEST 2

DIRECTIONS: Each question or incomplete statement is followed by several suggested answers or completions. Select the one that BEST answers the question or completes the statement. *PRINT THE LETTER OF THE CORRECT ANSWER IN THE SPACE AT THE RIGHT.*

Questions 1-10.

DIRECTIONS: In each of Questions 1 through 10, a pair of related words written in capital letters is followed by four other pairs of words. For each question, select the pair of words which MOST closely expresses a relationship similar to that of the pair in capital letters.

SAMPLE QUESTION:

BOAT - DOCK
A. airplane - hangar
B. rain - snow
C. cloth - cotton
D. hunger - food

Choice A is the answer to this sample question since, of the choices given, the relationship between airplane and hangar is most similar to the relationship between boat and dock.

1. AUTOMOBILE - FACTORY 1.____
   A. tea - lemon
   B. wheel - engine
   C. pot - flower
   D. paper - mill

2. GIRDER - BRIDGE 2.____
   A. petal - flower
   B. street - sidewalk
   C. meat - vegetable
   D. sun - storm

3. RADIUS - CIRCLE 3.____
   A. brick - building
   B. tie - tracks
   C. spoke - wheel
   D. axle - tire

4. DISEASE - RESEARCH 4.____
   A. death - poverty
   B. speech - audience
   C. problem - conference
   D. invalid - justice

5. CONCLUSION - INTRODUCTION 5.____
   A. commencement - beginning
   B. housing - motor
   C. caboose - engine
   D. train - cabin

6. SOCIETY - LAW 6.____
   A. baseball - rules
   B. jury - law
   C. cell - prisoner
   D. sentence - jury

7. PLAN - ACCOMPLISHMENT 7.____
   A. deed - fact
   B. method - success
   C. graph - chart
   D. rules - manual

8. ORDER - GOVERNMENT 8.____

A. chaos - administration
B. confusion - pandemonium
C. rule - stability
D. despair - hope

9. TYRANNY - FREEDOM 9.____

A. despot - mob
B. wealth - poverty
C. nobility - commoners
D. dictatorship - democracy

10. FAX - LETTER 10.____

A. hare - tortoise
B. lie - truth
C. number - word
D. report - research

Questions 11-16.

DIRECTIONS: Answer Questions 11 through 16 SOLELY on the basis of the information given in the passage below.

Inherent in all organized endeavors is the need to resolve the individual differences involved in conflict. Conflict may be either a positive or negative factor, since it may lead to creativity, innovation, and progress, on the one hand, or it may result, on the other hand, in a deterioration or even destruction of the organization. Thus, some forms of conflict are desirable, whereas others are undesirable and ethically wrong.

There are three management strategies which deal with interpersonal conflict. In the "divide-and-rule strategy", management attempts to maintain control by limiting the conflict to those directly involved and preventing their disagreement from spreading to the larger group. The "suppression-of-differences strategy" entails ignoring conflicts or pretending they are irrelevant. In the "working-through-differences strategy", management actively attempts to solve or resolve intergroup or interpersonal conflicts. Of the three strategies, only the last directly attacks and has the potential for eliminating the causes of conflict. An essential part of this strategy, however, is its employment by a committed and relatively mature management team.

11. According to the above passage, the *divide-and-rule strategy* for dealing with conflict is the attempt to 11.____

A. involve other people in the conflict
B. restrict the conflict to those participating in it
C. divide the conflict into positive and negative factors
D. divide the conflict into a number of smaller ones

12. The word *conflict* is used in relation to both positive and negative factors in this passage. Which one of the following words is MOST likely to describe the activity which the word *conflict*, in the sense of the passage, implies? 12.____

A. Competition
B. Cooperation
C. Confusion
D. Aggression

13. According to the above passage, which one of the following characteristics is shared by both the *suppression-of-differences strategy* and the *divide-and-rule strategy?* 13.____

A. Pretending that conflicts are irrelevant
B. Preventing conflicts from spreading to the group situation

C. Failure to directly attack the causes of conflict
D. Actively attempting to resolve interpersonal conflict

14. According to the above passage, the successful resolution of interpersonal conflict requires 14.____

A. allowing the group to mediate conflicts between two individuals
B. division of the conflict into positive and negative factors
C. involvement of a committed, mature management team
D. ignoring minor conflicts until they threaten the organization

15. Which can be MOST reasonably inferred from the above passage? 15.____
A conflict between two individuals is LEAST likely to continue when management uses

A. the *working-through-differences strategy*
B. the *suppression-of-differences strategy*
C. the *divide-and-rule strategy*
D. a combination of all three strategies

16. According to the above passage, a desirable result of conflict in an organization is when conflict 16.____

A. exposes production problems in the organization
B. can be easily ignored by management
C. results in advancement of more efficient managers
D. leads to development of new methods

Questions 17-23.

DIRECTIONS: Answer Questions 17 through 23 SOLELY on the basis of the information given in the passage below.

Modern management places great emphasis on the concept of communication. The communication process consists of the steps through which an idea or concept passes from its inception by one person, the sender, until it is acted upon by another person, the receiver. Through an understanding of these steps and some of the possible barriers that may occur, more effective communication may be achieved. The first step in the communication process is ideation by the sender. This is the formation of the intended content of the message he wants to transmit. In the next step, encoding, the sender organizes his ideas into a series of symbols designed to communicate his message to his intended receiver. He selects suitable words or phrases that can be understood by the receiver, and he also selects the appropriate media to be used-for example, memorandum, conference, etc. The third step is transmission of the encoded message through selected channels in the organizational structure. In the fourth step, the receiver enters the process by tuning in to receive the message. If the receiver does not function, however, the message is lost. For example, if the message is oral, the receiver must be a good listener. The fifth step is decoding of the message by the receiver, as for example, by changing words into ideas. At this step, the decoded message may not be the same idea that the sender originally encoded because the sender and receiver have different perceptions regarding the meaning of certain words.

Finally, the receiver acts or responds. He may file the information, ask for more information, or take other action. There can be no assurance, however, that communication has taken place unless there is some type of feedback to the sender in the form of an acknowledgement that the message was received.

17. According to the above passage, *ideation* is the process by which the 17.____

A. sender develops the intended content of the message
B. sender organizes his ideas into a series of symbols
C. receiver tunes in to receive the message
D. receiver decodes the message

18. In the last sentence of the passage, the word *feedback* refers to the process by which the sender is assured that the 18.____

A. receiver filed the information
B. receiver's perception is the same as his own
C. message was received
D. message was properly interpreted

19. Which one of the following BEST shows the order of the steps in the communication process as described in the passage? 19.____

A. 1- ideation 2- encoding
3- decoding 4- transmission
5- receiving 6- action
7- feedback to the sender

B. 1- ideation 2- encoding
3- transmission 4- decoding
5- receiving 6- action
7- feedback to the sender

C. 1- ideation 2- decoding
3- transmission 4- receiving
5- encoding 6- action
7- feedback to the sender

D. 1- ideation 2- encoding
3- transmission 4- receiving
5- decoding 6- action
7- feedback to the sender

20. Which one of the following BEST expresses the main theme of the passage? 20.____

A. Different individuals have the same perceptions regarding the meaning of words.
B. An understanding of the steps in the communication process may achieve better communication.
C. Receivers play a passive role in the communication process.
D. Senders should not communicate with receivers who transmit feedback.

21. The above passage implies that a receiver does NOT function properly when he 21.____

A. transmits feedback
B. files the information
C. is a poor listener
D. asks for more information

22. Which of the following, according to the above passage, is included in the SECOND step of the communication process? 22.____

A. Selecting the appropriate media to be used in transmission
B. Formulation of the intended content of the message
C. Using appropriate media to respond to the receiver's feedback
D. Transmitting the message through selected channels in the organization

23. The above passage implies that the *decoding process* is MOST NEARLY the reverse of the ______ process. 23.____

A. transmission B. receiving
C. feedback D. encoding

Questions 24-27.

DIRECTIONS: Answer Questions 24 through 27 SOLELY on the basis of the information given in the paragraph below.

A personnel researcher has at his disposal various approaches for obtaining information, analyzing it, and arriving at conclusions that have value in predicting and affecting the behavior of people at work. The type of method to be used depends on such factors as the nature of the research problem, the available data, and the attitudes of those people being studied to the various kinds of approaches. While the experimental approach, with its use of control groups, is the most refined type of study, there are others that are often found useful in personnel research. Surveys, in which the researcher obtains facts on a problem from a variety of sources, are employed in research on wages, fringe benefits, and labor relations. Historical studies are used to trace the development of problems in order to understand them better and to isolate possible causative factors. Case studies are generally developed to explore all the details of a particular problem that is representative of other similar problems. A researcher chooses the most appropriate form of study for the problem he is investigating. He should recognize, however, that the experimental method, commonly referred to as the scientific method, if used validly and reliably, gives the most conclusive results.

24. The above statement discusses several approaches used to obtain information on particular problems. 24.____
Which of the following may be MOST reasonably concluded from the paragraph?
A(n)

A. historical study cannot determine causative factors
B. survey is often used in research on fringe benefits
C. case study is usually used to explore a problem that is unique and unrelated to other problems
D. experimental study is used when the scientific approach to a problem fails

25. According to the above paragraph, all of the following are factors that may determine the type of approach a researcher uses EXCEPT 25.____

A. the attitudes of people toward being used in control groups
B. the number of available sources
C. his desire to isolate possible causative factors
D. the degree of accuracy he requires

26. The words *scientific method*, used in the last sentence of the paragraph, refer to a type of study which, according to the paragraph, 26.____

   A. uses a variety of sources
   B. traces the development of problems
   C. uses control groups
   D. analyzes the details of a representative problem

27. Which of the following can be MOST reasonably concluded from the above paragraph? In obtaining and analyzing information on a particular problem, a researcher employs the method which is the 27.____

   A. most accurate
   B. most suitable
   C. least expensive
   D. least time-consuming

Questions 28-31.

DIRECTIONS: The graph below indicates at 5-year intervals the number of citations issued for various offenses from the year 1990 to the year 2010. Answer Questions 28 through 31 according to the information given in this graph.

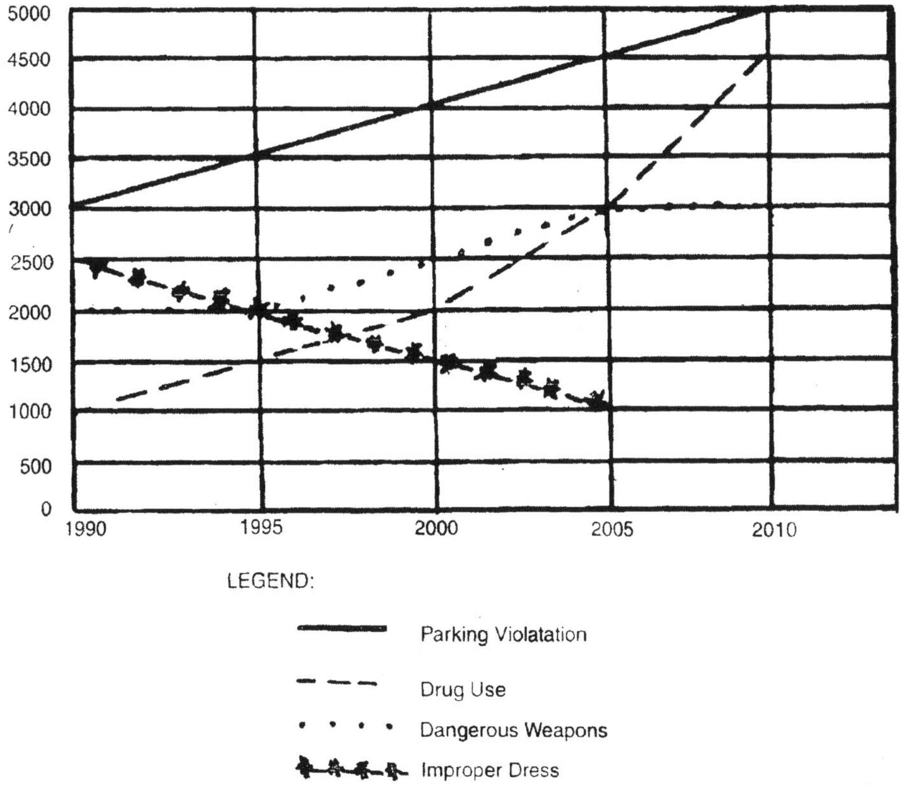

28. Over the 20-year period, which offense shows an AVERAGE rate of increase of more than 150 citations per year? 28.____

   A. Parking Violations
   B. Dangerous Weapons
   C. Drug Use
   D. None of the above

29. Over the 20-year period, which offense shows a CONSTANT rate of increase or decrease? 29.____

A. Parking Violations
B. Drug Use
C. Dangerous Weapons
D. Improper Dress

30. Which offense shows a TOTAL INCREASE OR DECREASE of 50% for the full 20-year period? 30.____

A. Parking Violations
B. Drug Use
C. Dangerous Weapons
D. Improper Dress

31. The percentage increase in total citations issued from 1995 to 2000 is MOST NEARLY 31.____

A. 7%
B. 11%
C. 21%
D. 41%

Questions 32-35.

DIRECTIONS: The chart below shows the annual average number of administrative actions completed for the four divisions of a bureau. Assume that the figures remain stable from year to year.

Answer Questions 32 through 35 SOLELY on the basis of information given in the chart.

	DIVISIONS				
Administrative Actions	W	X	Y	Z	Totals
Telephone Inquiries Answered	8,000	6,800	7,500	4,800	27,100
Interviews Conducted	500	630	550	500	2,180
Applications Processed	15,000	18,000	14,500	9,500	57,000
Letters Typed	2,500	4,400	4,350	3,250	14,500
Reports Completed	200	250	100	50	600
Totals	26,200	30,080	27,000	18,100	101,380

32. In which division is the number of Applications Processed the GREATEST percentage of the total Administrative Actions for that division? 32.____

A. W
B. X
C. Y
D. Z

33. The bureau chief is considering a plan that would consolidate the typing of letters in a separate unit. This unit would be responsible for the typing of letters for all divisions in which the number of letters typed exceeds 15% of the total number of Administrative Actions. Under this plan, which of the following divisions would CONTINUE to type its own letters? 33.____

A. W and X
B. W, X, and Y
C. X and Y
D. X and Z

34. The setting up of a central information service that would be capable of answering 25% of the whole bureau's telephone inquiries is under consideration. Under such a plan, the divisions would gain for other activities that time previously spent on telephone inquiries. Approximately how much total time would such a service gain for all four divisions if it requires 5 minutes to answer the average telephone inquiry? ______ hours. 34.____

A. 500 B. 515 C. 565 D. 585

35. Assume that the rate of production shown in the table can be projected as accurate for the coming year and that monthly output is constant for each type of administrative action within a division. Division Y is scheduled to work exclusively on a 4-month long special project during that year. During the period of the project, Division Y's regular workload will be divided evenly among the remaining divisions. 35.____
Using the figures in the table, what would be MOST NEARLY the percentage increase in the total Administrative Actions completed by Division Z for the year?

A. 8% B. 16% C. 25% D. 50%

36. You have conducted a traffic survey at 10 two-lane bridges and find the traffic between 4:30 and 5:30 P.M. averages 665 cars per bridge that hour. You can't find the tabulation sheet for Bridge #7, but you know that 6066 cars were counted at the other 9 bridges. Determine from this how many must have been counted at Bridge #7. 36.____

A. 584 B. 674 C. 665 D. 607

37. You pay temporary help $11.20 per hour and regular employees $12.00 per hour. Your workload is temporarily heavy, so you need 20 hours of extra regular employees' time to catch up. If you do this on overtime, you must pay time-and-a-half. If you use temporary help, it takes 25% more time to do the job. 37.____
What is the difference in cost between the two alternatives?

A. $20 more for temporary
B. $40 more for temporary
C. $80 more for regular
D. $136 more for regular

38. An experienced clerk can process the mailing of annual forms in 9 days. A new clerk takes 14 days to process them. 38.____
If they work together, how many days MOST NEARLY will it take to do the processing?

A. $4\frac{1}{2}$ B. $5\frac{1}{2}$ C. $6\frac{1}{2}$ D. 7

39. A certain administrative aide is usually able to successfully handle 27% of all telephone inquiries without assistance. In a particular month, he receives 1200 inquiries and handles 340 of them successfully on his own. How many more inquiries has he handled successfully in that month than would have been expected of him based on his usual rate? 39.____

A. 10 B. 16 C. 24 D. 44

40. Suppose that on a scaled drawing of an office building floor, 1/2 inch represents three feet of actual floor dimensions. 40.____
A floor which is, in fact, 75 feet wide and 132 feet long has which of the following dimensions on this scaled drawing? ______ inches wide and ______ inches long.

A. 9.5; 20.5
B. 12.5; 22
C. 17; 32
D. 25; 44

41. In a division of clerks and stenographers, 15 people are currently employed, 20% of whom are stenographers. 41.____
If management plans are to maintain the current number of stenographers, but to increase the clerical staff to the point where 12% of the total staff are stenographers, what is the MAXIMUM number of additional clerks that should be hired to meet these plans?

A. 3 B. 8 C. 10 D. 12

42. Suppose that a certain agency had a 2005 budget of $1,100,500. The 2006 budget was 7% higher than that of 2005, and the 2007 budget was 8% higher than that of 2006. Of the following, which one is MOST NEARLY that agency's budget for 2007? 42.____

A. $1,117,624 B. $1,261,737
C. $1,265,575 D. $1,271,738

Question's 43-50.

DIRECTIONS: Your office keeps a file card record of the work assignments for all the employees in a certain bureau. On each card is the employee's name, a work assignment code number, and the date of this assignment. In this filing system, the employee's name is filed alphabetically, the work assignment code is filed numerically, and the date of the assignment is filed chronologically (earliest date first).

Each of Questions 43 through 50 represents five cards to be filed, numbered (1) through (5) shown in Column I. Each card is made up of the employee's name, a work assignment code number shown in parentheses, and the date of this assignment. The cards are to be filed according to the following rules:

First: File in alphabetical order;
Second: When two or more cards have the same employee's name, file according to the work assignment number, beginning with the lowest number.
Third: When two or more cards have the same employee's name and same assignment number, file according to the assignment date beginning with earliest date.

Column II shows the cards arranged in four different orders. Pick the answer (A, B, C, or D) in Column II which shows the cards arranged correctly according to the above filing rules.

SAMPLE QUESTION:

	Column I			Column II
(1) Cluney	(486503)	6/17/07	A.	2, 3, 4, 1, 5
(2) Roster	(246611)	5/10/06	B.	2, 5, 1, 3, 4
(3) Altool	(711433)	10/15/07	C.	3, 2, 1, 4, 5
(4) Cluney	(527610)	12/18/06	D.	3, 5, 1, 4, 2
(5) Cluney	(486500)	4/8/07		

The correct way to file the cards is:

(3) Altool	(711433)	10/15/07
(5) Cluney	(486500)	4/8/07
(1) Cluney	(486503)	6/17/07
(4) Cluney	(527610)	12/18/06
(2) Roster	(246611)	5/10/06

The correct filing order is shown by the numbers in front of each name (3, 5, 1, 4, 2). The answer to the sample question is the letter in Column II in front of the numbers 3, 5, 1, 4, 2. This answer is D.

43. 43.____

	Column I				Column II
(1)	Prichard	(013469)	4/6/06	A.	5, 4, 3, 2, 1
(2)	Parks	(678941)	2/7/06	B.	1, 2, 5, 3, 4
(3)	Williams	(551467)	3/6/05	C.	2, 1, 5, 3, 4
(4)	Wilson	(551466)	8/9/02	D.	1, 5, 4, 3, 2
(5)	Stanhope	(300014)	8/9/02		

44. 44.____

(1)	Ridgeway	(623809)	8/11/06	A.	5, 1, 3, 4, 2
(2)	Travers	(305439)	4/5/02	B.	5, 1, 3, 2, 4
(3)	Tayler	(818134)	7/5/03	C.	1, 5, 3, 2, 4
(4)	Travers	(305349)	5/6/05	D.	1, 5, 4, 2, 3
(5)	Ridgeway	(623089)	10/9/06		

45. 45.____

(1)	Jaffe	(384737)	2/19/06	A.	3, 5, 2, 4, 1
(2)	Inez	(859176)	8/8/07	B.	3, 5, 2, 1, 4
(3)	Ingrahm	(946460)	8/6/04	C.	2, 3, 5, 1, 4
(4)	Karp	(256146)	5/5/05	D.	2, 3, 5, 4, 1
(5)	Ingrahm	(946460)	6/4/05		

46. 46.____

(1)	Marrano	(369421)	7/24/04	A.	1, 5, 3, 4, 2
(2)	Marks	(652910)	2/23/06	B.	3, 5, 4, 2, 1
(3)	Netto	(556772)	3/10/07	C.	2, 4, 1, 5, 3
(4)	Marks	(652901)	2/17/07	D.	4, 2, 1, 5, 3
(5)	Netto	(556772)	6/17/05		

47. 47.____

(1)	Abernathy	(712467)	6/23/05	A.	5, 3, 1, 2, 4
(2)	Acevedo	(680262)	6/23/03	B.	5, 4, 2, 3, 1
(3)	Aaron	(967647)	1/17/04	C.	1, 3, 5, 2, 4
(4)	Acevedo	(680622)	5/14/02	D.	2, 4, 1, 5, 3
(5)	Aaron	(967647)	4/1/00		

48. 48.____

(1)	Simon	(645219)	8/19/05	A.	4, 1, 2, 5, 3
(2)	Simon	(645219)	9/2/03	B.	4, 5, 2, 1, 3
(3)	Simons	(645218)	7/7/05	C.	3, 5, 2, 1, 4
(4)	Simms	(646439)	10/12/06	D.	5, 1, 2, 3, 4
(5)	Simon	(645219)	10/16/02		

49. 49.____

(1)	Rappaport	(312230)	6/11/06	A.	4, 3, 1, 2, 5
(2)	Rascio	(777510)	2/9/05	B.	4, 3, 1, 5, 2
(3)	Rappaport	(312230)	7/3/02	C.	3, 4, 1, 5, 2
(4)	Rapaport	(312330)	9/6/05	D.	5, 2, 4, 3, 1
(5)	Rascio	(777501)	7/7/05		

50. 50.____

(1)	Johnson	(843250)	6/8/02	A.	1, 3, 2, 4, 5
(2)	Johnson	(843205)	4/3/05	B.	1, 3, 2, 5, 4
(3)	Johnson	(843205)	8/6/02	C.	3, 2, 1, 4, 5
(4)	Johnson	(843602)	3/8/06	D.	3, 2, 1, 5, 4
(5)	Johnson	(843602)	8/3/05		

KEY (CORRECT ANSWERS)

1. D	11. B	21. C	31. B	41. C
2. A	12. A	22. A	32. B	42. D
3. C	13. C	23. D	33. A	43. C
4. C	14. C	24. B	34. C	44. A
5. C	15. A	25. D	35. B	45. C
6. A	16. D	26. C	36. A	46. D
7. B	17. A	27. B	37. C	47. A
8. C	18. C	28. C	38. B	48. B
9. D	19. D	29. A	39. B	49. B
10. A	20. B	30. C	40. B	50. D

EXAMINATION SECTION
TEST 1

DIRECTIONS: Each question or incomplete statement is followed by several suggested answers or completions. Select the one that BEST answers the question or completes the statement. *PRINT THE LETTER OF THE CORRECT ANSWER IN THE SPACE AT THE RIGHT.*

1. The MOST important reason for a supervisor to encourage his staff to make suggestions for improving the work of the unit is that such suggestions may 1.____

   A. indicate who is the most efficient employee in the unit
   B. increase the productivity of the unit
   C. raise the morale of the employees who make the suggestions
   D. reduce the amount of supervision necessary to perform the work of the unit

2. The PRIMARY purpose of a probationary period for a new employee is to 2.____

   A. thoroughly train the new employee in his job duties
   B. permit the new employee to become adjusted to his duties
   C. determine the fitness of the new employee for the job
   D. acquaint the new employee fully with the objectives of his agency

3. A unit supervisor finds that he is spending too much time on routine tasks, and not enough time on coordinating the work of his employees. 3.____
   It would be MOST advisable for this supervisor to

   A. delegate the task of work coordination to a capable subordinate
   B. eliminate some of the routine tasks that the unit is required to perform
   C. assign some of the routine tasks to his subordinates
   D. postpone the performance of routine tasks until he has achieved proper coordination of his employees' work

4. Of the following, the MOST important reason for having an office manual in looseleaf form rather than in permanent binding is that the looseleaf form 4.____

   A. facilitates the addition of new material and the removal of obsolete material
   B. permits several people to use different sections of the manual at the same time
   C. is less expensive to prepare than permanent binding
   D. is more durable than permanent binding

5. In his first discussion with an employee newly appointed to the title of Clerk in an agency, the LEAST important of the following topics for a supervisor of a clerical unit to include is the 5.____

   A. duties the subordinate is expected to perform on the job
   B. functions of the unit
   C. methods of determining standards of clerical performance
   D. nature and duration of the training the subordinate will receive on the job

6. Assume that you have been assigned to organize the files so that all the records now located in the various units in your bureau will be centrally located in a separate files unit. In setting up this system of centrally located files, you should be concerned LEAST with making certain that 6.____

   A. the material stored in the files has been checked for accuracy of content
   B. the filing system will be flexible enough to allow for possible future expansion
   C. material stored in the files can be located readily when needed
   D. the filing system will be readily understood by employees assigned to maintaining the files

7. A supervisor of a unit in a city department has just been told by a subordinate, Mr. Jones, that another employee, Mr. Smith, deliberately disobeyed an important rule of the department by taking home some confidential departmental material. Of the following courses of action, it would be MOST advisable for the supervisor first to 7.____

   A. discuss the matter privately with both Mr. Jones and Mr. Smith at the same time
   B. call a meeting of the entire unit and discuss the matter generally without mentioning any employee by name
   C. arrange to supervise Mr. Smith's activities more closely
   D. discuss the matter privately with Mr. Smith

8. A clerk who has the choice of sending a business letter either by certified mail or by registered mail should realize that 8.____

   A. it is less expensive to send letters by certified mail than by registered mail
   B. it is safer to send letters by certified mail than by registered mail
   C. letters sent by certified mail reach their destinations faster than those sent by registered mail
   D. the person to whom a certified letter is sent is not asked to acknowledge receipt of the letter

9. If the management of a public agency wishes to retain the elasticity of youth among employees who have been with the agency for a long time, it must furnish variety and novelty of work. To carry out the above recommendation, the BEST course of action for an agency to take is to 9.____

   A. encourage older employees to retire at the minimum retirement age
   B. vary its employees' assignments from time to time
   C. assign the routine tasks to newer and younger employees
   D. provide its employees with varied recreational activities

10. The one of the following actions which would be MOST efficient and economical for a supervisor to take to minimize the effect of seasonal fluctuations in the work load of his unit is to 10.____

   A. increase his permanent staff until it is large enough to handle the work of the busy season
   B. request the purchase of time and labor saving equipment to be used primarily during the busy season

C. lower, temporarily, the standards for quality of work performance during peak loads
D. schedule for the slow season work that it is not essential to perform during the busy season

11. A clerk in an agency should realize that each letter he sends out in response to a letter of inquiry from the public represents an expenditure of time and money by his agency. 11.____
The one of the following which is the MOST valid implication of this statement is that such a clerk should

A. use the telephone to answer letters of inquiry directly and promptly
B. answer mail inquiries with lengthy letters to eliminate the need for further correspondence
C. prevent the accumulation of a large number of similar inquiries by answering each of these letters promptly
D. use simple, concise language in answer to letters of inquiry

12. The forms and methods of discipline used in public agencies are as varied as the offenses which prompt disciplinary action, and range in severity from a frown of disapproval to dismissal from the service and even to prosecution in the courts. 12.____
On the basis of this sentence, the MOST accurate of the following statements is that

A. the severity of disciplinary measures varies directly with the seriousness of the offenses
B. dismissal from the service is the most severe action that can be taken by a public agency
C. public agencies use a variety of disciplinary measures to cope with offenses
D. public agencies sometimes administer excessive punishments

13. A well-planned training program can assist new employees to acquire the information they need to work effectively. Of the following, the information that a newly-appointed clerk would need LEAST in order to perform his work effectively is knowledge of the 13.____

A. acceptable ways of taking and recording telephone messages
B. techniques of evaluating the effectiveness of office forms used in the agency
C. methods of filing papers used in his bureau
D. proper manner of handling visitors to the agency

14. A supervisor of a unit who is not specific when making assignments creates a dangerous source of friction, misunderstanding, and inefficiency. 14.____
The MOST valid implication of this statement is that

A. supervisors are usually unaware that they are creating sources of friction
B. it is often difficult to remove sources of friction and misunderstanding
C. a competent supervisor attempts to find a solution to each problem facing him
D. employees will perform more efficiently if their duties are defined clearly

15. The employees' interest in the subject matter of a training course must be fully aroused if they are to derive the maximum benefits from the training. 15.____
Of the following, the LEAST effective method of arousing such interest is to

A. state to the employees that the subject matter of the training course will be of interest to mature, responsible workers
B. point out to the employees that the training course may help them to win promotion

C. explain to the employees how the training course will help them to perform their work better
D. relate the training course to the employees' interests and previous experiences

16. The control of clerical work in a public agency appears impossible if the clerical work is regarded merely as a series of duties unrelated to the functions of the agency. However, this control becomes feasible when it is realized that clerical work links and coordinates the functions of the agency. 16.____
On the basis of this statement, the MOST accurate of the following statements is that the

A. complexity of clerical work may not be fully understood by those assigned to control it
B. clerical work can be readily controlled if it is coordinated by other work of the agency
C. number of clerical tasks may be reduced by regarding coordination as the function of clerical work
D. purposes of clerical work must be understood to make possible its proper control

17. Assume that as supervisor of a unit you are to prepare a vacation schedule for the employees in your unit. 17.____
Of the following, the factor which is LEAST important for you to consider in setting up this schedule is

A. the vacation preferences of each employee in the unit
B. the anticipated work load in the unit during the vacation period
C. how well each employee has performed his work
D. how essential a specific employee's services will be during the vacation period

18. In order to promote efficiency and economy in an agency, it is advisable for the management to systematize and standardize procedures and relationships insofar as this can be done; however, excessive routinizing which does not permit individual contributions or achievements should be avoided. 18.____
On the basis of this statement, it is MOST accurate to state that

A. systematized procedures should be designed mainly to encourage individual achievements
B. standardized procedures should allow for individual accomplishments
C. systematization of procedures may not be possible in organizations which have a large variety of functions
D. individual employees of an organization must fully accept standardized procedures if the procedures are to be effective

19. Trained employees work most efficiently and with a minimum expenditure of time and energy. Suitable equipment and definite, well-developed procedures are effective only when employees know how to use the equipment and procedures. This statement means MOST NEARLY that 19.____

A. employees can be trained most efficiently when suitable equipment and definite procedures are used
B. training of employees is a costly but worthwhile investment

C. suitable equipment and definite procedures are of greatest value when employees have been properly trained to use them
D. the cost of suitable equipment and definite procedures is negligible when the saving in time and energy that they bring is considered

20. Assume that your supervisor has asked you to present to him comprehensive, periodic reports on the progress that your unit is making in meeting its work goals. 20.____
For you to give your superior oral reports rather than written ones is

A. *desirable*; it will be easier for him to transmit your oral report to his superiors
B. *undesirable*; the oral reports will provide no permanent record to which he may refer
C. *undesirable;* there will be less opportunity for you to discuss the oral reports with him than the written ones
D. *desirable;* the oral reports will require little time and effort to prepare

21. Assume that an employee under your supervision complains to you that your evaluation of his work is too low. 21.____
The MOST appropriate action for you to take FIRST is to

A. explain how you arrived at the evaluation of his work
B. encourage him to improve the quality of his work by pointing out specifically how he can do so
C. suggest that he appeal to an impartial higher authority if he disagrees with your evaluation
D. point out to him specific instances in which his work has been unsatisfactory

22. The nature of the experience and education that are made a prerequisite to employment determines in large degree the training job to be done after employment begins. 22.____
On the basis of this statement, it is MOST accurate to state that

A. the more comprehensive the experience and education required for employment the more extensive the training that is usually given after appointment
B. the training that is given to employees depends upon the experience and education required of them before appointment
C. employees who possess the experience and education required for employment should need little additional training after appointment
D. the nature of the work that employees are expected to perform determines the training that they will need

23. Assume that you are preparing a report evaluating the work of a clerk who was transferred to your unit from another unit in the agency about a year ago. 23.____
Of the following, the method that would probably be MOST helpful to you in making this evaluation is to

A. consult the evaluations this employee received from his former supervisors
B. observe this employee at his work for a week shortly before you prepare the report
C. examine the employee's production records and compare them with the standards set for the position
D. obtain tactfully from his fellow employees their frank opinions of his work

24. Of the following, the CHIEF value of a flow-of-work chart to the management of an organization is its usefulness in 24.____

A. locating the causes of delay in carrying out an operation
B. training new employees in the performance of their duties
C. determining the effectiveness of the employees in the organization
D. determining the accuracy of its organization chart

25. Assume that a procedure for handling certain office forms has just been extensively revised. As supervisor of a small unit, you are to instruct your subordinates in the use of the new procedure, which is rather complicated. 25.____
Of the following, it would be LEAST helpful to your subordinates for you to

A. compare the revised procedure with the one it has replaced
B. state that you believe the revised procedure to be better than the one it has replaced
C. tell them that they will probably find it difficult to learn the new procedure
D. give only a general outline of the revised procedure at first and then follow with more detailed instructions

26. A supervisor may make assignments to his subordinates in the form of a command, a request, or a call for volunteers. It is LEAST desirable for a supervisor to make an assignment in the form of a command when 26.____

A. a serious emergency has risen
B. an employee objects to carrying out an assignment
C. the assignment must be completed immediately
D. the assignment is an unpleasant one

27. For an office supervisor to confer periodically with his subordinates in order to anticipate job problems which are likely to arise is desirable MAINLY because 27.____

A. there will be fewer problems for which hasty decisions will have to be made
B. some problems which are anticipated may not arise
C. his subordinates will learn to refer the problems arising in the unit to him
D. constant anticipation of future problems tends to raise additional problems

28. A methods improvement program might be called a war against habit. 28.____
The MOST accurate implication of this statement is that

A. routine handling of routine office assignments should be discouraged
B. standardization of office procedures may encourage employees to form inefficient work habits
C. employees tend to continue the use of existing procedures, even when such procedures are inefficient
D. procedures should be changed constantly to prevent them from becoming habits

29. An office supervisor may give either a written or an oral order to his subordinates when making an assignment. 29.____
Of the following, it would be MOST appropriate for a supervisor to issue an order in writing when

A. a large number of two-page reports must be stapled together before the end of the day
B. the assignment is to be completed within two hours after it is issued to his subordinates

C. his subordinates have completed an identical assignment the day before
D. several entries must be made on a form at varying intervals of time by different clerks

30. A supervisor should always remember that the instruction or training of new employees is most effective if it is given when and where it is needed. 30.____
On the basis of this statement, it is MOST appropriate to conclude that

A. the new employee should be trained to handle any aspect of his work at the time he starts his job
B. the new employee should be given the training essential to get him started and additional training when he requires it
C. an employee who has received excessive training will be just as ineffective as one who has received inadequate training
D. a new employee is trained most effectively by his own supervisor

31. Some employees see an agency training program as a threat. Of the following, the MOST likely reason for such an employee attitude toward training is that the employees involved feel that 31.____

A. some trainers are incompetent
B. training rarely solves real work-a-day problems
C. training may attempt to change comfortable behavior patterns
D. training sessions are boring

32. Of the following, the CHIEF characteristic which distinguishes a good supervisor from a poor supervisor is the good supervisor's 32.____

A. ability to favorably impress others
B. unwillingness to accept monotony or routine
C. ability to deal constructively with problem situations
D. strong drive to overcome opposition

33. Of the following, the MAIN disadvantage of on-the-job training is that, generally, 33.____

A. special equipment may be needed
B. production may be slowed down
C. the instructor must maintain an individual relationship with the trainee
D. the on-the-job instructor must be better qualified than the classroom instructor

34. All of the following are correct methods for a supervisor to use in connection with employee discipline EXCEPT: 34.____

A. Trying not to be too lenient or too harsh
B. Informing employees of the rules and the penalties for violations of the rules
C. Imposing discipline immediately after the violation is discovered
D. Making sure, when you apply discipline, that the employee understands that you do not want to do it

35. Of the following, the MAIN reason for a supervisor to establish standard procedures for his unit is to 35.____

A. increase the motivation of his subordinates
B. make it easier for the subordinates to submit to authority

C. reduce the number of times that his subordinates have to consult him
D. reduce the number of mistakes that his subordinates will make

36. When delegating responsibility for an assignment to a subordinate, it is MOST important that you 36.____

A. retain all authority necessary to complete the assignment
B. make yourself generally available for consultation with the subordinate
C. inform your superiors that you are no longer responsible for the assignment
D. decrease the number of subordinates whom you have to supervise

37. You, as a unit head, have been asked to submit budget estimates of staff, equipment, and supplies in terms of programs for your unit for the coming fiscal year. 37.____
In addition to their use in planning, such unit budget estimates can be BEST used to

A. reveal excessive costs in operations
B. justify increases in the debt limit
C. analyze employee salary adjustments
D. predict the success of future programs

38. Because higher status is important to many employees, they will often make an effort to achieve it as an end in itself. 38.____
Of the following, the BEST course of action for the supervisor to take on the basis of the preceding statement is to

A. attach higher status to that behavior of subordinates which is directed toward reaching the goals of the organization
B. avoid showing sympathy toward subordinates' wishes for increased wages, improved working conditions, or other benefits
C. foster interpersonal competitiveness among subordinates so that personal friendliness is replaced by the desire to protect individual status
D. reprimand subordinates whenever their work is in some way unsatisfactory in order to adjust their status accordingly

39. Assume that a large office in a certain organization operates long hours and is thus on two shifts with a slight overlap. Those employees, including supervisors, who are most productive are given their choice of shifts. The earlier shift is considered preferable by most employees. 39.____
As a result of this method of assignment, which of the following is MOST likely to result?

A. Most non-supervisory employees will be assigned to the late shift; most supervisors will be assigned to the early shift.
B. Most supervisors will be assigned to the late shift; most non-supervisory employees will be assigned to the early shift.
C. The early shift will be more productive than the late shift.
D. The late shift will be more productive than the early shift.

40. Assume that a supervisor of a unit in which the employees are of average friendliness tells a newly hired employee on her first day that her co-workers are very friendly. The other employees hear his remarks to the new employee. Which of the following is the MOST likely result of this action of the supervisor? The 40.____

A. newly hired employee will tend to feel less friendly than if the supervisor had said nothing
B. newly hired employee will tend to believe that her co-workers are very friendly
C. other employees will tend to feel less friendly toward one another
D. other employees will tend to see the newly hired employee as insincerely friendly

41. A recent study of employee absenteeism showed that, although unscheduled absence for part of a week is relatively high for young employees, unscheduled absence for a full week is low. However, although full-week unscheduled absence is least frequent for the youngest employees, the frequency of such absence increases as the age of employees increases. 41.____
Which of the following statements is the MOST logical explanation for the greater full-week absenteeism among older employees?

A. Older employees are more likely to be males.
B. Older employees are more likely to have more relatively serious illnesses.
C. Younger employees are more likely to take longer vacations.
D. Younger employees are more likely to be newly hired.

42. An employee can be motivated to fulfill his needs as he sees them. He is not motivated by what others think he ought to have, but what he himself wants. 42.____
Which of the following statements follows MOST logically from the foregoing viewpoint?

A. A person's different traits may be separately classified, but they are all part of one system comprising a whole person.
B. Every job, however simple, entitles the person who does it to proper respect and recognition of his unique aspirations and abilities.
C. No matter what equipment and facilities an organization has, they cannot be put to use except by people who have been motivated.
D. To an observer, a person's needs may be unrealistic, but they are still controlling.

43. Assume that you are a supervisor of a unit which is about to start work on an urgent job. One of your subordinates starts to talk to you about the urgent job but seems not to be saying what is really on his mind. 43.____
What is the BEST thing for you to say under these circumstances?

A. I'm not sure I understand. Can you explain that?
B. Please come to the point. We haven't got all day.
C. What is it? Can't you see I'm busy?
D. Haven't you got work to do? What do you want?

44. Assume that you have recently been assigned to a new subordinate. You have explained to this subordinate how to fill out certain forms which will constitute the major portion of her job. After the first day, you find that she has filled out the forms correctly but has not completed as many as most other workers normally complete in a day. 44.____
Of the following, the MOST appropriate action for you to take is to

A. tell the subordinate how many forms she is expected to complete
B. instruct the subordinate in the correct method of filling out the forms
C. monitor the subordinate's production to see if she improves
D. reassign the job of filling out the forms to a more experienced worker in the unit

45. One of the problems commonly met by the supervisor is the *touchy* employee who imagines slights when none is intended. 45.____
Of the following, the BEST way to deal with such an employee is to

A. ignore him until he sees the error of his behavior
B. frequently reassure him of his value as a person
C. advise him that oversensitive people rarely get promoted
D. issue written instructions to him to avoid misinterpretation

46. The understanding supervisor should recognize that a certain amount of anxiety is common to all newly hired employees. 46.____
If you are a supervisor of a unit and a newly-hired employee has been assigned to you, you can usually assume that the LEAST likely worry that the new employee has is worry about

A. the job and the standards required in the job
B. his acceptance by the other people in your unit
C. the difficulty of advancing to top positions in the agency
D. your fairness in evaluating his work

47. In assigning work to subordinates, it is often desirable for you to tell them the overall or ultimate objective of the assignment. 47.____
Of the following, the BEST reason for telling them the objective is that it will

A. assure them that you know what you are doing
B. eliminate most of the possible complaints about the assignment
C. give them confidence in their ability to do the assignment
D. help them to make decisions consistent with the objective

48. Assume that the regular 8-hour working day of a laborer is from 8 A.M. to 5 P.M., with an hour off for lunch. He earns a regular hourly rate of pay for these 8 hours and is paid at the rate of time-and-a-half for each hour worked after his regular working day. 48.____
If, on a certain day, he works from 8 A.M. to 6 P.M., with an hour off for lunch, and earns $99.76, his regular hourly rate of pay is

A. $8.50 B. $9.00 C. $10.50 D. $11.50

49. Two clerical units, X and Y, each having a different number of clerks, are assigned to file registration cards. It takes Unit X, which contains 8 clerks, 21 days to file the same number of cards that Unit Y can file, in 28 days. It is also a fact that Unit X can file 174,528 cards in 72 days. 49.____
Assuming that all the clerks in both units work at the same rate of speed, the number of cards which can be filed by Unit Y in 144 days, if 4 more clerks are added to the staff of Unit Y, is MOST NEARLY

A. 349,000 B. 436,000 C. 523,000 D. 669,000

50. Each side of a square room which is being used as an office measures 66 feet. The floor of the room is divided by six traffic aisles, each aisle being six feet wide. Three of the aisles run parallel to the east and west sides of the room and the other three run parallel to the north and south sides of the room, so that the remaining floor space is divided into 16 equal sections. 50.____
If all of the floor space which is not being used for traffic aisles is occupied by desk and chair sets, and each set takes up 24 square feet of floor space, the number of desk and chair sets in the room is

A. 80   B. 64   C. 36   D. 96

KEY (CORRECT ANSWERS)

1. B	11. D	21. A	31. C	41. B
2. C	12. C	22. B	32. C	42. D
3. C	13. B	23. C	33. B	43. A
4. A	14. D	24. A	34. D	44. C
5. C	15. A	25. C	35. C	45. B
6. A	16. B	26. D	36. B	46. C
7. D	17. C	27. A	37. A	47. D
8. A	18. B	28. C	38. A	48. C
9. B	19. C	29. D	39. C	49. B
10. D	20. B	30. B	40. B	50. D

TEST 2

DIRECTIONS: Each question or incomplete statement is followed by several suggested answers or completions. Select the one that BEST answers the question or completes the statement. *PRINT THE LETTER OF THE CORRECT ANSWER IN THE SPACE AT THE RIGHT.*

Questions 1-6.

DIRECTIONS: Each of Questions 1 through 6 consists of statements which contains one word that is incorrectly used because it is not in keeping with the meaning that the statement is evidently intended to convey. For each of these questions, you are to select the incorrectly used word and substitute for it one of the words lettered A, B, C, D, or E, which helps BEST to convey the meaning of the quotation. In the space at the right, write the letter preceding the word which should be substituted for the incorrectly used word.

1. The determination of the value of the employees in an organization is fundamental not only as a guide to the administration of salary schedules, promotion, demotion, and transfer, but also as a means of keeping the working force on its toes and of checking the originality of selection methods. 1.____

   A. effectiveness B. initiation C. increasing
   D. system E. none of these

2. No training course can operate to full advantage without job descriptions which indicate training requirements so that those parts of the job requiring the most training can be carefully analyzed before the training course is completed. 2.____

   A. improved B. started C. least
   D. meet E. predict

3. The criticism that supervisors are discriminatory in their treatment of subordinates is to some extent untrue, for the subjective nature of many supervisory decisions makes it probable that many employees who have not progressed will attribute their lack of success to supervisory favoritism. 3.____

   A. knowledge B. unavoidable C. detrimental
   D. deny E. indifferent

4. Some demands of employees will, if satisfied, result in a decrease in production. Some supervisors largely ignore such demands on the part of their subordinates, and instead, concentrate on the direction and production of work; others yield to such requests and thereby emphasize the production goals and objectives set by higher levels of authority. 4.____

   A. responsibility B. increase C. neglect
   D. value E. morale

5. It is generally accepted that when a supervisor is at least as well informed about the work of his unit as are his subordinates, he will fail to win their approval, which is essential to him if he is to supervise the unit effectively. 5.____

   A. unimportant B. preferable C. unless
   D. attention E. poorly

6. The laws of almost every state permit certain classes of persons to vote despite their absence from home at election time. Sometimes this privilege is given only to members of the armed forces of the United States, though more commonly it is extended to all voters whose occupations make absence preventable. 6.____

A. prohibition B. sanction C. intangible
D. avoidable E. necessary

Questions 7-25.

DIRECTIONS: Each of Questions 7 through 25 consists of a word in capitals followed by four suggested meanings of the word. Print in the space at the right the number preceding the word which means MOST NEARLY the same as the word in capitals.

7. ALLEVIATE 7.____

A. soothe B. make difficult
C. introduce gradually D. complicate

8. OSTENSIBLE 8.____

A. intelligent B. successful
C. necessary D. apparent

9. REDUNDANT 9.____

A. excessive B. sufficient
C. logical D. unpopular

10. TANTAMOUNT 10.____

A. superior B. opposed
C. equivalent D. disturbing

11. EXPUNGE 11.____

A. leap over B. erase
C. exploit D. concede fully

12. VESTIGE 12.____

A. ancestor B. basis C. choice D. remnant

13. CONTENTION 13.____

A. modification B. controversy
C. cooperation D. sight

14. PROSCRIBE 14.____

A. recommend B. avoid C. provide D. prohibit

15. URBANE 15.____

A. polite B. adjacent to a city
C. modern D. common

16. INADVERTENT 16.____

A. unknown
B. public
C. deliberate
D. unintentional

17. EVINCE 17.____

A. enlarge B. conceal C. display D. evade

18. SIMULATE 18.____

A. attempt B. imitate C. elude D. arouse

19. PRECLUDE 19.____

A. prevent
B. contribute generously
C. simplify
D. prepare gradually

20. REMISS 20.____

A. careless B. absent C. guilty D. thorough

21. CONTRIVE 21.____

A. contract B. restrict C. scheme D. contribute

22. MALIGN 22.____

A. mislead deliberately
B. slander
C. flatter excessively
D. disturb

23. CONTINGENT 23.____

A. loose
B. intentional
C. dependent
D. forceful

24. SPORADIC 24.____

A. quick B. alert C. destroyed D. scattered

25. COALESCE 25.____

A. unite B. reveal C. abate D. freeze

Questions 26-33.

DIRECTIONS: Each of Questions 26 through 33 consists of three sentences lettered A, B, and C. In each of these questions, one of the sentences may contain an error in grammar, sentence structure, or punctuation, or all three sentences may be correct. If one of the sentences in a question contains an error in grammar, sentence structure, or punctuation, write in the space at the right, the letter preceding the sentence which contains the error. If all three sentences are correct, write the letter D.

26. 26.____
A. Mr. Smith appears to be less competent than I in performing these duties.
B. The supervisor spoke to the employee, who had made the error, but did not reprimand him.
C. When he found the book lying on the table, he immediately notified the owner.

27. A. Being locked in the desk, we were certain that the papers would not be taken. 27.____
B. It wasn't I who dictated the telegram; I believe it was Eleanor.
C. You should interview whoever comes to the office today.

28. A. The clerk was instructed to set the machine on the table before summoning the manager. 28.____
B. He said that he was not familiar with those kind of activities.
C. A box of pencils, in addition to erasers and blotters, was included in the shipment of supplies.

29. A. The supervisor remarked, "Assigning an employee to the proper type of work is not always easy." 29.____
B. The employer found that each of the applicants were qualified to perform the duties of the position.
C. Any competent student is permitted to take this course if he obtains the consent of the instructor.

30. A. The prize was awarded to the employee whom the judges believed to be most deserving. 30.____
B. Since the instructor believes this book is the better of the two, he is recommending it for use in the school.
C. It was obvious to the employees that the completion of the task by the scheduled date would require their working overtime.

31. A. These reports have been typed by employees who were trained by a capable supervisor. 31.____
B. This employee is as old, if not older, than any other employee in the department.
C. Running rapidly down the street, the manager soon reached the office.

32. A. It is believed, that if these terms are accepted, the building can be constructed at a reasonable cost. 32.____
B. The typists are seated in the large office; the stenographers, in the small office.
C. Either the operators or the machines are at fault.

33. A. Mr. Jones, who is the head of the agency, will come today to discuss the plans for the new training program. 33.____
B. The reason the report is not finished is that the supply of paper is exhausted.
C. It is now obvious that neither of the two employees is able to handle this type of assignment.

Questions 34-40.

DIRECTIONS: Each of Questions 34 through 40 consists of four words. In each question, one of the words may be spelled incorrectly or all four words may be spelled correctly. If one of the words in a question is spelled incorrectly, print in the space at the right the letter preceding the word which is spelled incorrectly. If all four words are spelled correctly, print the letter E.

34. A. guarantee B. committment 34.____
C. mitigate D. publicly

35. A. prerogative B. apprise 35.____
C. extrordinary D. continual

36. A. arrogant B. handicapped 36.____
C. judicious D. perennial

37. A. permissable B. deceive 37.____
C. innumerable D. retrieve

38. A. notable B. allegiance 38.____
C. reimburse D. illegal

39. A. interceed B. benefited 39.____
C. analogous D. altogether

40. A. seizure B. irrelevant 40.____
C. inordinate D. dissapproved

Questions 41-50.

DIRECTIONS: Questions 41 through 50 are based on the Production Record table shown on the following page for the Information Unit in Agency X for the work week ended Friday, December 6. The table shows, for each employee, the quantity of each type of work performed and the percentage of the work week spent in performing each type of work.

NOTE: Assume that each employee works 7 hours a day and 5 days a week, making a total of 35 hours for the work week.

PRODUCTION RECORD - INFORMATION UNIT IN AGENCY X
(For the work week ended Friday, December 6)

	Number of			
	Papers Filed	Sheets Proofread	Visitors Received	Envelopes Addressed
Miss Agar	3120	33	178	752
Mr . Brun	1565	59	252	724
Miss Case	2142	62	214	426
Mr. Dale	4259	29	144	1132
Miss Earl	2054	58	212	878
Mr. Farr	1610	69	245	621
Miss Glen	2390	57	230	790
Mr . Hope	3425	32	176	805
Miss Iver	3736	56	148	650
Mr. Joad	3212	55	181	495

Percentage of Work Week Spent On

	Filing Papers	Proof-reading	Receiving Visitors	Addressing Envelopes	Performing Miscellaneous Work
Miss Agar	30%	9%	34%	11%	16%
Mr . Brun	13%	15%	52%	10%	10%
Miss Case	23%	18%	38%	6%	15%
Mr. Dale	50%	7%	17%	16%	10%
Miss Earl	24%	14%	37%	14%	11%
Mr. Farr	16%	19%	48%	8%	9%
Miss Glen	27%	12%	42%	12%	7%
Mr . Hope	38%	8%	32%	13%	9%
Miss Iver	43%	13%	24%	9%	11%
Mr. Joad	33%	11%	36%	7%	13%

41. For the week, the average amount of time which the employees spent in proofreading was MOST NEARLY ______ hours. 41.____

A. 3.1 B. 3.6 C. 4.4 D. 5.1

42. The average number of visitors received daily by an employee was MOST NEARLY 42.____

A. 40 B. 57 C. 198 D. 395

43. Of the following employees, the one who addressed envelopes at the FASTEST rate was 43.____

A. Miss Agar
B. Mr. Brun
C. Miss Case
D. Mr. Dale

44. Mr. Farr's rate of filing papers was MOST NEARLY ______ pages per minute. 44.____

A. 2 B. 1.7 C. 5 D. 12

45. The average number of hours that Mr. Brun spent daily on receiving visitors exceeded the average number of hours that Miss Iver spent daily on the same type of work by MOST NEARLY ______ hours. 45.____

A. 2 B. 3 C. 4 D. 5

46. Miss Earl worked at a faster rate than Miss Glen in 46.____

A. filing papers
B. proofreading sheets
C. receiving visitors
D. addressing envelopes

47. Mr. Joad's rate of filing papers ______ Miss Iver's rate of filing papers by approximately ______%. 47.____

A. was less than; 10
B. exceeded; 33
C. C. was less than; 16
D. exceeded; 12

48. Assume that in the following week, Miss Case is instructed to increase the percentage of her time spent in filing papers to 35%. 48.____
If she continued to file papers at the same rate as she did for the week ended December 6, the number of additional papers that she filed the following week was MOST NEARLY

A. 3260 B. 5400 C. 250 D. 1120

49. Assume that in the following week, Mr. Hope increased his weekly total of envelopes addressed to 1092. 49.____
If he continued to spend the same amount of time on this assignment as he did for the week ended December 6, the increase in his rate of addressing envelopes the following week was MOST NEARLY ______ envelopes per hour.

A. 15 B. 65 C. 155 D. 240

50. Assume that in the following week, Miss Agar and Mr. Dale spent 3 and 9 hours less, respectively, on filing papers than they had spent for the week ended December 6, without changing their rates of work. 50.____
The total number of papers filed during the following week by both Miss Agar and Mr. Dale was MOST NEARLY

A. 4235 B. 4295 C. 4315 D. 4370

KEY (CORRECT ANSWERS)

1. A	11. B	21. C	31. B	41. C
2. B	12. D	22. B	32. A	42. A
3. B	13. B	23. C	33. D	43. B
4. C	14. D	24. D	34. B	44. C
5. C	15. A	25. A	35. C	45. A
6. E	16. D	26. B	36. E	46. C
7. A	17. C	27. A	37. A	47. D
8. D	18. B	28. B	38. E	48. D
9. A	19. A	29. B	39. A	49. B
10. C	20. A	30. D	40. D	50. B

READING COMPREHENSION
UNDERSTANDING AND INTERPRETING WRITTEN MATERIAL

COMMENTARY

The ability to read, understand, and interpret written materials texts, publications, newspapers, orders, directions, expositions, legal passages is a skill basic to a functioning democracy and to an efficient business or viable government.

That is why almost all examinations – for beginning, middle, and senior levels – test reading comprehension, directly or indirectly.

The reading test measures how well you understand what you read. This is how it is done: You read a paragraph and several statements based on a question. From the statements, you choose the *one* statement, or answer, that is *BEST* supported by, or *BEST* matches, what is said in the paragraph.

SAMPLE QUESTIONS

DIRECTIONS: Each question has five suggested answers, lettered A, B, C, D, and E. Decide which one is the *BEST* answer. *PRINT THE LETTER OF THE CORRECT ANSWER IN THE SPACE AT THE RIGHT.*

1. The prevention of accidents makes it necessary not only that safety devices be used to guard exposed machinery but also that mechanics be instructed in safety rules which they must follow for their own protection and that the light in the plant be adequate.
The paragraph BEST supports the statement that industrial accidents

A. are always avoidable
B. may be due to ignorance
C. usually result from inadequate machinery
D. cannot be entirely overcome
E. result in damage to machinery

ANALYSIS

Remember what you have to do -

First - Read the paragraph.
Second - Decide what the paragraph means.
Third - Read the five suggested answers.
Fourth - Select the one answer which *BEST* matches what the paragraph says or is *BEST* supported by something in the paragraph. (Sometimes you may have to read the paragraph again in order to be sure which suggested answer is best.)

This paragraph is talking about three steps that should be taken to prevent industrial accidents:

1. use safety devices on machines
2. instruct mechanics in safety rules
3. provide adequate lighting

SELECTION

With this in mind, let's look at each suggested answer. Each one starts with "Industrial accidents ..."

SUGGESTED ANSWER A.

Industrial accidents (A) are always avoidable.

(The paragraph talks about how to avoid accidents but does not say that accidents are always avoidable.)

SUGGESTED ANSWER B.

Industrial accidents (B) may be due to ignorance.

(One of the steps given in the paragraph to prevent accidents is to instruct mechanics on safety rules. This suggests that lack of knowledge or ignorance of safety rules causes accidents. This suggested answer sounds like a good possibility for being the right answer.)

SUGGESTED ANSWER C.

Industrial accidents (C) usually result from inadequate machinery.

(The paragraph does suggest that exposed machines cause accidents, but it doesn't say that it is the usual cause of accidents. The word *usually* makes this a wrong answer.)

SUGGESTED ANSWER D.

Industrial accidents (D) cannot be entirely overcome.

(You may know from your own experience that this is a true statement. But that is not what the paragraph is talking about. Therefore, it is NOT the correct answer.)

SUGGESTED ANSWER E.

Industrial accidents (E) result in damage to machinery.

(This is a statement that may or may not be true, but, in any case, it is NOT covered by the paragraph.)

Looking back, you see that the one suggested answer of the five given that *BEST* matches what the paragraph says is

Industrial accidents (B) may be due to ignorance.

The *CORRECT* answer then is B.

Be sure you read *ALL* the possible answers before you make your choice. You may think that none of the five answers is really good, but choose the *BEST* one of the five.

---

2. Probably few people realize, as they drive on a concrete road, that steel is used to keep the surface flat in spite of the weight of the busses and trucks. Steel bars, deeply embedded in the concrete, provide sinews to take the stresses so that the stresses cannot crack the slab or make it wavy.
   The paragraph BEST supports the statement that a concrete road

A. is expensive to build
B. usually cracks under heavy weights
C. looks like any other road
D. is used only for heavy traffic
E. is reinforced with other material

ANALYSIS

This paragraph is commenting on the fact that -

1. few people realize, as they drive on a concrete road, that steel is deeply embedded
2. steel keeps the surface flat
3. steel bars enable the road to take the stresses without cracking or becoming wavy

SELECTION

Now read and think about the possible answers:

A. A concrete road is expensive to build.
(Maybe so but that is not what the paragraph is about.)
B. A concrete road usually cracks under heavy weights.
(The paragraph talks about using steel bars to prevent heavy weights from cracking concrete roads. It says nothing about how usual it is for the roads to crack. The word *usually* makes this suggested answer wrong.)
C. A concrete road looks like any other road.
(This may or may not be true. The important thing to note is that it has nothing to do with what the paragraph is about.)
D. A concrete road is used only for heavy traffic.
(This answer at least has something to do with the paragraph–concrete roads are used with heavy traffic but it does not say "used only.")
E. A concrete road is reinforced with other material.
(This choice seems to be the correct one on two counts: *First,* the paragraph does suggest that concrete roads are made stronger by embedding steel bars in them. This is another way of saying "concrete roads are reinforced with steel bars." *Second,* by the process of elimination, the other four choices are ruled out as correct answers simply because they do not apply.)

You can be sure that not all the reading questions will be so easy as these.

SUGGESTIONS FOR ANSWERING READING QUESTIONS

1. Read the paragraph carefully. Then read each suggested answer carefully. Read every word, because often one word can make the difference between a right and a wrong answer.
2. Choose that answer which is supported in the paragraph itself. Do not choose an answer which is a correct statement unless it is based on information in the paragraph.
3. Even though a suggested answer has many of the words used in the paragraph, it may still be wrong.
4. Look out for words – such as *always, never, entirely, or only*–which tend to make a suggested answer wrong.

5. Answer first those questions which you can answer most easily. Then work on the other questions.
6. If you can't figure out the answer to the question, guess.

READING COMPREHENSION
UNDERSTANDING AND INTERPRETING WRITTEN MATERIAL

EXAMINATION SECTION
TEST 1

DIRECTIONS: Each question or incomplete statement is followed by several suggested answers or completions. Select the one that BEST answers the question or completes the statement. *PRINT THE LETTER OF THE CORRECT ANSWER IN THE SPACE AT THE RIGHT.*

Questions 1-5.

DIRECTIONS: The following selection is to be used as the SOLE basis for answering Questions 1 through 5. Read the selection carefully and base your answers ONLY on the information contained therein.

As an example of the importance of social psychological concepts to law enforcement, let us consider stereotypes. Police officers must deal with stereotypes in a number of kinds of situations. First they are themselves the victims of a vicious kind of stereotyping which runs the range from "idiot" to "sadist."

Secondly, they themselves have stereotypes of others in their minds, as a result of their backgrounds and socialization; these they must examine in the light of reason and experience, or they may be led into expressions of prejudice to the permanent destruction of their proper role in the community.

Finally, they need to do all that is possible to prevent the stereotyping of minority groups by others, and the stereotyping of others by minority groups–for here lie the seeds of civil disturbances, as stereotyping feeds prejudice, and prejudice creates tension.

The difficulty in trying to change such stereotypes is that there often seems to be a "kernel of truth" in most of them when they are drawn out of people who have firsthand knowledge of the group being stereotyped. It is this surface validity which cries out for more thorough assessment, otherwise a permanent prejudice may be created for the lack of true facts and the failure to appreciate the reason behind the attitude that was born in ignorance.

People who cherish stereotypes can be changed and they can be influenced to discard them. There are many social reinforcements that can be used to defeat the unwholesome stereotypes (and the behaviors they generate) that are omens of trouble.

Techniques for the control of human behavior have been developed by psychologists who have probed deeply into the science of behavior modification. Conditioning, modeling procedures, and insights into the learning process all offer meaningful measures to invoke the power of scientific knowledge toward human behavior modification.

For example, Watson has developed an approach called the process of reconditioning. Working with a small child in his crib, he conditioned the fear of anything furry by making a loud noise whenever he put a furry object in the crib with the child.

Then he reversed this by reconditioning the child to accept the furry object. Slowly, by placing the object across the room until the child could exist without fear of it, Watson would move the two closer together. Now, if the child is taken to represent a prejudiced person and the furry object, the "object" of his prejudice, one can easily see how this technique could be applied in a wide variety of situations, and with people of all age levels.

The effectiveness of behavior modification, involving manipulation, influence, and control of the environment, is such that the police should be concerned – if only from a negative standpoint. What is this new power that has been created by man, how might we use it and how do we prevent its abuse? These are questions to which law enforcement personnel might well address themselves.

Interpersonal contact between persons and groups helps to develop mutual attitudes of understanding. Whether favorable or unfavorable stereotypes will develop depends upon the perceptions of the participants and the testing of these perceptions against reality, but it has been demonstrated through scientific research that the proper degree of contact with many different races, nationalities, and cultures helps to break down the barriers of unwholesome stereotypes and prejudices.

Discussion groups with police and citizens from a variety of ethnic backgrounds have proven effective in combatting stereotypes. It is best in such groups not to talk about race, religion, politics, or other controversial topics; rather, topics of conversation should be of common interest to all participants. Crime problems, conditions in the community that encourage crime, and ways to protect against crime are topics which provide the proper environment for lively interaction, which in turn leads people toward a better understanding of their similarities and individual differences.

1. The phrase *kernel of truth* appears in the fourth paragraph of the selection. Which one of the following phrases from that same paragraph means MOST NEARLY the same thing as *kernel of truth?* 1.____

   A. True facts
   B. Surface validity
   C. Firsthand knowledge
   D. Thorough assessment
   E. Reason behind the attitude

2. According to the conditioning principle set forth in the selection, which one of the following MOST accurately describes how stereotypes are formed? 2.____
   People

   A. are born uninformed, and stereotypes result from a failure to learn
   B. learn to fear others when, as youths, they have contact with them
   C. learn to fear others because they do not have the opportunity to get together with them
   D. learn to fear others when they have contact with them under unpleasant circumstances
   E. learn to fear others as a result of getting into an argument during which they are shouting at one another

3. A certain police department is conducting group discussions with Black, Hispanic, and White civilians, all participating along with several police officers. These discussions are aimed at combatting stereotypes and developing mutual understanding. 3.____
According to the selection, which one of the following topics of conversation is MOST likely to be effective in achieving this goal?

   A. *Gun Registration and Control*
   B. Keeping Burglars Out of your Home
   C. *Know Good English, Get a Good Job*
   D. *What Your City Councilman Can Do For You*
   E. *Contributions of Black Men in American History*

4. According to the selection, which one of the following results is MOST likely to occur if police officers show that they themselves are prejudiced? The police 4.____

   A. will be called *idiots* or *sadists*
   B. will be subjected to behavior modification
   C. will create tensions leading to a civil disorder
   D. generally will become stereotyped by citizen groups
   E. will be unable to fulfill their proper community role

5. According to the selection, which one of the following is the MOST serious obstacle encountered in trying to eliminate unwholesome stereotypes? 5.____

   A. Psychologists have not yet developed techniques for changing stereotypes.
   B. Stereotypes develop as a result of uncontrollable environmental influences.
   C. Such stereotypes are basically accurate because they are based on first-hand knowledge.
   D. Such stereotypes are generally inborn, or learned very young, and, in such cases, cannot be changed.
   E. Such stereotypes have an appearance of truth which makes people less likely to examine the stereotypes closely.

Questions 6-10.

DIRECTIONS: The following selection is to be used as the sole basis for answering Questions 6 through 10. Read the selection carefully and base your answers ONLY on the information contained therein.

Programs designed to reduce delinquency have been many and varied in approach. One can almost say that the pre-Lombroso era was one characterized as a total community approach.

Prior to the emergence of the Positive School of Criminology in 19th century Italy, criminology as a distinct scientific discipline did not exist. Crime was looked upon as one of the problems of the community, no different from the rest. Essentially, what the great doctor did was create a specialty, one which viewed the criminal among us as "different," a biologically distinct kind of human being, a "throwback" to earlier types of man.

From that point forward, in the history of man, wherever criminologists have gathered and organized themselves as separate from students of society in general, they have tended to study criminals as a type of group essentially different from other members in our society. Special ways of knowing tend to create special things to be known: new scientific disciplines generate new facts.

Lombrosoism has never completely died. It is still with us today, in a somewhat changed form, but nevertheless still there. The criminologist in the early 1900s changed the model of operation from the positivist school of thought, in which the idea of sin and willful corruption was stressed, to the individualistic or analytical school. The emphasis was shifted to single causes: physical disabilities, mental defects, etc. As one would suspect, our efforts at the art of crime prevention followed these theories. Coming full circle, we are now in the era of multiple causation3 or a school that by and large places the blame for crime and delinquency back on the community.

6. According to the selection, which one of the following choices MOST accurately describes the succession of schools of criminological thought? 6.____
   First the

   A. *analytical school and,* most recently, the positivistic school
   B. *positivistic school* and, most recently, the analytical school
   C. *analytical school,* followed by the positivistic school and, most recently, the multiple causation school
   D. *positivistic school,* followed by the individualistic school and, most recently, the multiple causation school
   E. *multiple causation school,* followed by the individualistic school, both of which superseded the positivistic school

7. Following are three statements about the history of Lombrosoism that might possibly be accurate: 7.____
   I. Lombrosoism replaced the Positive School of Criminology in the 19th century
   II. Lombrosoism served as the beginning point for criminology
   III. Some remainders of Lombrosoism still are left in modern theories of criminology

   Which one of the following choices MOST accurately classifies the above statements into those which are accurate and those which are not?

   A. I and II are accurate, but III is not.
   B. I and III are accurate, but II is not.
   C. II and III are accurate, but I is not.
   D. II is accurate, but I and III are not.
   E. All of I, II, and III are accurate.

8. Which one of the following was the MOST important belief held by the Positive School of Criminology? 8.____

   A. There is a single cause for criminal behavior.
   B. Blame for crime rests with the community.
   C. Criminology is not a distinct scientific discipline.
   D. Criminals are *throwbacks* to an earlier type of man.
   E. Crime results from a combination of causes which are present in every community.

9. The term *scientific discipline* appears near the end of the third paragraph of the selection. 9.____
Which one of the following words or phrases from that same paragraph means MOST NEARLY the same thing as *scientific discipline*?

A. Ways of knowing
B. Criminologists
C. Generate new facts
D. Things to be known
E. Students of society

10. A certain criminologist believes strongly that the theories of the analytical school of criminology are right. 10.____
Which one of the following factors or combinations of factors is this person MOST likely to blame for crime?

A. Heredity
B. Sinfulness
C. Mental illness
D. Community attitudes
E. Unemployment and poverty

KEY (CORRECT ANSWERS)

1.	B	6.	D
2.	D	7.	C
3.	B	8.	D
4.	E	9.	A
5.	E	10.	C

TEST 2

DIRECTIONS: Each question or incomplete statement is followed by several suggested answers or completions. Select the one that BEST answers the question or completes the statement. *PRINT THE LETTER OF THE CORRECT ANSWER IN THE SPACE AT THE RIGHT.*

Questions 1-6.

DIRECTIONS: Questions 1 through 6 are to be answered on the basis of the following situation.

Lieutenant X has just been assigned as the commanding officer of a small departmental unit in which important administrative services are performed in the handling of departmental property and equipment records. Before assuming his new duties, Lieutenant X is informed by his superior officer that he has not been satisfied with the operation of this office under the previous commanding officer. Specifically, this superior officer informs the lieutenant that some, but not all, of the office personnel, consisting entirely of uniformed personnel, did not perform their work accurately enough nor did they produce the amount of work that could reasonably be expected of them. Further, the superior feels that the office routine in the handling of records was somewhat inefficient.

The first day in his new assignment, Lieutenant X calls the entire staff together for a meeting and proceeds to outline to them a completely revised office procedure which he has personally developed within the past few days and which is to be effective immediately. The lieutenant requests all staff members to give him their reactions to the revised procedure. The revised procedure is not in conflict with official departmental procedures. He also states that the office personnel will have to be more accurate in their work and not devote any of their working time to personal matters or needless conversation.

Sergeant Y, next in the line of command in the unit, hearing of the revisions in procedure for the first time at the meeting, feels that the revisions are too drastic and should be modified since, in his opinion, most of the previous inefficiency was due to the quality of work performed by some personnel in need of additional training and not to poor procedures as such. The sergeant, however, decides not to mention his views to the lieutenant since he thinks it may appear that he is trying to establish a personal defense of the previous procedures because he was involved in their operation.

Patrolman Z is disturbed by the lieutenant's statement concerning the need for greater attention to duty and speaks up vigorously at the meeting. He states that he has personally been very conscientious in the performance of his duties and implies that this may not hold true for everyone else in the office, glancing toward the sergeant as he talks. The lieutenant, in an attempt to forestall a possible exchange of words between this patrolman and the sergeant, proceeds to take up some other matter. However, Sergeant Y feels compelled to defend himself and states that Patrolman Z is probably the individual most guilty of inattention to duty and that he spends a substantial part of the day in conversation of a personal nature with other office personnel. The lieutenant, feeling that the meeting is getting out of hand, states that this meeting is over, but that future meetings will be held regularly once every week.

1. The action taken by Lieutenant X's superior officer in informing him of the reasons for his dissatisfaction with the operation of the records office under the previous commanding officer was 1.____

   A. *improper*, giving such information constitutes an unnecessary personal criticism of the previous commanding officer
   B. *proper;* the operation of the office is more likely to be improved by Lieutenant X if he has some specific indications of the previously prevailing conditions
   C. *improper*, the lieutenant is more likely to correct poor procedures if he is allowed to discover for himself the reason that such procedures were employed
   D. *proper;* it is an effective method of mildly disciplining the previous commanding officer

2. Lieutenant X's method of instituting the completely revised office procedure was 2.____

   A. *good;* the old procedures were not effective and had to be changed
   B. *poor;* he should have waited until he had established a friendly relationship with each of his subordinates
   C. *good;* the poor work performance of his subordinates is a clear indication that it would be a waste of time to obtain their views on the revision of procedures
   D. *poor;* the revisions are likely to be more effective and more acceptable to his subordinates if their views were considered before putting the revisions into effect

3. Lieutenant X's remarks at the meeting concerning the poor work performance of the office personnel and their devoting working time to personal matters were 3.____

   A. *appropriate;* Lieutenant X's superior officer knows definitely that some of the personnel did not perform their work in an acceptable manner
   B. *inappropriate;* these remarks serve to handicap supervisory relationships
   C. *appropriate;* staff morale is less likely to suffer if no particular individual is singled out
   D. *inappropriate;* any negative remarks concerning the work performance of the unit as a whole should be made privately to staff members

4. Sergeant Y's decision NOT to inform the lieutenant at this time of his opinion that the revisions of procedure are too drastic was 4.____

   A. *improper*, the sergeant should express his doubts concerning the revised procedure despite possible misinterpretation by the lieutenant
   B. *proper*, a sergeant must wait until a lieutenant addresses a question to him personally
   C. *improper*, the lieutenant's revisions of procedure should be reviewed and approved by all those affected before such changes are adopted
   D. *proper*, the sergeant's belief that the lieutenant does not really expect an expression of views is a realistic appraisal of the situation

5. The lieutenant's immediate action when Patrolman Z implies that the sergeant has not been very conscientious in the performance of his duties was 5.____

   A. *good;* the patrolman's statement is clearly biased and merits no further consideration
   B. *poor;* this situation provides a good opportunity for the lieutenant to determine to what extent the sergeant was responsible for the unit's poor performance

C. *good;* an exchange of words between the officers is likely to become highly personal and tend to undermine unit discipline
D. *poor;* the patrolman should be required to give details to support his implications of neglect of duty by the sergeant

6. Sergeant Y's answer to the charge of the patrolman was 6.____

A. *appropriate;* an officer is justified in defending himself against unjust charges whatever their source may be
B. *inappropriate;* the patrolman did not identify the sergeant by name as not being conscientious in the performance of his duties
C. *appropriate;* a patrolman is never justified in criticizing the behavior of a superior in the presence of other staff members
D. *inappropriate;* such a detailing of the patrolman's alleged misconduct should not be undertaken in the presence of other staff members

Questions 7-9.

DIRECTIONS: Questions 7 through 9 are to be answered SOLELY on the basis of the following paragraphs.

Perhaps the most difficult administrative problem of the police records unit is the maintenance of cooperative relationships with the operating units in the department. Unless these relationships are completely accepted by the operating units, some records activities will result in friction. The records system is a tool of the chief administrative officer and the various supervising officers in managing personnel; police operations and procedures. However, the records unit must constantly check on the records activities of all members of the department if the records system is to serve as a really effective tool for these supervisory officers.

The first step in avoiding conflict between the records and the operating units is to develop definite policies and regulations governing the records system. These regulations should be prepared jointly by the head of the records unit and the heads of the operating units under the leadership of the chief administrative officer of the department. Once the records policies and regulations have been agreed upon, the task is to secure conformity. Theoretically, if a patrolman fails to prepare a report of an investigation, his commanding officer should be notified by the records unit and he in turn should take appropriate measures to secure the report. Practically, this line of command must be cut across in the case of such routine matters, or the commanding officer will spend time in keeping the records system going that should be devoted to the other police duties which comprise the major work of the department. However, if the patrolman is persistently negligent, or if a new policy or procedure is being initiated, the records unit must deal through the commanding officer.

7. According to the above paragraphs, the one of the following situations in which the records unit would MOST likely contact a commanding officer of an operating unit is when 7.____

A. a patrolman has expressed disagreement with a records unit policy and suggests a modification of the policy
B. an important record, which involves more than one operating unit, has been carelessly prepared by a patrolman

C. the commanding officer of the operating unit devotes little time to police duties which comprise the major work of the department
D. the records unit has received orders from the chief administrative officer to institute several changes in previous records procedures

8. According to the above paragraphs, obtaining agreement as to definite policies and regulations governing the records system 8.____

A. guarantees the avoidance of conflict between the records and operating divisions
B. is of lesser importance than the maintenance of cooperative relationships thereafter
C. should precede any active records division efforts to gain compliance with such policies and regulations
D. should be preceded by an evaluation of the extent to which supervisory officers consider the system an effective management tool

9. According to the above paragraph, conflict between the records division and the operating divisions is MOST likely to result when the 9.____

A. chief administrative officer denies to the records division the authority to check on the records activities of all members of the department
B. operating divisions are not convinced that their work contacts with the records division are useful and desirable
C. records division voluntarily attempts to establish productive relationships with operating divisions
D. operating divisions understand the specific nature of records division duties

Questions 10-12.

DIRECTIONS: Questions 10 through 12 are to be answered SOLELY on the basis of the following paragraph.

Early in the development of police service, legislators granted powers and authority to policemen beyond their inherent rights as citizens in order that they would be able to act effectively in the discharge of their duties. The law makers also recognized the fact that unless policemen were excused from complete obedience to certain laws and regulations they would be seriously encumbered in the effective discharge of their duties. The exemptions were specifically provided for by legislative action because of the danger of abuse of power involved in granting blanket privileges and powers. The public, however, has not been so discriminating and has gone well beyond the law in excusing policemen, from full obedience to regulatory measures. The liberal interpretation that the public has placed upon the right of police officers to disobey the law has been motivated in part by public confidence in law enforcement and in part by a sincere desire of the public to assist the police in every way in the performance of their duties. Further, the average citizen is not interested in the technicalities of law enforcement nor is he aware of the legal limitations that are placed upon the authority of policemen. It is a regrettable fact that many policemen assume so-called rights of law that either do not exist or that are subject to well-defined legal limitations, because the public generally is unaware of the limitations placed by law upon policemen.

10. According to the above paragraph, the one of the following statements which BEST explains the reason for granting special legal powers to policemen is that such powers were granted 10._____

A. because the exercise of their inherent rights by citizens frequently conflicted with efficient law enforcement
B. because the public has not been sufficiently vigilant in objecting to blanket grants of power
C. in order to excuse policemen from full obedience to laws and regulations which they are unable to enforce
D. in order to remove certain handicaps experienced by policemen in law enforcement operations

11. According to the above paragraph, specific legislative exemptions for policemen from complete obedience to certain laws and regulations 11._____

A. are based largely on so-called rights of law that either do not exist or are misinterpreted by the public
B. have not been abused by the police even though most individual policemen ignore proper legal limitations
C. have not provided a fully effective limitation on the exercise of unwarranted police authority
D. have been misunderstood by the police and the public partly because they are based on unduly technical laws

12. According to the above paragraph, the one of the following statements which BEST explains the liberal attitude of the public toward the special powers of policemen is that the public 12._____

A. believes that the police are justified in disregarding the technicalities of law enforcement and also wants to assist the police in the performance of their duties
B. feels that the laws restricting police authority are overly strict and also believes that the police are performing their duties in a proper manner
C. is not aware of the legal restrictions on police authority and also believes that the police are performing their duties in a proper manner
D. wants to assist the police in the performance of their duties and also feels that the laws on police authority are sufficiently restrictive

Questions 13-15.

DIRECTIONS: Questions 13 through 15 are to be answered SOLELY on the basis of the following paragraph.

The use of modem scientific methods in the examination of physical evidence often provides information to the investigator which he could not otherwise obtain. This applies particularly to small objects and materials present in minute quantities or trace evidence because the quantities here are such that they may be overlooked without methodical searching, and often special means of detection are needed. Whenever two objects come in contact with one another, there is a transfer of material, however slight. Usually, the softer object will transfer to the harder, but the transfer may be mutual. The quantity of material transferred differs with the type of material involved and the more violent the contact the greater the degree of transferrence. Through scientific methods of determining physical properties and chemical composition, we can add to the facts observable by the investigator's unaided senses, and thereby increase the chances of identification.

13. According to the above paragraph, the amount of material transferred whenever two objects come in contact with one another 13.____

    A. varies directly with the softness of the objects involved
    B. varies directly with the violence of the contact of the objects
    C. is greater when two soft, rather than hard, objects come into violent contact with each other
    D. is greater when coarse-grained, rather than smooth-grained, materials are involved

14. According to the above paragraph, the PRINCIPAL reason for employing scientific methods in obtaining trace evidence is that 14.____

    A. other methods do not involve a methodical search of the crime scene
    B. scientific methods of examination frequently reveal physical evidence which did not previously exist
    C. the amount of trace evidence may be so sparse that other methods are useless
    D. trace evidence cannot be properly identified unless special means of detection are employed

15. According to the above paragraph, the one of the following statements which BEST describes the manner in which scientific methods of analyzing physical evidence assists the investigator is that such methods 15.____

    A. add additional valuable information to the investigator's own knowledge of complex and rarely occurring materials found as evidence
    B. compensate for the lack of important evidential material through the use of physical and chemical analyses
    C. make possible an analysis of evidence which goes beyond the ordinary capacity of the investigator's senses
    D. identify precisely those physical characteristics of the individual which the untrained senses of the investigator are unable to discern

---

KEY (CORRECT ANSWERS)

1.	B	6.	D	11.	C
2.	D	7.	D	12.	C
3.	B	8.	C	13.	B
4.	A	9.	B	14.	C
5.	C	10.	D	15.	C

PREPARING WRITTEN MATERIAL

PARAGRAPH REARRANGEMENT COMMENTARY

The sentences which follow are in scrambled order. You are to rearrange them in proper order and indicate the letter choice containing the correct answer at the space at the right.

Each group of sentences in this section is actually a paragraph presented in scrambled order. Each sentence in the group has a place in that paragraph; no sentence is to be left out. You are to read each group of sentences and decide upon the best order in which to put the sentences so as to form as well-organized paragraph.

The questions in this section measure the ability to solve a problem when all the facts relevant to its solution are not given.

More specifically, certain positions of responsibility and authority require the employee to discover connections between events sometimes, apparently, unrelated. In order to do this, the employee will find it necessary to correctly infer that unspecified events have probably occurred or are likely to occur. This ability becomes especially important when action must be taken on incomplete information.

Accordingly, these questions require competitors to choose among several suggested alternatives, each of which presents a different sequential arrangement of the events. Competitors must choose the MOST logical of the suggested sequences.

In order to do so, they may be required to draw on general knowledge to infer missing concepts or events that are essential to sequencing the given events. Competitors should be careful to infer only what is essential to the sequence. The plausibility of the wrong alternatives will always require the inclusion of unlikely events or of additional chains of events which are NOT essential to sequencing the given events.

It's very important to remember that you are looking for the best of the four possible choices, and that the best choice of all may not even be one of the answers you're given to choose from.

There is no one right way to solve these problems. Many people have found it helpful to first write out the order of the sentences, as they would have arranged them, on their scrap paper before looking at the possible answers. If their optimum answer is there, this can save them some time. If it isn't, this method can still give insight into solving the problem. Others find it most helpful to just go through each of the possible choices, contrasting each as they go along. You should use whatever method feels comfortable, and works, for you.

While most of these types of questions are not that difficult, we've added a higher percentage of the difficult type, just to give you more practice. Usually there are only one or two questions on this section that contain such subtle distinctions that you're unable to answer confidently, and you then may find yourself stuck deciding between two possible choices, neither of which you're sure about.

PREPARING WRITTEN MATERIAL
EXAMINATION SECTION
TEST 1

DIRECTIONS: The sentences that follow are in scrambled order. You are to rearrange them in proper order and indicate the letter choice containing the CORRECT answer. *PRINT THE LETTER OF THE CORRECT ANSWER IN THE SPACE AT THE RIGHT.*

1. Police Officer Jenner responds to the scene of a burglary at 2106 La Vista Boulevard. He is approached by an elderly man named Richard Jenkins, whose account of the incident includes the following five sentences: 1.____

   I. I saw that the lock on my apartment door had been smashed and the door was open.
   II. My apartment was a shambles; my belongings were everywhere and my television set was missing.
   III. As I walked down the hallway toward the bedroom, I heard someone opening a window.
   IV. I left work at 5:30 P.M. and took the bus home.
   V. At that time, I called the police.

   The MOST logical order for the above sentences to appear in the report is

   A. I, V, IV, II, III
   B. IV, I, II, III, V
   C. I, V, II, III, IV
   D. IV, III, II, V, I

2. Police Officer LaJolla is writing an Incident Report in which back-up assistance was required. The report will contain the following five sentences: 2.____

   I. The radio dispatcher asked what my location was and he then dispatched patrol cars for back-up assistance.
   II. At approximately 9:30 P.M., while I was walking my assigned footpost, a gunman fired three shots at me.
   III. I quickly turned around and saw a white male, approximately 5'10", with black hair, wearing blue jeans, a yellow T-shirt, and white sneakers, running across the avenue carrying a handgun.
   IV. When the back-up officers arrived, we searched the area but could not find the suspect.
   V. I advised the radio dispatcher that a gunman had just fired a gun at me, and then I gave the dispatcher a description of the man.

   The MOST logical order for the above sentences to appear in the report is

   A. III, V, II, IV, I
   B. II, III, V, I, IV
   C. III, II, IV, I, V
   D. II, V, I, III, IV

3. Police Officer Durant is completing a report of a robbery and assault. The report will contain the following five sentences: 3.____

   I. I went to Mount Snow Hospital to interview a man who was attacked and robbed of his wallet earlier that night.
   II. An ambulance arrived at 82nd Street and 3rd Avenue and took an intoxicated, wounded man to Mount Snow Hospital.
   III. Two youths attacked the man and stole his wallet.
   IV. A well-dressed man left Hanratty's Bar very drunk, with his wallet hanging out of his back pocket.
   V. A passerby dialed 911 and requested police and ambulance assistance.

The MOST logical order for the above sentences to appear in the report is

A. I, II, IV, III, V
B. IV, III, V, II, I
C. IV, V, II, III, I
D. V, IV, III, II, I

4. Police Officer Boswell is preparing a report of an armed robbery and assault which will contain the following five sentences: 4.____

I. Both men approached the bartender and one of them drew a gun.
II. The bartender immediately went to grab the phone at the bar.
III. One of the men leaped over the counter and smashed a bottle over the bartender's head.
IV. Two men in a blue Buick drove up to the bar and went inside.
V. I found the cash register empty and the bartender unconscious on the floor, with the phone still dangling off the hook.

The MOST logical order for the above sentences to appear in the report is

A. IV, I, II, III, V
B. V, IV, III, I, II
C. IV, III, II, V, I
D. II, I, III, IV, V

5. Police Officer Mitzler is preparing a report of a bank robbery, which will contain the following five sentences: 5.____

I. The teller complied with the instructions on the note, but also hit the silent alarm.
II. The perpetrator then fled south on Broadway.
III. A suspicious male entered the bank at approximately 10:45 A.M.
IV. At this time, an undetermined amount of money has been taken.
V. He approached the teller on the far right side and handed her a note.

The MOST logical order for the above sentences to appear in the report is

A. III, V, I, II, IV
B. I, III, V, II, IV
C. III, V, IV, I, II
D. III, V, II, IV, I

6. A Police Officer is preparing an Accident Report for an accident which occurred at the intersection of East 119th Street and Lexington Avenue. The report will include the following five sentences: 6.____

I. On September 18, 1990, while driving ten children to school, a school bus driver passed out.
II. Upon arriving at the scene, I notified the dispatcher to send an ambulance.
III. I notified the parents of each child once I got to the station house.
IV. He said the school bus, while traveling west on East 119th Street, struck a parked Ford which was on the southwest corner of East 119th Street.
V. A witness by the name of John Ramos came up to me to describe what happened.

The MOST logical order for the above sentences to appear in the Accident Report is

A. I, II, V, III, IV
B. I, II, V, IV, III
C. II, V, I, III, IV
D. II, V, I, IV, III

7. A Police Officer is preparing a report concerning a dispute. The report will contain the following five sentences: 7.____

I. The passenger got out of the back of the taxi and leaned through the front window to complain to the driver about the fare.
II. The driver of the taxi caught up with the passenger and knocked him to the ground; the passenger then kicked the driver and a scuffle ensued.
III. The taxi drew up in front of the high-rise building and stopped.
IV. The driver got out of the taxi and followed the passenger into the lobby of the apartment building.
V. The doorman tried but was unable to break up the fight, at which point he called the precinct.

The MOST logical order for the above sentences to appear in the report is

A. III, I, IV, II, V
B. III, IV, I, II, V
C. III, IV, II, V, I
D. V, I, III, IV, II

8. Police Officer Morrow is writing an Incident Report. The report will include the following four sentences: 8.____

I. The man reached into his pocket and pulled out a gun.
II. While on foot patrol, I identified a suspect, who was wanted for six robberies in the area, from a wanted picture I was carrying.
III. I drew my weapon and fired six rounds at the suspect, killing him instantly.
IV. I called for back-up assistance and told the man to put his hands up.

The MOST logical order for the above sentences to appear in the report is

A. II, III, IV, I
B. IV, I, III, II
C. IV, I, II, III
D. II, IV, I, III

9. Sergeant Allen responds to a call at 16 Grove Street regarding a missing child. At the scene, the Sergeant is met by Police Officer Samuels, who gives a brief account of the incident consisting of the following five sentences: 9.____

I. I transmitted the description and waited for you to arrive before I began searching the area.
II. Mrs. Banks, the mother, reports that she last saw her daughter Julie about 7:30 A.M. when she took her to school.
III. About 6 P.M., my partner and I arrived at this location to investigate a report of a missing 8 year-old girl.
IV. When Mrs. Banks left her, Julie was wearing a red and white striped T-shirt, blue jeans, and white sneakers.
V. Mrs. Banks dropped her off in front of the playground of P.S. 11.

The MOST logical order for the above sentences to appear in the report is

A. III, V, IV, II, I
B. III, II, V, IV, I
C. III, IV, I, II, V
D. III, II, IV, I, V

10. Police Officer Franco is completing a report of an assault. The report will contain the following five sentences: 10.____

I. In the park I observed an elderly man lying on the ground, bleeding from a back wound.
II. I applied first aid to control the bleeding and radioed for an ambulance to respond.

III. The elderly man stated that he was sitting on the park bench when he was attacked from behind by two males.
IV. I received a report of a man's screams coming from inside the park, and I went to investigate.
V. The old man could not give a description of his attackers.

The MOST logical order for the above sentences to appear in the report is

A. IV, I, II, III, V
B. V, III, I, IV, II
C. IV, III, V, II, I
D. II, I, V, IV, III

11. Police Officer Williams is completing a Crime Report. The report contains the following five sentences: 11.____

I. As Police Officer Hanson and I approached the store, we noticed that the front door was broken.
II. After determining that the burglars had fled, we notified the precinct of the burglary.
III. I walked through the front door as Police Officer Hanson walked around to the back.
IV. At approximately midnight, an alarm was heard at the Apex Jewelry Store.
V. We searched the store and found no one.

The MOST logical order for the above sentences to appear in the report is

A. I, IV, II, III, V
B. I, IV, III, V, II
C. IV, I, III, II, V
D. IV, I, III, V, II

12. Police Officer Clay is giving a report to the news media regarding someone who has jumped from the Empire State Building. His report will include the following five sentences: 12.____

I. I responded to the 86th floor, where I found the person at the edge of the roof.
II. A security guard at the building had reported that a man was on the roof at the 86th floor.
III. At 5:30 P.M., the person jumped from the building.
IV. I received a call from the radio dispatcher at 4:50 P.M. to respond to the Empire State Building.
V. I tried to talk to the person and convince him not to jump.

The MOST logical order for the above sentences to appear in the report is

A. I, II, IV, III, V
B. III, IV, I, II, V
C. II, IV, I, III, V
D. IV, II, I, V, III

13. The following five sentences are part of a report of a burglary written by Police Officer Reed: 13.____

I. When I arrived at 2400 1st Avenue, I noticed that the door was slightly open.
II. I yelled out, *Police, don't move!*
III. As I entered the apartment, I saw a man with a TV set passing it through a window to another man standing on a fire escape.
IV. While on foot patrol, I was informed by the radio dispatcher that a burglary was in progress at 2400 1st Avenue.
V. However, the burglars quickly ran down the fire escape.

The MOST logical order for the above sentences to appear in the report is

A. I, III, IV, V, II
B. IV, I, III, V, II
C. IV, I, III, II, V
D. I, IV, III, II, V

14. Police Officer Jenkins is preparing a report for Lost or Stolen Property. The report will include the following five sentences: 14.____

I. On the stairs, Mr. Harris slipped on a wet leaf and fell on the landing.
II. It wasn't until he got to the token booth that Mr. Harris realized his wallet was no longer in his back pants pocket.
III. A boy wearing a football jersey helped him up and brushed off the back of Mr. Harris' pants.
IV. Mr. Harris states he was walking up the stairs to the elevated subway at Queensborough Plaza.
V. Before Mr. Harris could thank him, the boy was running down the stairs to the street.

The MOST logical order for the above sentences to appear in the report is

A. IV, III, V, I, II
B. IV, I, III, V, II
C. I, IV, II, III, V
D. I, II, IV, III, V

15. Police Officer Hubbard is completing a report of a missing person. The report will contain the following five sentences: 15.____

I. I visited the store at 7:55 P.M. and asked the employees if they had seen a girl fitting the description I had been given.
II. She gave me a description and said she had gone into the local grocery store at about 6:15 P.M.
III. I asked the woman for a description of her daughter.
IV. The distraught woman called the precinct to report that her daughter, aged 12, had not returned from an errand.
V. The storekeeper said a girl matching the description had been in the store earlier, but he could not give an exact time.

The MOST logical order for the above sentences to appear in the report is

A. I, III, II, V, IV
B. IV, III, II, I, V
C. V, I, II, III, IV
D. III, I, II, IV, V

16. A police officer is completing an entry in his Daily Activity Log regarding traffic summonses which he issued. The following five sentences will be included in the entry: 16.____

I. I was on routine patrol parked 16 yards west of 170th Street and Clay Avenue.
II. The summonses were issued for unlicensed operator and disobeying a steady red light.
III. At 8 A.M. hours, I observed an auto traveling westbound on 170th Street not stop for a steady red light at the intersection of Clay Avenue and 170th Street.
IV. I stopped the driver of the auto and determined that he did not have a valid driver's license.
V. After a brief conversation, I informed the motorist that he was receiving two summonses.

The MOST logical order for the above sentences to appear in the report is

A. I, III, IV, V, II
B. III, IV, II, V, I
C. V, II, I, III, IV
D. IV, V, II, I, III

17. The following sentences appeared on an Incident Report: 17.____

I. Three teenagers who had been ejected from the theater were yelling at patrons who were now entering.
II. Police Officer Dixon told the teenagers to leave the area.
III. The teenagers said that they were told by the manager to leave the theater because they were talking during the movie.
IV. The theater manager called the precinct at 10:20 P.M. to report a disturbance outside the theater.
V. A patrol car responded to the theater at 10:42 P.M. and two police officers went over to the teenagers.

The MOST logical order for the above sentences to appear in the Incident Report

A. I, V, IV, III, II
B. IV, I, V, III, II
C. IV, I, III, V, II
D. IV, III, I, V, II

18. Activity Log entries are completed by police officers. Police Officer Samuels has written an entry concerning vandalism and part of it contains the following five sentences: 18.____

I. The man, in his early twenties, ran down the block and around the corner.
II. A man passing the store threw a brick through a window of the store.
III. I arrived on the scene and began to question the witnesses about the incident.
IV. Malcolm Holmes, the owner of the Fast Service Shoe Repair Store, was working in the back of the store at approximately 3 P.M.
V. After the man fled, Mr. Holmes called the police.

The MOST logical order for the above sentences to appear in the Activity Log is

A. IV, II, I, V, III
B. II, IV, I, III, V
C. II, I, IV, III, V
D. IV, II, V, III, I

19. Police Officer Buckley is preparing a report concerning a dispute in a restaurant. The report will contain the following five sentences: 19.____

I. The manager, Charles Chin, and a customer, Edward Green, were standing near the register arguing over the bill.
II. The manager refused to press any charges providing Green pay the check and leave.
III. While on foot patrol, I was informed by a passerby of a disturbance in the Dragon Flame Restaurant.
IV. Green paid the $7.50 check and left the restaurant.
V. According to witnesses, the customer punched the owner in the face when Chin asked him for the amount due.

The MOST logical order for the above sentences to appear in the report is

A. III, I, V, II, IV
B. I, II, III, IV, V
C. V, I, III, II, IV
D. III, V, II, IV, I

20. Police Officer Wilkins is preparing a report for leaving the scene of an accident. The report will include the following five sentences: 20.____

    I. The Dodge struck the right rear fender of Mrs. Smith's 1980 Ford and continued on its way.
    II. Mrs. Smith stated she was making a left turn from 40th Street onto Third Avenue.
    III. As the car passed, Mrs. Smith noticed the dangling rear license plate #412AEJ.
    IV. Mrs. Smith complained to police of back pains and was removed by ambulance to Bellevue Hospital.
    V. An old green Dodge traveling up Third Avenue went through the red light at 40th Street and Third Avenue.

    The MOST logical order for the above sentences to appear in the report is

    A. V, III, I, II, IV
    B. I, III, II, V, IV
    C. IV, V, I, II, III
    D. II, V, I, III, IV

21. Detective Simon is completing a Crime Report. The report contains the following five sentences: 21.____

    I. Police Officer Chin, while on foot patrol, heard the yelling and ran in the direction of the man.
    II. The man, carrying a large hunting knife, left the High Sierra Sporting Goods Store at approximately 10:30 A.M.
    III. When the man heard Police Officer Chin, he stopped, dropped the knife, and began to cry.
    IV. As Police Officer Chin approached the man, he drew his gun and yelled, *Police, freeze.*
    V. After the man left the store, he began yelling, over and over, *I am going to 'kill myself!*

    The MOST logical order for the above sentences to appear in the report is

    A. V, II, I, IV, III
    B. II, V, I, IV, III
    C. II, V, IV, I, III
    D. II, I, V, IV, III

22. Police Officer Miller is preparing a Complaint Report which will include the following five sentences: 22.____

    I. From across the lot, he yelled to the boys to get away from his car.
    II. When he came out of the store, he noticed two teenage boys trying to break into his car.
    III. The boys fled as Mr. Johnson ran to his car.
    IV. Mr. Johnson stated that he parked his car in the municipal lot behind Tams Department Store.
    V. Mr. Johnson saw that the door lock had been broken, but nothing was missing from inside the auto.

    The MOST logical order for the above sentences to appear in the report is

    A. IV, I, II, V, III
    B. II, III, I, V, IV
    C. IV, II, I, III, V
    D. I, II, III, V, IV

23. Police Officer O'Hara completes a Universal Summons for a motorist who has just passed a red traffic light. The Universal Summons includes the following five sentences: 23.____

I. As the car passed the light, I followed in the patrol car.
II. After the driver stopped the car, he stated that the light was yellow, not red.
III. A blue Cadillac sedan passed the red light on the corner of 79th Street and 3rd Avenue at 11:25 P.M.
IV. As a result, the driver was informed that he did pass a red light and that his brake lights were not working.
V. The driver in the Cadillac stopped his car as soon as he saw the patrol car, and I noticed that the brake lights were not working.

The MOST logical order for the above sentences to appear in the Universal Summons is

A. I, III, V, II, IV
B. III, I, V, II, IV
C. Iil, I, V, IV, II
D. I, III, IV, II, V

24. Detective Egan is preparing a follow-up report regarding a homicide on 170th Street and College Avenue. An unknown male was found at the scene. The report will contain the following five sentences: 24.____

I. Police Officer Gregory wrote down the names, addresses, and phone numbers of the witnesses.
II. A 911 operator received a call of a man shot and dispatched Police Officers Worth and Gregory to the scene.
III. They discovered an unidentified male dead on the street.
IV. Police Officer Worth notified the Precinct Detective Unit immediately.
V. At approximately 9:00 A.M., an unidentified male shot another male in the chest during an argument.

The MOST logical order for the above sentences to appear in the report is

A. V, II, III, IV, I
B. II, III, V, IV, I
C. IV, I, V, II, III
D. V, III, II, IV, I

25. Police Officer Tracey is preparing a Robbery Report which will include the following five sentences: 25.____

I. I ran around the corner and observed a man pointing a gun at a taxidriver.
II. I informed the man I was a police officer and that he should not move.
III. I was on the corner of 125th Street and Park Avenue when I heard a scream coming from around the corner.
IV. The man turned around and fired one shot at me.
V. I fired once, shooting him in the arm and causing him to fall to the ground.

The MOST logical order for the above sentences to appear in the report is

A. I, III, IV, II, V
B. IV, V, II, I, III
C. III, I, II, IV, V
D. III, I, V, II, IV

KEY (CORRECT ANSWERS)

1. B
2. B
3. B
4. A
5. A
6. B
7. A
8. D
9. B
10. A
11. D
12. D
13. C
14. B
15. B
16. A
17. B
18. A
19. A
20. D
21. B
22. C
23. B
24. A
25. C

TEST 2

DIRECTIONS: The sentences that follow are in scrambled order. You are to rearrange them in proper order and indicate the letter choice containing the CORRECT answer. *PRINT THE LETTER OF THE CORRECT ANSWER IN THE SPACE AT THE RIGHT.*

1. Police Officer Weiker is completing a Complaint Report which will contain the following- five sentences: 1.____
   I. Mr. Texlor was informed that the owner of the van would receive a parking ticket and that the van would be towed away.
   II. The police tow truck arrived approximately one half hour after Mr. Texlor complained.
   III. While on foot patrol on West End Avenue, I saw the owner of Rand's Restaurant arrive to open his business.
   IV. Mr. Texlor, the owner, called to me and complained that he could not receive deliveries because a van was blocking his driveway.
   V. The van's owner later reported to the precinct that his van had been stolen, and he was then informed that it had been towed.

   The MOST logical order for the above sentences to appear in the report is

   A. III, V, I, II, IV
   B. III, IV, I, II, V
   C. IV, III, I, II, V
   D. IV, III, II, I, V

2. Police Officer Ames is completing an entry in his Activity Log. The entry contains the following five sentences: 2.____
   I. Mr. Sands gave me a complete description of the robber.
   II. Alvin Sands, owner of the Star Delicatessen, called the precinct to report he had just been robbed.
   III. I then notified all police patrol vehicles to look for a white male in his early twenties wearing brown pants and shirt, a black leather jacket, and black and white sneakers.
   IV. I arrived on the scene after being notified by the precinct that a robbery had just occurred at the Star Delicatessen.
   V. Twenty minutes later, a man fitting the description was arrested by a police officer on patrol six blocks from the delicatessen.

   The MOST logical order for the above sentences to appear in the Activity Log is

   A. II, I, IV, III, V
   B. II, IV, III, I, V
   C. II, IV, I, III, V
   D. II, IV, I, V, III

3. Police Officer Benson is completing a Complaint Report concerning a stolen taxicab, which will include the following five sentences: 3.____
   I. Police Officer Benson noticed that a cab was parked next to a fire hydrant.
   II. Dawson *borrowed* the cab for transportation purposes since he was in a hurry.
   III. Ed Dawson got into his car and tried to start it, but the battery was dead.
   IV. When he reached his destination, he parked the cab by a fire hydrant and placed the keys under the seat.
   V. He looked around and saw an empty cab with the engine running.

   The MOST logical order for the above sentences to appear in the report is

A. I, III, II, IV, V
B. III, I, II, V, IV
C. III, V, II, IV, I
D. V, II, IV, III, I

4. Police Officer Hatfield is reviewing his Activity Log entry prior to completing a report. The entry contains the following five sentences: 4.____

I. When I arrived at Zand's Jewelry Store, I noticed that the door was slightly open.
II. I told the burglar I was a police officer and that he should stand still or he would be shot.
III. As I entered the store, I saw a man wearing a ski mask attempting to open the safe in the back of the store.
IV. On December 16, 1990, at 1:38 A.M., I was informed that a burglary was in progress at Zand's Jewelry Store on East 59th Street.
V. The burglar quickly pulled a knife from his pocket when he saw me.

The MOST logical order for the above sentences to appear in the report is

A. IV, I, III, V, II
B. I, IV, III, V, II
C. IV, III, II, V, I
D. I, III, IV, V, II

5. Police Officer Lorenz is completing a report of a murder. The report will contain the following five statements made by a witness: 5.____

I. I was awakened by the sound of a gunshot coming from the apartment next door, and I decided to check.
II. I entered the apartment and looked into the kitchen and the bathroom.
III. I found Mr. Hubbard's body slumped in the bathtub.
IV. The door to the apartment was open, but I didn't see anyone.
V. He had been shot in the head.

The MOST logical order for the above sentences to appear in the report is

A. I, III, II, IV, V
B. I, IV, II, III, V
C. IV, II, I, III, V
D. III, I, II, IV, V

6. Police Officer Baldwin is preparing an accident report which will include the following five sentences: 6.____

I. The old man lay on the ground for a few minutes, but was not physically hurt.
II. Charlie Watson, a construction worker, was repairing some brick work at the top of a building at 54th Street and Madison Avenue.
III. Steven Green, his partner, warned him that this could be dangerous, but Watson ignored him.
IV. A few minutes later, one of the bricks thrown by Watson smashed to the ground in front of an old man, who fainted out of fright.
V. Mr. Watson began throwing some of the bricks over the side of the building.

The MOST logical order for the above sentences to appear in the report is

A. II, V, III, IV, I
B. I, IV, II, V, III
C. III, II, IV, V, I
D. II, III, I, IV, V

7. Police Officer Porter is completing an incident report concerning her rescue of a woman being held hostage by a former boyfriend. Her report will contain the following five sentences: 7.____

I. I saw a man holding .25 caliber gun to a woman's head, but he did not see me.
II. I then broke a window and gained access to the house.
III. As I approached the house on foot, a gunshot rang out and I heard a woman scream.
IV. A decoy van brought me as close as possible to the house where the woman was being held hostage.
V. I ordered the man to drop his gun, and he released the woman and was taken into custody.

The MOST logical order for the above sentences to appear in the report is

A. I, III, II, IV, V
B. IV, III, II, I, V
C. III, II, I, IV, V
D. V, I, II, III, IV

8. Police Officer Byrnes is preparing a crime report concerning a robbery. The report will consist of the following five sentences: 8.____

I. Mr. White, following the man's instructions, opened the car's hood, at which time the man got out of the auto, drew a revolver, and ordered White to give him all the money in his pockets.
II. Investigation has determined there were no witnesses to this incident.
III. The man asked White to check the oil and fill the tank.
IV. Mr. White, a gas attendant, states that he was working alone at the gas station when a black male pulled up to the gas pump in a white Mercury.
V. White was then bound and gagged by the male and locked in the gas station's rest room.

The MOST logical order for the above sentences to appear in the report is

A. IV, I, III, II, V
B. III, I, II, V, IV
C. IV, III, I, V, II
D. I, III, IV, II, V

9. Police Officer Gale is preparing a report of a crime committed against Mr. Weston. The report will consist of the following five sentences: 9.____

I. The man, who had a gun, told Mr. Weston not to scream for help and ordered him back into the apartment.
II. With Mr. Weston disposed of in this fashion, the man proceeded to ransack the apartment.
III. Opening the door to see who was there, Mr. Weston was confronted by a tall white male wearing a dark blue jacket and white pants.
IV. Mr. Weston was at home alone in his living room when the doorbell rang.
V. Once inside, the man bound and gagged Mr. Weston and locked him in the bathroom.

The MOST logical order for the above sentences to appear in the report is

A. III, V, II, I, IV
B. IV, III, I, V, II
C. III, V, IV, II, I
D. IV, III, V, I, II

10. A police officer is completing a report of a robbery, which will contain the following five sentences: 10.____

I. Two police officers were about to enter the Red Rose Coffee Shop on 47th Street and 8th Avenue.
II. They then noticed a male running up the street carrying a brown paper bag.
III. They heard a woman standing outside the Broadway Boutique yelling that her store had just been robbed by a young man, and she was pointing up the street.
IV. They caught up with him and made an arrest.
V. The police officers pursued the male, who ran past them on 8th Avenue.

The MOST logical order for the above sentences to appear in the report is

A. I, III, II, V, IV
B. III, I, II, V, IV
C. IV, V, I, II, III
D. I, V, IV, III, II

11. Police Officer Capalbo is preparing a report of a bank robbery. The report will contain the following five statements made by a witness: 11.____

I. Initially, all I could see were two men, dressed in maintenance uniforms, sitting in the area reserved for bank officers.
II. I was passing the bank at 8 P.M. and noticed that all the lights were out, except in the rear section.
III. Then I noticed two other men in the bank, coming from the direction of the vault, carrying a large metal box.
IV. At this point, I decided to call the police.
V. I knocked on the window to get the attention of the men in the maintenance uniforms, and they chased the two men carrying the box down a flight of steps.

The MOST logical order for the above sentences to appear in the report is

A. IV, I, II, V, III
B. I, III, II, V, IV
C. II, I, III, V, IV
D. II, III, I, V, IV

12. Police Officer Roberts is preparing a crime report concerning an assault and a stolen car. The report will contain the following five sentences: 12.____

I. Upon leaving the store to return to his car, Winters noticed that a male unknown to him was sitting in his car.
II. The man then re-entered Winters' car and drove away, fleeing north on 2nd Avenue.
III. Mr. Winters stated that he parked his car in front of 235 East 25th Street and left the engine running while he went into the butcher shop at that location.
IV. Mr. Robert Gering, a witness, stated that the male is known in the neighborhood as Bobby Rae and is believed to reside at 323 East 114th Street.
V. When Winters approached the car and ordered the man to get out, the man got out of the auto and struck Winters with his fists, knocking him to the ground.

The MOST logical order for the above sentences to appear in the report is

A. III, II, V, I, IV
B. III, I, V, II, IV
C. I, IV, V, II, III
D. III, II, I, V, IV

13. Police Officer Robinson is preparing a crime report concerning the robbery of Mr. Edwards' store. The report will consist of the following five sentences: 13.____

I. When the last customer left the store, the two men drew revolvers and ordered Mr. Edwards to give them all the money in the cash register.
II. The men proceeded to the back of the store as if they were going to do some shopping.
III. Janet Morley, a neighborhood resident, later reported that she saw the men enter a green Ford station wagon and flee northbound on Albany Avenue.
IV. Edwards complied after which the gunmen ran from the store.
V. Mr. Edwards states that he was stocking merchandise behind the store counter when two white males entered the store.

The MOST logical order for the above sentences to appear in the report is

A. V, II, III, I, IV
B. V, II, I, IV, III
C. II, I, V, IV, III
D. III, V, II, I, IV

14. Police Officer Wendell is preparing an accident report for a 6-car accident that occurred at the intersection of Bath Avenue and Bay Parkway. The report will consist of the following five sentences: 14.____

I. A 2006 Volkswagen Beetle, traveling east on Bath Avenue, swerved to the left to avoid the Impala, and struck a 2004 Ford station wagon which was traveling west on Bath Avenue.
II. The Seville then mounted the curb on the northeast corner of Bath Avenue and Bay Parkway and struck a light pole.
III. A 2003 Buick Lesabre, traveling northbound on Bay Parkway directly behind the Impala, struck the Impala, pushing it into the intersection of Bath Avenue and Bay Parkway.
IV. A 2005 Chevy Impala, traveling northbound on Bay Parkway, had stopped for a red light at Bath Avenue.
V. A 2007 Toyota, traveling westbound on Bath Avenue, swerved to the right to avoid hitting the Ford station wagon, and struck a 2007 Cadillac Seville double-parked near the corner.

The MOST logical order for the above sentences to appear in the report is

A. IV, III, V, II, I
B. III, IV, V, II, I
C. IV, III, I, V, II
D. III, IV, V, I, II

15. The following five sentences are part of an Activity Log entry Police Officer Rogers made regarding an explosion, 15.____

I. I quickly treated the pedestrian for the injury.
II. The explosion caused a glass window in an office building to shatter.
III. After the pedestrian was treated, a call was placed to the precinct requesting additional police officers to evacuate the area.
IV. After all the glass settled to the ground, I saw a pedestrian who was bleeding from the arm
V. While on foot patrol near 5th Avenue and 53rd Street, I heard a loud explosion.

The MOST logical order for the above sentences to appear in the report is

A. II, V, IV, I, III
B. V, II, IV, III, I
C. V, II, I, IV, III
D. V, II, IV, I, III

16. Police Officer David is completing a report regarding illegal activity near the entrance to Madison Square Garden during a recent rock concert. The report will contain the following five sentences: 16.____

I. As I came closer to the man, he placed what appeared to be tickets in his pocket and began to walk away.
II. After the man stopped, I questioned him about *scalping* tickets.
III. While on assignment near the Madison Square Garden entrance, I observed a man apparently selling tickets.
IV. I stopped the man by stating that I was a police officer.
V. The man was then given a summons, and he left the area.

The MOST logical order for the above sentences to appear in the report is

A. I, III, IV, II, V
B. III, I, IV, V, II
C. III, IV, I, II, V
D. III, I, IV, II, V

17. Police Officer Sampson is preparing a report concerning a dispute in a bar. The report will contain the following five sentences: 17.____

I. John Evans, the bartender, ordered the two men out of the bar.
II. Two men dressed in dungarees entered the C and D Bar at 5:30 P.M.
III. The two men refused to leave and began to beat up Evans.
IV. A customer in the bar saw me on patrol and yelled to me to come separate the three men.
V. The two men became very drunk and loud within a short time.

The MOST logical order for the above sentences to appear in the report is

A. II, I, V, III, IV
B. II, III, IV, V, I
C. III, I, II, V, IV
D. II, V, I, III, IV

18. A police officer is completing a report concerning the response to a crime in progress. The report will include the following five sentences: 18.____

I. The officers saw two armed men run out of the liquor store and into a waiting car.
II. Police Officers Lunty and Duren received the call and responded to the liquor store.
III. The robbers gave up without a struggle.
IV. Lunty and Duren blocked the getaway car with their patrol car.
V. A call came into the precinct concerning a robbery in progress at Jane's Liquor Store.

The MOST logical order for the above sentences to appear in the report is

A. V, II, I, IV, III
B. II, V, I, III, IV
C. V, I, IV, II, III
D. I, V, II, III, IV

19. Police Officer Jenkins is preparing a Crime Report which will consist of the following five sentences: 19.____

I. After making inquiries in the vicinity, Smith found out that his next door neighbor, Viola Jones, had seen two local teenagers, Michael Heinz and Vincent Gaynor, smash his car's windshields with a crowbar.
II. Jones told Smith that the teenagers live at 8700 19th Avenue.
III. Mr. Smith heard a loud crash at approximately 11:00 P.M., looked out his apartment window, and saw two white males running away from his car.
IV. Smith then reported the incident to the precinct, and Heinz and Gaynor were arrested at the address given.

V. Leaving his apartment to investigate further, Smith discovered that his car's front and rear windshields had been smashed.

The MOST logical order for the above sentences to appear in the report is

A. III, IV, V, I, II
B. III, V, I, II, IV
C. III, I, V, II, IV
D. V, III, I, II, IV

20. Sergeant Nancy Winston is reviewing a Gun Control Report which will contain the following five sentences: 20.____

I. The man fell to the floor when hit in the chest with three bullets from 22 caliber gun.
II. Merriam'22 caliber gun was seized, and he wasgiven a summons for not having a pistol permit.
III. Christopher Merriam, the owner of A-Z Grocery, shot a man who attempted to rob him.
IV. Police Officer Franks responded and asked Merriam for his pistol permit, which he could not produce.
V. Merriam phoned the police to report he had just shot a man who had attempted to rob him.

The MOST logical order for the above sentences to appear in the report is

A. III, I, V, IV, II
B. I, III, V, IV, II
C. III, I, V, II, IV
D. I, III, II, V, IV

21. Detective John Manville is completing a report for his superior regarding the murder of an unknown male who was shot in Central Park. The report will contain the following five sentences: 21.____

I. Police Officers Langston and Cavers responded to the scene.
II. I received the assignment to investigate the murder in Central Park from Detective Sergeant Rogers.
III. Langston notified the Detective Bureau after questioning Jason.
IV. An unknown male, apparently murdered, was discovered in Central Park by Howard Jason, a park employee, who immediately called the police.
V. Langston and Cavers questioned Jason.

The MOST logical order for the above sentences to appear in the report is

A. I, IV, V, III, II
B. IV, I, V, II, III
C. IV, I, V, III, II
D. IV, V, I, III, II

22. A police officer is completing a report concerning the arrest of a juvenile. The report will contain the following five sentences: 22.____

I. Sanders then telephoned Jay's parents from the precinct to inform them of their son's arrest.
II. The store owner resisted, and Jay then shot him and ran from the store.
III. Jay was transported directly to the precinct by Officer Sanders.
IV. James Jay, a juvenile, walked into a candy store and announced a hold-up.
V. Police Officer Sanders, while on patrol, arrested Jay a block from the candy store.

The MOST logical order for the above sentences to appear in the report is

A. IV, V, II, I, III
B. IV, II, V, III, I
C. II, IV, V, III, I
D. V, IV, II, I, III

23. Police Officer Olsen prepared a crime report for a robbery which contained the following five sentences: 23.____

I. Mr. Gordon was approached by this individual who then produced a gun and demanded the money from the cash register.
II. The man then fled from the scene on foot, southbound on 5th Avenue.
III. Mr. Gordon was working at the deli counter when a white male, 5'6", 150-160 lbs., wearing a green jacket and blue pants, entered the store.
IV. Mr. Gordon complied with the man's demands and handed him the daily receipts.
V. Further investigation has determined there are no other witnesses to this robbery.

The MOST logical order for the above sentences to appear in the report is

A. I, III, IV, V, II
B. I, IV, II, III, V
C. III, IV, I, V, II
D. III, I, IV, , II, V

24. Police Officer Bryant responded to 285 E. 31st Street to take a crime report of a burglary of Mr. Bond's home. The report will contain a brief description of the incident, consisting of the following five sentences: 24.____

I. When Mr. Bond attempted to stop the burglar by grabbing him, he was pushed to the floor.
II. The burglar had apparently gained access to the home by forcing open the 2nd floor bedroom window facing the fire escape.
III. Mr. Bond sustained a head injury in the scuffle, and the burglar exited the home through the front door.
IV. Finding nothing in the dresser, the burglar proceeded downstairs to the first floor, where he was confronted by Mr. Bond who was reading in the dining room.
V. Once inside, he searched the drawers of the bedroom dresser.

The MOST logical order for the above sentences to appear in the report is

A. V, IV, I, II, III
B. II, V, IV, I, III
C. II, IV, V, III, I
D. III, II, I, V, IV

25. Police Officer Derringer responded to a call of a rape-homicide case in his patrol area and was ordered to prepare an incident report, which will contain the following five sentences: 25.____

I. He pushed Miss Scott to the ground and forcibly raped her.
II. Mary Scott was approached from behind by a white male, 5'7", 150-160 lbs. wearing dark pants and a white jacket.
III. As Robinson approached the male, he ordered him to stop.
IV. Screaming for help, Miss Scott alerted one John Robinson, a local grocer, who chased her assailant as he fled the scene.
V. The male turned and fired two shots at Robinson, who fell to the ground mortally wounded.

The MOST logical order for the above' sentences to appear in the report is

A. IV, III, I, II, V
B. II, IV, III, V, I
C. II, IV, I, V, III
D. II, I, IV, III, V

KEY (CORRECT ANSWERS)

1. B
2. C
3. C
4. A
5. B
6. A
7. B
8. C
9. B
10. A
11. C
12. B
13. B
14. C
15. D
16. D
17. D
18. A
19. B
20. A
21. C
22. B
23. D
24. B
25. D

PREPARING WRITTEN MATERIAL

EXAMINATION SECTION
TEST 1

DIRECTIONS: Each question or incomplete statement is followed by several suggested answers or completions. Select the one that BEST answers the question or completes the statement. *PRINT THE LETTER OF THE CORRECT ANSWER IN THE SPACE AT THE RIGHT.*

Questions 1-4.

DIRECTIONS: Questions 1 through 4 each consist of a sentence which may or may not be an example of good English. The underlined parts of each sentence may be correct or incorrect. Examine each sentence, considering grammar, punctuation, spelling, and capitalization. If the English usage in the underlined parts of the sentence given is better than any of the changes in the underlined words suggested in options B, C, or D, choose option A. If the changes in the underlined words suggested in options B, C, or D would make the sentence correct, choose the correct option. Do not choose an option that will change the meaning of the sentence.

1. This Fall, the office will be closed on Columbus Day, October 9th. 1.____

   A. Correct as is
   B. fall...Columbus Day, October
   C. Fall...columbus day, October
   D. fall...Columbus Day, October

2. There weren't no paper in the supply closet. 2.____

   A. Correct as is
   B. weren't any
   C. wasn't any
   D. wasn't no

3. The alphabet, or A to Z sequence are the basis of most filing systems. 3.____

   A. Correct as is
   B. alphabet, or A to Z sequence, is
   C. alphabet, or A to Z sequence, are
   D. alphabet, or A too Z sequence, is

4. The Office Aide checked the register and finding the date of the meeting. 4.____

   A. Correct as is
   B. regaster and finding
   C. register and found
   D. regaster and found

Questions 5-10.

DIRECTIONS: Questions 5 through 10 consist of sentences which contain examples of correct or incorrect English usage. Examine each sentence with reference to grammar, spelling, punctuation, and capitalization. Choose one of the following options that would be BEST for correct English usage:

A. The sentence is correct
B. There is one mistake
C. There are two mistakes
D. There are three mistakes

5. Mrs. Fitzgerald came to the 59th Precinct to retreive her property which were stolen earlier in the week. 5.____

6. The two officer's responded to the call, only to find that the perpatrator and the victim have left the scene. 6.____

7. Mr. Coleman called the 61st Precinct to report that, upon arriving at his store, he discovered that there was a large hole in the wall and that three boxes of radios were missing. 7.____

8. The Administrative Leiutenant of the 62nd Precinct held a meeting which was attended by all the civilians, assigned to the Precinct. 8.____

9. Three days after the robbery occured the detective apprahended two suspects and recovered the stolen items. 9.____

10. The Community Affairs Officer of the 64th Precinct is the liaison between the Precinct and the community; he works closely with various community organizations, and elected officials. 10.____

Questions 11-18.

DIRECTIONS: Questions 11 through 18 are to be answered on the basis of the following paragraph, which contains some deliberate errors in spelling and/or grammar and/or punctuation. Each line of the paragraph is preceded by a number. There are 9 lines and 9 numbers.

Line No.	Paragraph Line
1	The protection of life and proporty are, one of
2	the oldest and most important functions of a city.
3	New York city has it's own full-time police Agency.
4	The police Department has the power an it shall
5	be there duty to preserve the Public piece,
6	prevent crime detect and arrest offenders, supress
7	riots, protect the rites of persons and property, etc.
8	The maintainance of sound relations with the community they
9	serve is an important function of law enforcement officers

11. How many errors are contained in line one? 11.____

A. One B. Two C. Three D. None

12. How many errors are contained in line two? 12.____

A. One B. Two C. Three D. None

13. How many errors are contained in line three? 13.____

A. One B. Two C. Three D. None

14. How many errors are contained in line four? 14.____

    A. One B. Two C. Three D. None

15. How many errors are contained in line five? 15.____

    A. One B. Two C. Three D. None

16. How many errors are contained in line six? 16.____

    A. One B. Two C. Three D. None

17. How many errors are contained in line seven? 17.____

    A. One B. Two C. Three D. None

18. How many errors are contained in line eight? 18.____

    A. One B. Two C. Three D. None

19. In the sentence, *The candidate wants to file his application for preference before it is too late,* the word *before* is used as a(n) 19.____

    A. preposition
    B. subordinating conjunction
    C. pronoun
    D. adverb

20. The one of the following sentences which is grammatically PREFERABLE to the others is: 20.____

    A. Our engineers will go over your blueprints so that you may have no problems in construction.
    B. For a long time he had been arguing that we, not he, are to blame for the confusion.
    C. I worked on this automobile for two hours and still cannot find out what is wrong with it.
    D. Accustomed to all kinds of hardships, fatigue seldom bothers veteran policemen.

KEY (CORRECT ANSWERS)

1.	A	11.	C
2.	C	12.	D
3.	B	13.	C
4.	C	14.	B
5.	C	15.	C
6.	D	16.	B
7.	A	17.	A
8.	C	18.	A
9.	C	19.	B
10.	B	20.	A

TEST 2

DIRECTIONS: Each question or incomplete statement is followed by several suggested answers or completions. Select the one that BEST answers the question or completes the statement. *PRINT THE LETTER OF THE CORRECT ANSWER IN THE SPACE AT THE RIGHT.*

1. The plural of 1.____

   A. turkey is turkies
   B. cargo is cargoes
   C. bankruptcy is bankruptcys
   D. son-in-law is son-in-laws

2. The abbreviation *viz.* means MOST NEARLY 2.____

   A. namely
   B. for example
   C. the following
   D. see

3. In the sentence, *A man in a light-grey suit waited thirty-five minutes in the ante-room for the all-important document,* the word IMPROPERLY hyphenated is 3.____

   A. light-grey
   B. thirty-five
   C. ante-room
   D. all-important

4. The MOST accurate of the following sentences is: 4.____

   A. The commissioner, as well as his deputy and various bureau heads, were present.
   B. A new organization of employers and employees have been formed.
   C. One or the other of these men have been selected.
   D. The number of pages in the book is enough to discourage a reader.

5. The MOST accurate of the following sentences is: 5.____

   A. Between you and me, I think he is the better man.
   B. He was believed to be me.
   C. Is it us that you wish to see?
   D. The winners are him and her.

Questions 6-13.

DIRECTIONS: The sentences numbered 6 through 13 deal with some phase of police activity. They may be classified most appropriately under one of the following four categories.

A. Faulty because of incorrect grammar
B. Faulty because of incorrect punctuation
C. Faulty because of incorrect use of a word
D. Correct

Examine each sentence carefully. Then, in the space at the right, print the capital letter preceding the option which is the BEST of the four suggested above. All incorrect sentences contain only one type of error. Consider a sentence correct if it contains none of the types of errors mentioned, even though there may be other correct ways of expressing the same thought.

6. The Department Medal of Honor is awarded to a member of the Police Force who distinguishes himself inconspicuously in the line of police duty by the performance of an act of gallantry. 6.____

7. Members of the Detective Division are charged with the prevention of crime, the detection and arrest of criminals and the recovery of lost or stolen property. 7.____

8. Detectives are selected from the uniformed patrol forces after they have indicated by conduct, aptitude and performance that they are qualified for the more intricate duties of a detective. 8.____

9. The patrolman, pursuing his assailant, exchanged shots with the gunman and immortally wounded him as he fled into a nearby building. 9.____

10. The members of the Traffic Division has to enforce the Vehicle and Traffic Law, the Traffic Regulations and ordinances relating to vehicular and pedestrian traffic. 10.____

11. After firing a shot at the gunman, the crowd dispersed from the patrolman's line of fire. 11.____

12. The efficiency of the Missing Persons Bureau is maintained with a maximum of public personnel due to the specialized training given to its members. 12.____

13. Records of persons arrested for violations of Vehicle and Traffic Regulations are transmitted upon request to precincts, courts and other authorized agencies. 13.____

14. Following are two sentences which may or may not be written in correct English: 14.____
    I. Two clients assaulted the officer.
    II. The van is illegally parked.

    Which one of the following statements is CORRECT?

    A. Only Sentence I is written in correct English.
    B. Only Sentence II is written in correct English.
    C. Sentences I and II are both written in correct English.
    D. Neither Sentence I nor Sentence II is written in correct English.

15. Following are two sentences which may or may not be written in correct English: 15.____
    I. Security Officer Rollo escorted the visitor to the patrolroom.
    II. Two entry were made in the facility logbook.

    Which one of the following statements is CORRECT?

    A. Only Sentence I is written in correct English.
    B. Only Sentence II is written in correct English.
    C. Sentences I and II are both written in correct English.
    D. Neither Sentence I nor Sentence II is written in correct English.

16. Following are two sentences which may or may not be written in correct English: 16.____
    I. Officer McElroy putted out a small fire in the wastepaper basket.
    II. Special Officer Janssen told the visitor where he could obtained a pass.

    Which one of the following statements is CORRECT?

    A. Only Sentence I is written in correct English.
    B. Only Sentence II is written in correct English.
    C. Sentences I and II are both written in correct English.
    D. Neither Sentence I nor Sentence II is written in correct English.

17. Following are two sentences which may or may not be written in correct English: 17.____
    I. Security Officer Warren observed a broken window while he was on his post in Hallway C.
    II. The worker reported that two typewriters had been stoled from the office.

    Which one of the following statements is CORRECT?

    A. Only Sentence I is written in correct English.
    B. Only Sentence II is written in correct English.
    C. Sentences I and II are both written in correct English.
    D. Neither Sentence I nor Sentence II is written in correct English.

18. Following are two sentences which may or may not be written in correct English: 18.____
    I. Special Officer Cleveland was attempting to calm an emotionally disturbed visitor.
    II. The visitor did not stops crying and calling for his wife.

    Which one of the following statements is CORRECT?

    A. Only Sentence I is written in correct English.
    B. Only Sentence II is written in correct English.
    C. Sentences I and II are both written in correct English.
    D. Neither Sentence I nor Sentence II is written in correct English.

19. Following are two sentences that may or may not be written in correct English: 19.____
    I. While on patrol, I observes a vagrant loitering near the drug dispensary.
    II. I escorted the vagrant out of the building and off the premises.

    Which one of the following statements is CORRECT?

    A. Only Sentence I is written in correct English.
    B. Only Sentence II is written in correct English.
    C. Sentences I and II are both written in correct English.
    D. Neither Sentence I nor Sentence II is written in correct English.

20. Following are two sentences which may or may not be written in correct English: 20.____
    I. At 4:00 P.M., Sergeant Raymond told me to evacuate the waiting area immediately due to a bomb threat.
    II. Some of the clients did not want to leave the building.

    Which one of the following statements is CORRECT?

    A. Only Sentence I is written in correct English.
    B. Only Sentence II is written in correct English.
    C. Sentences I and II are both written in correct English.
    D. Neither Sentence I nor Sentence II is written in correct English.

KEY (CORRECT ANSWERS)

1.	B	11.	A
2.	A	12.	C
3.	C	13.	D
4.	D	14.	C
5.	A	15.	A
6.	C	16.	D
7.	B	17.	A
8.	D	18.	A
9.	C	19.	B
10.	A	20.	C

INTERPRETING STATISTICAL DATA GRAPHS, CHARTS AND TABLES

EXAMINATION SECTION

TEST 1

DIRECTIONS: Each question or incomplete statement is followed by several suggested answers or completions. Select the one that BEST answers the question or completes the statement. *PRINT THE LETTER OF THE CORRECT ANSWER IN THE SPACE AT THE RIGHT.*

Questions 1-4.

DIRECTIONS: Questions 1 through 4 are to be answered SOLELY on the basis of the following table.

STOLEN AND RECOVERED PROPERTY IN COMMUNITY X
2018-2019

Type of Property	Value of Property Stolen 2018	Value of Property Stolen 2019	Value of Property Recovered 2018	Value of Property Recovered 2019
Currency	$264,925	$204,534	$10,579	$13,527
Jewelry	165,317	106,885	20,913	20,756
Furs	10,007	24,028	105	1,620
Clothing	62,265	49,219	4,322 7	15,821
Automobiles	740,719	606,062	36,701	558,442
Miscellaneous	356,901	351,064	62,077	103,117
TOTAL	$1,600,134	$1,341,792	$834,697	$713,283

1. Of the following types of property, the one which shows the HIGHEST ratio of *value of property recovered* to *value of property stolen* is 1.____

   A. clothing for 2018
   B. currency for 2018
   C. jewelry for 2019
   D. miscellaneous for 2019

2. Of the types of property which show a decrease from 2018 to 2019 in the value of property stolen, the one which shows the GREATEST percentage decrease in the value of the property recovered is 2.____

   A. automobiles
   B. currency
   C. furs
   D. jewelry

3. According to the above table, the total value of currency and jewelry stolen in 2019, as compared to 2018, decreased APPROXIMATELY by 3.____

   A. 3%
   B. 20%
   C. 28%
   D. 38%

4. According to the above table, the TOTAL value of all types of property recovered was 4.____

A. a slightly lower percentage of the value of property stolen for 2018 than for 2019
B. less for the year 2018 than the value of any individual type of property recovered for the year 2019
C. approximately 60% of the value of all property stolen in 2018 and approximately 70% in 2019
D. greater for the year 2019 than the value of any individual type of property recovered for the year 2018

KEY (CORRECT ANSWERS)

1. D
2. A
3. C
4. A

TEST 2

Questions 1-6.

DIRECTIONS: Questions 1 through 6 are to be answered SOLELY on the basis of the information supplied in the chart below.

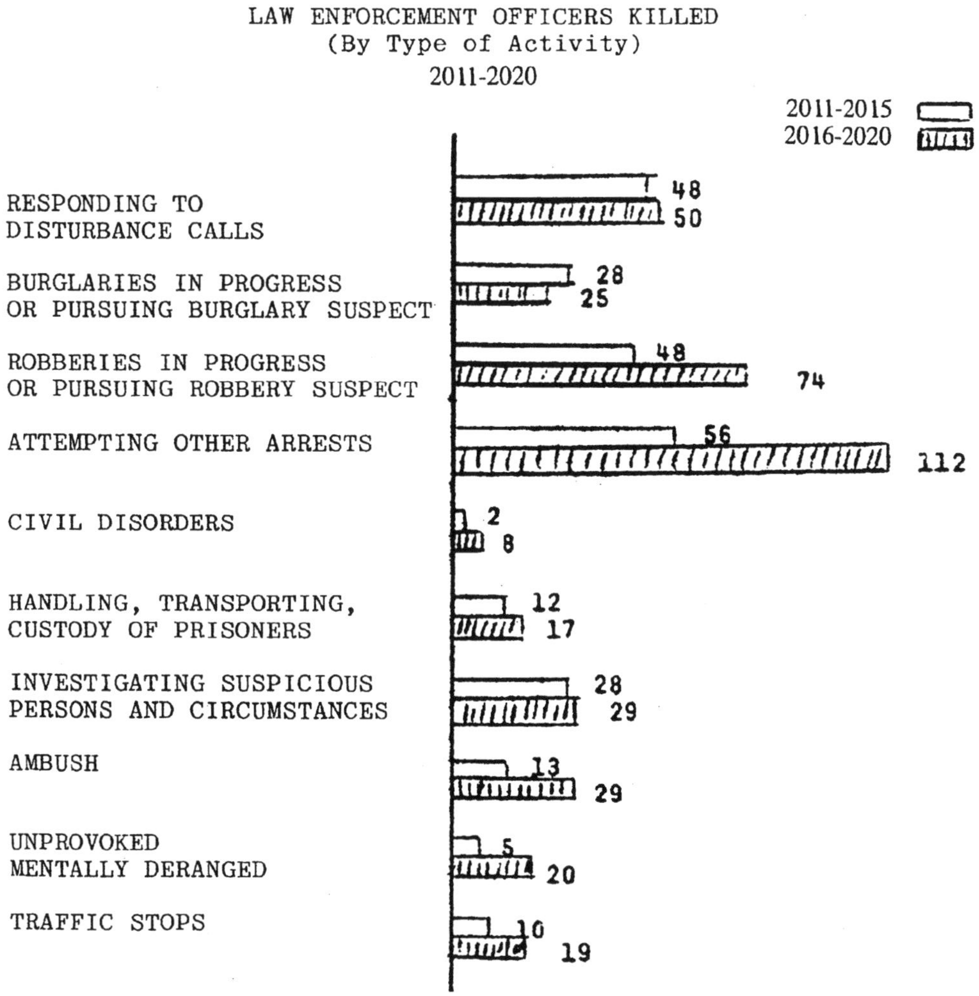

1. According to the above chart, the percent of the total number of law enforcement officers killed from 2011-2020 in activities related to burglaries and robberies is MOST NEARLY ______ percent. 1.____

   A. 8.4 B. 19.3 C. 27.6 D. 36.2

2. According to the above chart, the two of the following categories which increased from 2011-2015 to 2016-2020 by the SAME percent are 2.____

   A. ambush and traffic stops
   B. attempting other arrests and ambush

C. civil disorders and unprovoked mentally deranged
D. response to disturbance calls and investigating suspicious persons and circumstances

3. According to the above chart, the percentage increase in law enforcement officers killed from the 2011-2015 period to the 2016-2020 period is MOST NEARLY _______ percent. 3.____

A. 34 B. 53 C. 65 D. 100

4. According to the above chart, in which one of the following activities did the number of law enforcement officers killed increase by 100 percent? 4.____

A. Ambush
B. Attempting other arrests
C. Robberies in progress or pursuing robbery suspect
D. Traffic stops

5. According to the above chart, the two of the following activities during which the total number of law enforcement officers killed from 2011 to 2020 was the SAME are 5.____

A. burglaries in progress or pursuing burglary suspect and investigating suspicious persons and circumstances
B. handling, transporting, custody of prisoners and traffic stops
C. investigating suspicious persons and circumstances and ambush
D. responding to disturbance calls and robberies in progress or pursuing robbery suspect

6. According to the categories in the above chart, the one of the following statements which can be made about law enforcement officers killed from 2011 to 2015 is that 6.____

A. the number of law enforcement officers killed during civil disorders equals one-sixth of the number killed responding to disturbance calls
B. the number of law enforcement officers killed during robberies in progress or pursuing robbery suspect equals 25 percent of the number killed while handling or transporting prisoners
C. the number of law enforcement officers killed during traffic stops equals one-half the number killed for unprovoked reasons or by the mentally deranged
D. twice as many law enforcement officers were killed attempting other arrests as were killed during burglaries in progress or pursuing burglary suspect

KEY (CORRECT ANSWERS)

1. C
2. C
3. B
4. B
5. B
6. D

TEST 3

Questions 1-6.

DIRECTIONS: Questions 1 through 6 are to be answered SOLELY on the basis of the graph below.

YEARLY INCIDENCE OF MAJOR CRIMES FOR COMMUNITY Z
2017-2019

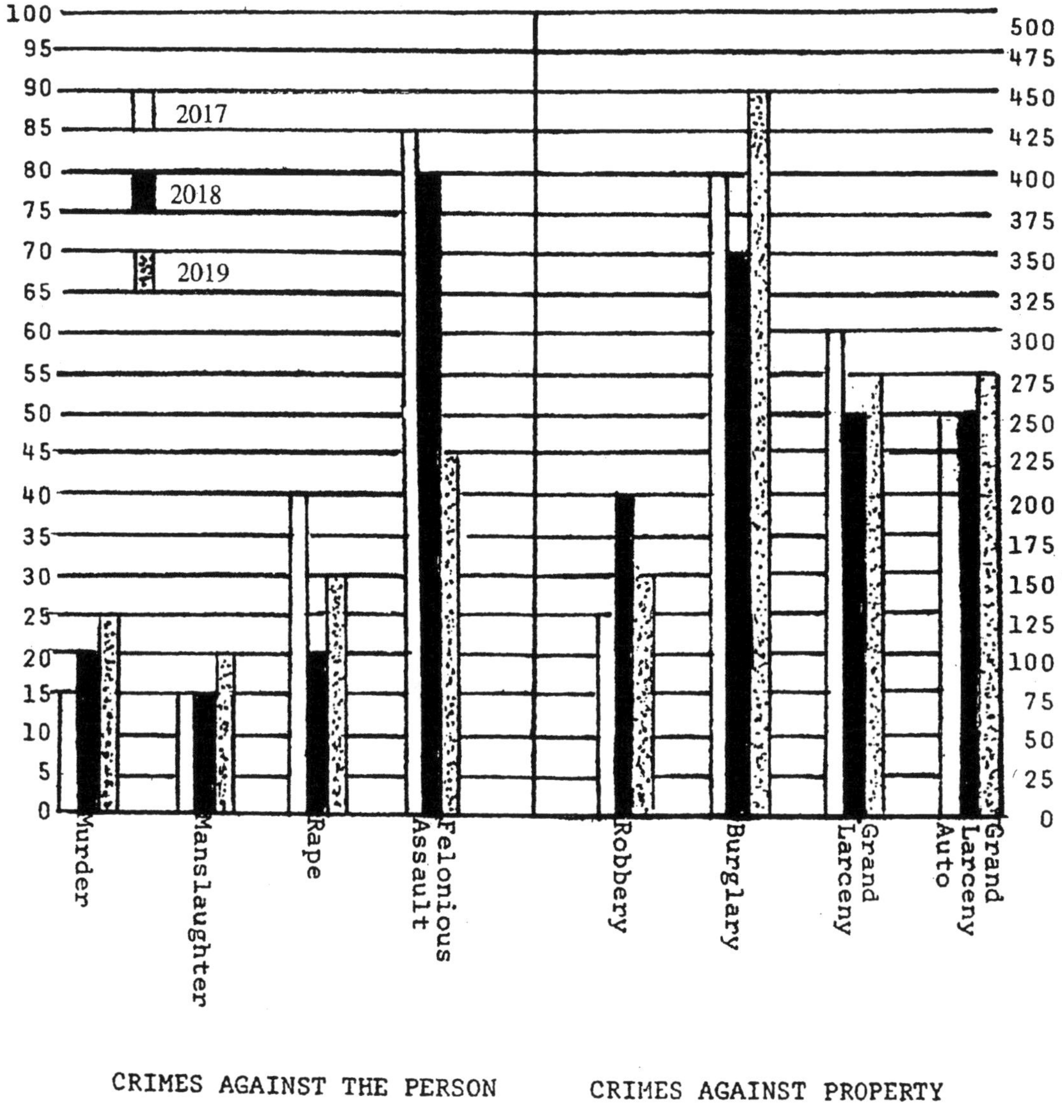

1. Of the following crimes, the one for which the 2019 figure was GREATER than the average of the previous two years was 1.____

   A. grand larceny
   B. manslaughter
   C. rape
   D. robbery

2. If the incidence of burglary in 2020 were to increase over 2019 by the same number as it increased in 2019 over 2018, then the average for this crime for the four-year period from 2017 through 2020 would be MOST NEARLY 2.____

   A. 100 B. 400 C. 415 D. 440

3. The above graph indicates that the percentage INCREASE in grand larceny auto over the previous year was 3.____

   A. greater in 2019 than in 2018
   B. greater in 2018 than in 2019
   C. greater in 2019 than in 2017
   D. the same in both 2018 and 2019

4. The one of the following which cannot be determined because there is not enough information in the above graph to do so is the 4.____

   A. percentage of *Crimes Against Property* for the three-year period which were committed in 2017
   B. percentage of *Crimes Against the Person* for the three-year period which were murders committed in 2018
   C. percentage of *Major Crimes* for the three-year period which were committed in the first six months of 2018
   D. major crimes which were following a pattern of continuing yearly increases for the three-year period

5. According to this graph, the ratio of *Crimes Against Property* to *Crimes Against the Person* for 2019, as compared to the ratio for 2018, is 5.____

   A. increasing
   B. decreasing
   C. about the same
   D. cannot be determined

6. Assume that it is desired to present information from the above graph to the public in a form most likely to gain their cooperation in a special police effort to reduce the incidence of grand larceny auto. 6.____
   The one of the following which is MOST likely to result in such cooperation is a public statement that

   A. in 2019, approximately .75 of an automobile was stolen every day
   B. in 2019, one automobile was stolen, on the average, about,32 hours hours
   C. the number of automobiles stolen per year will increase from year to year
   D. there were more crimes of grand larceny auto than crimes of robbery committed during the past three years

---

KEY (CORRECT ANSWERS)

1. B	4. C
2. D	5. A
3. B	6. B

TEST 4

Questions 1-7.

DIRECTIONS: Questions 1 through 7 are to be answered SOLELY on the basis of the information contained in the following tables and chart.

TABLE 1

Number of Murders bv Region, United States: 2014 and 2015

Region	Year	
	2014	2015
Northeastern States	2,521	2,849
North Central States	3,427	3,697
Southern States	6,577	7,055
Western States	2,062	2,211

Number in each case for given year and region represents total number (100%) of murders in that region for that year.

TABLE 2

Murder by Circumstance, U.S. - 2015
(Percent distribution by category)

Region	Total	Spouse Killing spouse	Parent Killing child	Other family killings	Romantic triangle and lovers' quarrels	Other arguments	Known Felony type	Suspected felony type
Northeastern States	100.0	9.6	3.7	6.1	7.9	38.4	25.4	8.9
North Central States	100.0	11.3	3.0	8.9	5.0	39.5	22.4	9.9
Southern States	100.0	13.8	2.2	8.8	8.4	46.0	13.9	6.9
Western States	100.0	12.5	4.9	7.0	6.4	32.2	28.0	9.0

CHART 1

Murder by Type of Weapon Used, U.S. - 2015
(Percent Distribution)

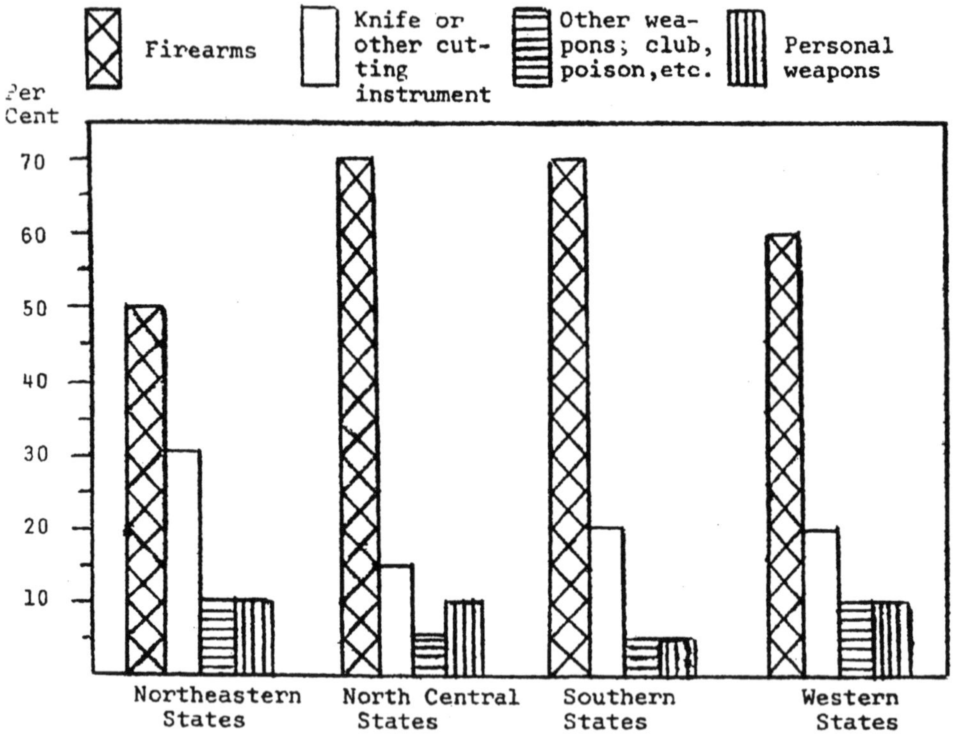

1. The number of persons murdered by firearms in the Western States in 2015 was MOST NEARLY 1.____

   A. 220 B. 445 C. 1235 D. 1325

2. In 2015, the number of murders in the category *Parent killing child* was GREATEST in the ______ States. 2.____

   A. Northeastern B. North Central
   C. Southern D. Western

3. The difference between the number of persons murdered with firearms and the number of persons murdered with other weapons (club, poison, etc.) in the North Central States in 2015 is MOST NEARLY 3.____

   A. 2200 B. 2400 C. 2600 D. 2800

4. In 2014, the ratio of the number of murders in the Western States to the total number of murders in the U.S. was MOST NEARLY 4.____

   A. 1 to 4 B. 1 to 5 C. 1 to 7 D. 1 to 9

5. The total number of murders in the U.S. in the category of *Romantic triangles and lovers' quarrels* in 2015 was MOST NEARLY 5.____

A. 850 B. 950 C. 1050 D. 1150

6. Which of the following represents the GREATEST number of murders in 2015? Persons murdered by 6.____

A. firearms in the Western States
B. knives or other cutting instruments in the Southern States
C. knives or other cutting instruments and persons murdered by other weapons (club, poison, etc.) in the Northeastern States
D. knives or other cutting instruments, persons murdered by other weapons (club, poison, etc.) and persons murdered by personal weapons in the North Central States

7. From 2014 to 2015, the total number of murders increased by the GREATEST percentage in the ______ States. 7.____

A. Northeastern
B. North Central
C. Southern
D. Western

KEY (CORRECT ANSWERS)

1. D
2. C
3. B
4. C
5. D
6. B
7. A

TEST 5

Questions 1-5.

DIRECTIONS: Questions 1 through 5 are to be answered SOLELY on the basis of the following.

DISTRIBUTION OF CITIZENS' RESPONSES TO STATEMENTS
CONCERNING SHERIFFS' ARRESTS
(Number of citizens responding = 1171)

	CATEGORIES				
	(A) Strongly Agree	(B) Agree	(C) Disagree	(D) Strongly Disagree	(E) Don't Know
I. Sheriffs act improperly in arresting defendants, even when these persons are rude and ill-mannered	12%	37%	36%	9%	6%
II. Sheriffs frequently use more force than necessary when making arrests	9%	19%	46%	19%	7%
III. Any defendant who insults or physically abuses a sheriff has no complaint if he is sternly handled in return	13%	44%	32%	7%	4%

1. The total percentage of responses to Statement III OTHER THAN *Strongly Agree* and *Disagree* is 1.____

   A. 45% B. 46% C. 55% D. 59%

2. The number of *Disagree* responses to Statement II is MOST NEARLY ' 2.____

   A. 71 B. 114 C. 539 D. 820

3. Assume that for Statement II the (B) percentage of responses were doubled and the (A) percentage increased one and a half times. 3.____
If the (D) and (E) percentages remained the same, the (C) percentage would then MOST NEARLY be

A. 23% B. 26% C. 39% D. 52%

4. The total number of *Don't Know* responses is MOST NEARLY 4.____

A. 17
B. 188
C. 200
D. a figure which cannot be determined from the table

5. If the percentage of Disagree responses to Statement III were 35% less, the resulting percentage would MOST NEARLY be 5.____

A. 11% B. 14% C. 15% D. 21%

KEY (CORRECT ANSWERS)

1. C
2. C
3. A
4. C
5. D

TEST 6

Questions 1-3.

DIRECTIONS: Questions 1 through 3 are to be answered SOLELY on the basis of the statistical report given below.

The following is a statistical report of the activities of the bureau during the current year as compared with the previous year.

	Current Year	Previous Year
Memoranda of law prepared	68	83
Legal matters forwarded to Corporation Counsel	122	144
Letters requesting legal information	756	807
Letters requesting departmental records	139	111
Matters for publication	17	26
Court appearances of members of bureau	4,678	4,621
Conferences	94	103
Lectures at Police Academy	30	33
Reports on proposed legislation	194	255
Deciphering of codes	79	27
Expert testimony	31	16
Notices to court witnesses	55	81
Briefs prepared	22	18
Court papers prepared	258	

1. According to the report, the percentage of bills prepared and sponsored by the Legal Bureau which were passed by the State Legislature and sent to the Governor for approval was APPROXIMATELY 1.____

   A. 3.1%
   B. 2.6%
   C. .5%
   D. not capable of determination from the data given

2. According to the statistical report, the activity showing the GREATEST percentage of *decrease* in the current year as compared with the previous year was 2.____

   A. matters for publication
   B. reports on proposed legislation

C. notices to court witnesses
D. memoranda of law prepared

3. According to the statistical report, the activity showing the GREATEST percentage of *increase* in the current year as compared with the previous year was 3.____

A. court appearances of members of the bureau
B. giving expert testimony
C. deciphering of codes
D. letters requesting departmental records

KEY (CORRECT ANSWERS)

1. D
2. A
3. C

TEST 7

Questions 1-5.

DIRECTIONS: Questions 1 through 5 are to be answered SOLELY on the basis of the information contained in Tables I and II that appear below and on the following page.

TABLE I
NUMBER OF ARRESTS FOR VARIOUS CRIMES AND DISPOSITION

OFFENSES	TOTAL ARRESTED	INVESTIGATED AND RELEASED	HELD FOR PROSECUTION	GUILTY AS CHARGED	GUILTY OF LESSER OFFENSES	DISPOSITION OTHER THAN CONVICTION
Murder	48	10	38	12	9	17
Rape	41	10	31	8	3	20
Aggravated assault	241	106	135	36	32	67
Robbery	351	177	174	98	35	41
Burglary	890	371	519	322	88	109
Larceny	1,665	466 78	1,199	929	58	212
Auto theft	464		386	278	46	62
TOTAL	3,700	1,218	2,482	1,683	271	528

TABLE II

ARRESTS FOR LARCENY - PERCENTAGE OF SUCH ARRESTS BY AGE AND SEX

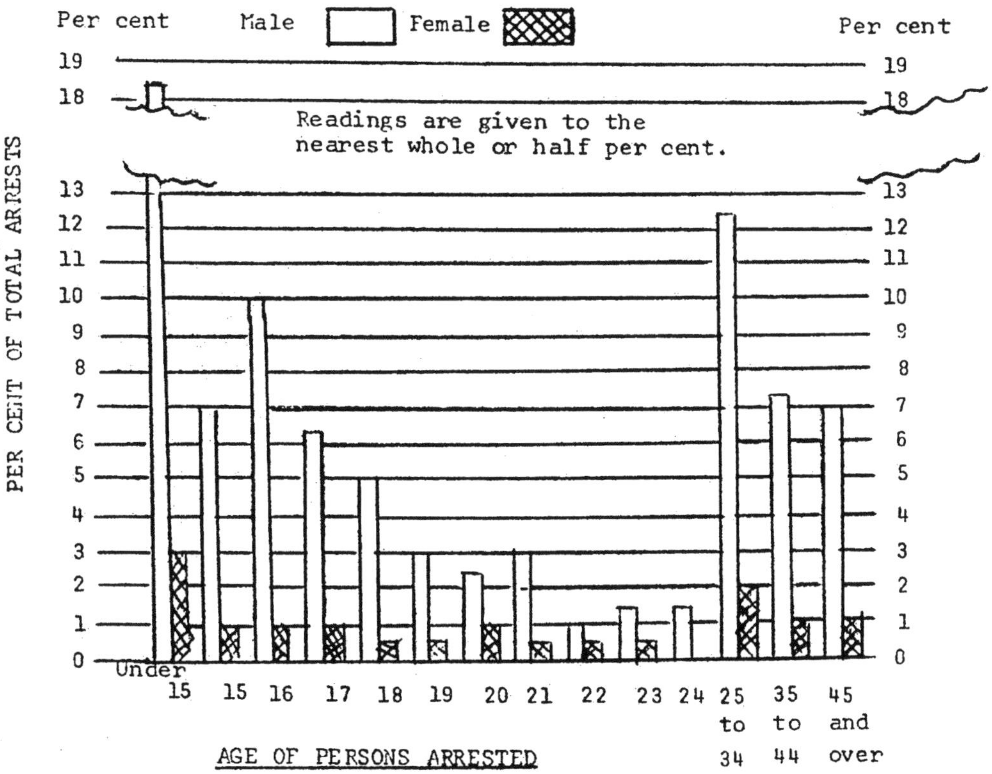

1. The category in which the HIGHEST percentage of those arrested were found guilty as charged was 1.____

   A. robbery B. burglary C. larceny D. auto theft

2. The number of 21-year-olds, both males and females, arrested for larceny is MOST NEARLY 2.____

   A. 29 B. 37 C. 42 D. 58

3. The total number of males arrested for larceny, as compared to the number of females arrested for larceny, is ______ times as great. 3.____

   A. 5 B. 6 C. 8 D. 10

4. Considering only the category of larceny, the one of the following statements which is INCORRECT is: 4.____

   A. The percentage of 25-year-old males arrested cannot be determined
   B. Twice as many 16-year-old males were arrested as 18-year-old males

C. The percentage of 16-year-old males arrested was twice as high as the percentage of 18-year-old males
D. Persons 19 years of age and younger accounted for exactly half of the total arrests for larceny

5. The one of the following which is the MOST accurate statement with respect to the disposition of arrests in each category is that in 5.____

A. no category was the number investigated and released greater than half the number arrested
B. no category was the number investigated and released less than one-fifth of those arrested
C. only two categories was the number found guilty of lesser offense greater than one-tenth of those arrested
D. only one category was the number found guilty as charged less than one-fourth of those arrested

---

KEY (CORRECT ANSWERS)

1. D
2. D
3. B
4. D
5. C

TEST 8

Questions 1-5.

DIRECTIONS: Questions 1 through 5 are to be answered SOLELY on the basis of the table below.

VALUE OF PROPERTY STOLEN - 2017 AND 2018
LARCENY

Category	2017		2018	
	Number of Offenses	Value of Stolen Property	Number of Offense	Value of Stolen Property
Pocket -picking	20	$1,950	10	$ 950
Purse- snatching	175	5,750	20	12,500
Shoplifting	155	7,950	225	17,350
Automobile thefts	1,040	127,050	860	108,000
Thefts of auto accessories	1,135	34,950	970	24,400
Bicycle thefts	355	8,250	240	6,350
All other thefts	1,375	187,150	1,300	153,150

1. Of the total number of larcenies reported for 2017, automobile thefts accounted for MOST NEARLY 1.____

   A. 5% B. 15% C. 25% D. 50%

2. The LARGEST percentage decrease in the value of the stolen property from 2017 to 2018 was in the category of 2.____

   A. pocket-picking
   B. automobile thefts
   C. thefts of automobile accessories
   D. bicycle thefts

3. In 2018, the average amount of each theft was LOWEST for the category of 3.____

   A. pocket-picking
   B. purse-snatching
   C. shoplifting
   D. thefts of auto accessories

4. The category which had the LARGEST numerical reduction in the number of offenses from 2017 to 2018 was 4.____

   A. pocket-picking
   B. automobile thefts
   C. thefts of auto accessories
   D. bicycle thefts

5. When the categories are ranked for each year according to the number of offenses committed in each category (largest number to rank first), the number of categories which will have the SAME rank in 2017 as in 2018 is 5.____

A. 3 B. 4 C. 5 D. 6

KEY (CORRECT ANSWERS)

1. C
2. A
3. D
4. B
5. C

TEST 9

Questions 1-5.

DIRECTIONS: Questions 1 through 5 are to be answered SOLELY on the basis of the graphs below.

2017

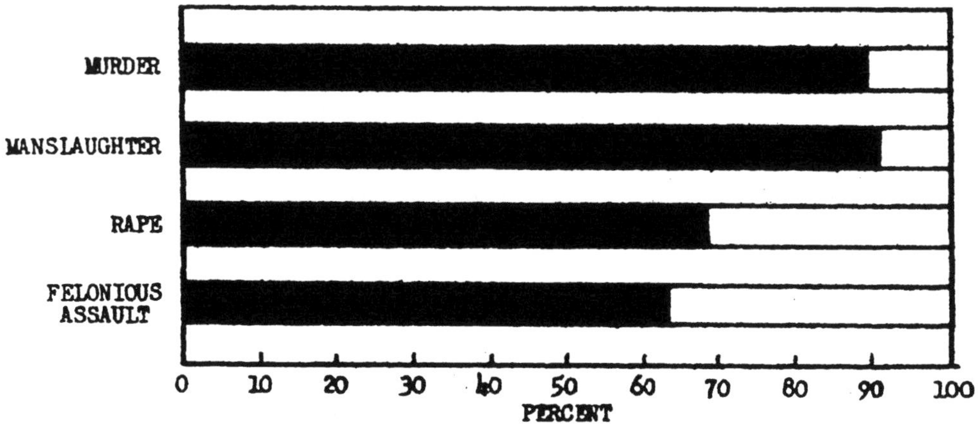

2018

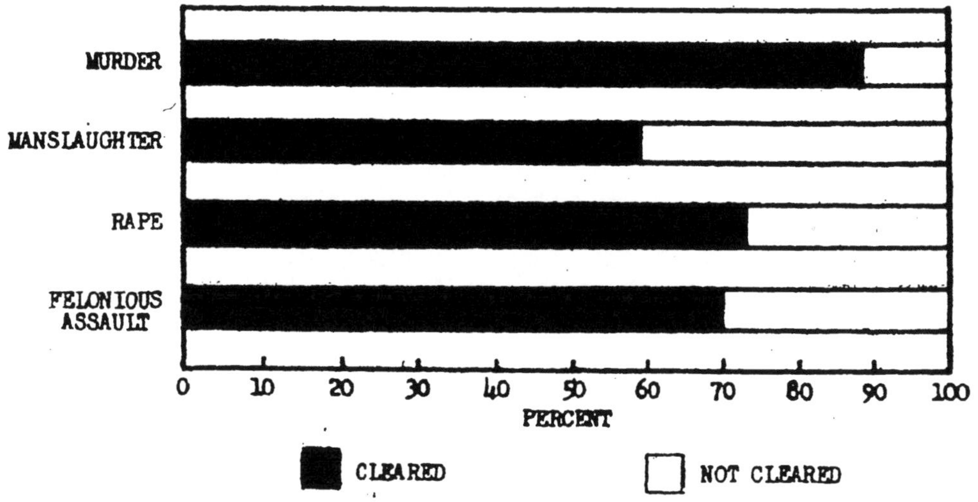

NOTE: The clearance rate is defined as the percentage of reported cases which were closed by the police through arrests or other means.

1. According to the above graphs, the AVERAGE clearance rate for all four crimes for 2018 1.____

   A. was greater than in 2017
   B. was less than in 2017

C. was the same as in 2017
D. cannot properly be compared to the 2017 figures

2. According to the above graphs, the crimes which did NOT show an increasing clearance rate from 2017 to 2018 were 2.____

A. manslaughter and murder
B. rape and felonious assault
C. manslaughter and felonious assault
D. rape and murder

3. According to the above graphs, the average clearance rate for the two-year period 2017-2018 was SMALLEST for the crime of 3.____

A. murder
B. manslaughter
C. rape
D. felonious assault

4. If, in 2018, 63 cases of reported felonious assault remained *not cleared,* then the total number of felonious assault cases reported that year was MOST NEARLY 4.____

A. 90 B. 150 C. 210 D. 900

5. In comparing the graphs for 2017 and 2018, it would be MOST accurate to state that 5.____

A. it is not possible to compare the total number of crimes cleared in 2017 with the total number cleared in 2018
B. the total number of crimes reported in 2017 is greater than the number in 2018
C. there were fewer manslaughter cases cleared during 2017 than in 2018
D. there were more rape cases cleared during 2018 than manslaughter cases cleared in the same year

---

KEY (CORRECT ANSWERS)

1. B
2. A
3. D
4. C
5. A

TEST 10

Questions 1-5.

DIRECTIONS: Questions 1 through 5 are to be answered SOLELY on the basis of the following chart.

FATAL HIGHWAY ACCIDENTS

	Drivers Over 18 Years of Age			Drivers 18 Years of Age And Under		
2018	Auto	Other Vehicles	Total	Auto	Other Vehicles	Total
January	43	0	43	4	0	4
February	52	0	52	10	0	10
March	36	0	36	8	0	8
April	50	0	50	17	0	17
May	40	2	42	5	0	5
June	26	0	26	8	0	8
July	29	0	29	6	0	6
August	29	1	30	3	0	3
September	36	0	36	4	0	4
October	45	1	46	2	1	3
November	54	1	55	3	0	3
December	66	1	67	3	0	6
TOTALS	506	6	512	76	1	77

1. The average number of fatal auto accidents per month during 2018 involving drivers older than eighteen was MOST NEARLY 1.____

   A. 42 B. 43 C. 44 D. 45

2. The TOTAL number of fatal highway accidents during 2018 was 2.____

   A. 506 B. 512 C. 582 D. 589

3. The month during which the LOWEST number of fatal highway accidents occurred was 3.____

   A. March B. June C. July D. August

4. Of the total number of fatal highway accidents during 2018 involving drivers older than eighteen, the percentage of accidents which took place during December is MOST NEARLY 4.____

A. 10 B. 13 C. 16 D. 19

5. The GREATEST percentage drop in fatal highway accidents occurred from 5.____

A. February to March
B. April to May
C. June to July
D. July to Augus

KEY (CORRECT ANSWERS)

1. A
2. D
3. D
4. B
5. B

PHILOSOPHY, PRINCIPLES, PRACTICES AND TECHNICS OF SUPERVISION, ADMINISTRATION, MANAGEMENT AND ORGANIZATION

TABLE OF CONTENTS

TABLE OF CONTENTS (CONTINUED)

PHILOSOPHY, PRINCIPLES, PRACTICES, AND TECHNICS OF SUPERVISION, ADMINISTRATION, MANAGEMENT AND ORGANIZATION

I. MEANING OF SUPERVISION

The extension of the democratic philosophy has been accompanied by an extension in the scope of supervision. Modern leaders and supervisors no longer think of supervision in the narrow sense of being confined chiefly to visiting employees, supplying materials, or rating the staff. They regard supervision as being intimately related to all the concerned agencies of society, they speak of the supervisor's function in terms of "growth", rather than the "improvement," of employees.

This modern concept of supervision may be defined as follows:

Supervision is leadership and the development of leadership within groups which are cooperatively engaged in inspection, research, training, guidance and evaluation.

II. THE OLD AND THE NEW SUPERVISION

TRADITIONAL

1. Inspection
2. Focused on the employee
3. Visitation
4. Random and haphazard
5. Imposed and authoritarian
6. One person usually

MODERN

1. Study and analysis
2. Focused on aims, materials, methods, supervisors, employees, environment
3. Demonstrations, intervisitation, workshops, directed reading, bulletins, etc.
4. Definitely organized and planned (scientific)
5. Cooperative and democratic
6. Many persons involved (creative)

III THE EIGHT (8) BASIC PRINCIPLES OF THE NEW SUPERVISION

1. *PRINCIPLE OF RESPONSIBILITY*

Authority to act and responsibility for acting must be joined.

a. If you give responsibility, give authority.
b. Define employee duties clearly.
c. Protect employees from criticism by others.
d. Recognize the rights as well as obligations of employees.
e. Achieve the aims of a democratic society insofar as it is possible within the area of your work.
f. Establish a situation favorable to training and learning.
g. Accept ultimate responsibility for everything done in your section, unit, office, division, department.
h. Good administration and good supervision are inseparable.

2. *PRINCIPLE OF AUTHORITY*

The success of the supervisor is measured by the extent to which the power of authority is not used.

a. Exercise simplicity and informality in supervision.
b. Use the simplest machinery of supervision.
c. If it is good for the organization as a whole, it is probably justified.
d. Seldom be arbitrary or authoritative.
e. Do not base your work on the power of position or of personality.
f. Permit and encourage the free expression of opinions.

3. *PRINCIPLE OF SELF-GROWTH*

The success of the supervisor is measured by the extent to which, and the speed with which, he is no longer needed.

a. Base criticism on principles, not on specifics.
b. Point out higher activities to employees.
c. Train for self-thinking by employees, to meet new situations.
d. Stimulate initiative, self-reliance and individual responsibility.
e. Concentrate on stimulating the growth of employees rather than on removing defects.

4. *PRINCIPLE OF INDIVIDUAL WORTH*

Respect for the individual is a paramount consideration in supervision.

a. Be human and sympathetic in dealing with employees.
b. Don't nag about things to be done.
c. Recognize the individual differences among employees and seek opportunities to permit best expression of each personality.

5. *PRINCIPLE OF CREATIVE LEADERSHIP*

The best supervision is that which is not apparent to the employee.

a. Stimulate, don't drive employees to creative action.
b. Emphasize doing good things.
c. Encourage employees to do what they do best.
d. Do not be too greatly concerned with details of subject or method.
e. Do not be concerned exclusively with immediate problems and activities.
f. Reveal higher activities and make them both desired and maximally possible.
g. Determine procedures in the light of each situation but see that these are derived from a sound basic philosophy.
h. Aid, inspire and lead so as to liberate the creative spirit latent in all good employees.

6. *PRINCIPLE OF SUCCESS AND FAILURE*

There are no unsuccessful employees, only unsuccessful supervisors who have failed to give proper leadership.

a. Adapt suggestions to the capacities, attitudes, and prejudices of employees.
b. Be gradual, be progressive, be persistent.
c. Help the employee find the general principle; have the employee apply his own problem to the general principle.
d. Give adequate appreciation for good work and honest effort.
e. Anticipate employee difficulties and help to prevent them.
f. Encourage employees to do the desirable things they will do anyway.
g. Judge your supervision by the results it secures.

7. *PRINCIPLE OF SCIENCE*

Successful supervision is scientific, objective, and experimental. It is based on facts, not on prejudices.

a. Be cumulative in results.
b. Never divorce your suggestions from the goals of training.
c. Don't be impatient of results.
d. Keep all matters on a professional, not a personal level.
e. Do not be concerned exclusively with immediate problems and activities.
f. Use objective means of determining achievement and rating where possible.

8. *PRINCIPLE OF COOPERATION*

Supervision is a cooperative enterprise between supervisor and employee.

a. Begin with conditions as they are.
b. Ask opinions of all involved when formulating policies.
c. Organization is as good as its weakest link.
d. Let employees help to determine policies and department programs.
e. Be approachable and accessible - physically and mentally.
f. Develop pleasant social relationships.

IV. WHAT IS ADMINISTRATION?

Administration is concerned with providing the environment, the material facilities, and the operational procedures that will promote the maximum growth and development of supervisors and employees. (Organization is an aspect, and a concomitant, of administration.)

There is no sharp line of demarcation between supervision and administration; these functions are intimately interrelated and, often, overlapping. They are complementary activities.

1. *PRACTICES COMMONLY CLASSED AS "SUPERVISORY"*

a. Conducting employees conferences
b. Visiting sections, units, offices, divisions, departments
c. Arranging for demonstrations
d. Examining plans
e. Suggesting professional reading
f. Interpreting bulletins
g. Recommending in-service training courses
h. Encouraging experimentation
i. Appraising employee morale
j. Providing for intervisitation

2. *PRACTICES COMMONLY CLASSIFIED AS "ADMINISTRATIVE"*

a. Management of the office
b. Arrangement of schedules for extra duties
c. Assignment of rooms or areas
d. Distribution of supplies
e. Keeping records and reports
f. Care of audio-visual materials
g. Keeping inventory records
h. Checking record cards and books
i. Programming special activities
j. Checking on the attendance and punctuality of employees

3. *PRACTICES COMMONLY CLASSIFIED AS BOTH "SUPERVISORY" AND "ADMINISTRATIVE"*
    a. Program construction
    b. Testing or evaluating outcomes
    c. Personnel accounting
    d. Ordering instructional materials

V. RESPONSIBILITIES OF THE SUPERVISOR

A person employed in a supervisory capacity must constantly be able to improve his own efficiency and ability. He represents the employer to the employees and only continuous self-examination can make him a capable supervisor.

Leadership and training are the supervisor's responsibility. An efficient working unit is one in which the employees work with the supervisor. It is his job to bring out the best in his employees. He must always be relaxed, courteous and calm in his association with his employees. Their feelings are important, and a harsh attitude does not develop the most efficient employees.

VI. COMPETENCIES OF THE SUPERVISOR

1. Complete knowledge of the duties and responsibilities of his position.
2. To be able to organize a job, plan ahead and carry through.
3. To have self-confidence and initiative.
4. To be able to handle the unexpected situation and make quick decisions.
5. To be able to properly train subordinates in the positions they are best suited for.
6. To be able to keep good human relations among his subordinates.
7. To be able to keep good human relations between his subordinates and himself and to earn their respect and trust.

VII. THE PROFESSIONAL SUPERVISOR-EMPLOYEE RELATIONSHIP

There are two kinds of efficiency: one kind is only apparent and is produced in organizations through the exercise of mere discipline; this is but a simulation of the second, or true, efficiency which springs from spontaneous cooperation. If you are a manager, no matter how great or small your responsibility, it is your job, in the final analysis, to create and develop this involuntary cooperation among the people whom you supervise. For, no matter how powerful a combination of money, machines, and materials a company may have, this is a dead and sterile thing without a team of willing, thinking and articulate people to guide it.

The following 21 points are presented as indicative of the exemplary basic relationship that should exist between supervisor and employee:

1. Each person wants to be liked and respected by his fellow employee and wants to be treated with consideration and respect by his superior.
2. The most competent employee will make an error. However, in a unit where good relations exist between the supervisor and his employees, tenseness and fear do not exist. Thus, errors are not hidden or covered up and the efficiency of a unit is not impaired.
3. Subordinates resent rules, regulations, or orders that are unreasonable or unexplained.
4. Subordinates are quick to resent unfairness, harshness, injustices and favoritism.
5. An employee will accept responsibility if he knows that he will be complimented for a job well done, and not too harshly chastised for failure; that his supervisor will check the cause of the failure, and, if it was the supervisor's fault, he will assume the blame therefore. If it was the employee's fault, his supervisor will explain the correct method or means of handling the responsibility.

6. An employee wants to receive credit for a suggestion he has made, that is used. If a suggestion cannot be used, the employee is entitled to an explanation. The supervisor should not say "no" and close the subject.
7. Fear and worry slow up a worker's ability. Poor working environment can impair his physical and mental health. A good supervisor avoids forceful methods, threats and arguments to get a job done.
8. A forceful supervisor is able to train his employees individually and as a team, and is able to motivate them in the proper channels.
9. A mature supervisor is able to properly evaluate his subordinates and to keep them happy and satisfied.
10. A sensitive supervisor will never patronize his subordinates.
11. A worthy supervisor will respect his employees' confidences.
12. Definite and clear-cut responsibilities should be assigned to each executive.
13. Responsibility should always be coupled with corresponding authority.
14. No change should be made in the scope or responsibilities of a position without a definite understanding to that effect on the part of all persons concerned.
15. No executive or employee, occupying a single position in the organization, should be subject to definite orders from more than one source.
16. Orders should never be given to subordinates over the head of a responsible executive. Rather than do this, the officer in question should be supplanted.
17. Criticisms of subordinates should, whoever possible, be made privately, and in no case should a subordinate be criticized in the presence of executives or employees of equal or lower rank.
18. No dispute or difference between executives or employees as to authority or responsibilities should be considered too trivial for prompt and careful adjudication.
19. Promotions, wage changes, and disciplinary action should always be approved by the executive immediately superior to the one directly responsible.
20. No executive or employee should ever be required, or expected, to be at the same time an assistant to, and critic of, another.
21. Any executive whose work is subject to regular inspection should, whever practicable, be given the assistance and facilities necessary to enable him to maintain an independent check of the quality of his work.

VIII. MINI-TEXT IN SUPERVISION, ADMINISTRATION, MANAGEMENT, AND ORGANIZATION

A. BRIEF HIGHLIGHTS

Listed concisely and sequentially are major headings and important data in the field for quick recall and review.

1. *LEVELS OF MANAGEMENT*

Any organization of some size has several levels of management. In terms of a ladder the levels are:

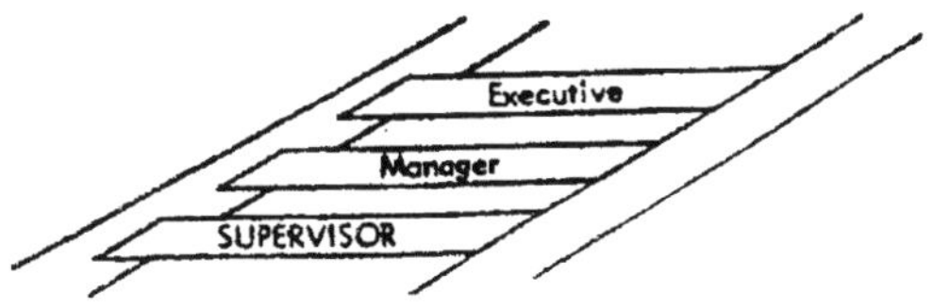

The first level is very important because it is the beginning point of management leadership.

2. *WHAT THE SUPERVISOR MUST LEARN*

A supervisor must learn to:

(1) Deal with people and their differences
(2) Get the job done through people
(3) Recognize the problems when they exist
(4) Overcome obstacles to good performance
(5) Evaluate the performance of people
(6) Check his own performance in terms of accomplishment

3. *A DEFINITION OF SUPERVISOR*

The term supervisor means any individual having authority, in the interests of the employer, to hire, transfer, suspend, lay-off, recall, promote, discharge, assign, reward, or discipline other employees or responsibility to direct them, or to adjust their grievances, or effectively to recommend such action, if, in connection with the foregoing, exercise of such authority is not of a merely routine or clerical nature but requires the use of independent judgment.

4. *ELEMENTS OF THE TEAM CONCEPT*

What is involved in teamwork? The component parts are:

(1) Members	(3) Goals	(5) Cooperation
(2) A leader	(4) Plans	(6) Spirit

5. *PRINCIPLES OF ORGANIZATION*

(1) A team member must know what his job is.
(2) Be sure that the nature and scope of a job are understood.
(3) Authority and responsibility should be carefully spelled out.
(4) A supervisor should be permitted to make the maximum number of decisions affecting his employees.
(5) Employees should report to only one supervisor.
(6) A supervisor should direct only as many employees as he can handle effectively.
(7) An organization plan should be flexible.
(8) Inspection and performance of work should be separate.
(9) Organizational problems should receive immediate attention.
(10) Assign work in line with ability and experience.

6. *THE FOUR IMPORTANT PARTS OF EVERY JOB*

(1) Inherent in every job is the *accountability* for results.
(2) A second set of factors in every job is *responsibilities.*
(3) Along with duties and responsibilities one must have the *authority* to act within certain limits without obtaining permission to proceed.
(4) No job exists in a vacuum. The supervisor is surrounded by key *relationships.*

7. *PRINCIPLES OF DELEGATION*

Where work is delegated for the first time, the supervisor should think in terms of these questions:

(1) Who is best qualified to do this?
(2) Can an employee improve his abilities by doing this?
(3) How long should an employee spend on this?
(4) Are there any special problems for which he will need guidance?
(5) How broad a delegation can I make?

8. PRINCIPLES OF EFFECTIVE COMMUNICATIONS

(1) Determine the media
(2) To whom directed?
(3) Identification and source authority
(4) Is communication understood?

9. *PRINCIPLES OF WORK IMPROVEMENT*

(1) Most people usually do only the work which is assigned to them
(2) Workers are likely to fit assigned work into the time available to perform it
(3) A good workload usually stimulates output
(4) People usually do their best work when they know that results will be reviewed or inspected
(5) Employees usually feel that someone else is responsible for conditions of work, workplace layout, job methods, type of tools/equipment, and other such factors
(6) Employees are usually defensive about their job security
(7) Employees have natural resistance to change
(8) Employees can support or destroy a supervisor
(9) A supervisor usually earns the respect of his people through his personal example of diligence and efficiency

10. *AREAS OF JOB IMPROVEMENT*

The areas of job improvement are quite numerous, but the most common ones which a supervisor can identify and utilize are:

(1) Departmental layout
(2) Flow of work
(3) Workplace layout
(4) Utilization of manpower
(5) Work methods
(6) Materials handling
(7) Utilization
(8) Motion economy

11. *SEVEN KEY POINTS IN MAKING IMPROVEMENTS*

(1) Select the job to be improved
(2) Study how it is being done now
(3) Question the present method
(4) Determine actions to be taken
(5) Chart proposed method
(6) Get approval and apply
(7) Solicit worker participation

12. *CORRECTIVE TECHNIQUES OF JOB IMPROVEMENT*

Specific Problems	General Improvement	Corrective Techniques
(1) Size of workload	(1) Departmental layout	(1) Study with scale model
(2) Inability to meet schedules	(2) Flow of work	(2) Flow chart study
(3) Strain and fatigue	(3) Work plan layout	(3) Motion analysis
(4) Improper use of men and skills	(4) Utilization of manpower	(4) Comparison of units produced to standard allowance
(5) Waste, poor quality, unsafe conditions	(5) Work methods	(5) Methods analysis
(6) Bottleneck conditions that hinder output	(6) Materials handling	(6) Flow chart & equipment study
(7) Poor utilization of equipment and machine	(7) Utilization of equipment	(7) Down time vs. running time
(8) Efficiency and productivity of labor	(8) Motion economy	(8) Motion analysis

13. A *PLANNING CHECKLIST*

(1) Objectives	(6) Resources	(11) Safety
(2) Controls	(7) Manpower	(12) Money
(3) Delegations	(8) Equipment	(13) Work
(4) Communications	(9) Supplies and materials	(14) Timing of improvements
(5) Resources	(10) Utilization of time	

14. *FIVE CHARACTERISTICS OF GOOD DIRECTIONS*

In order to get results, directions must be:

(1) Possible of accomplishment
(2) Agreeable with worker interests
(3) Related to mission
(4) Planned and complete
(5) Unmistakably clear

15. *TYPES OF DIRECTIONS*

(1) Demands or direct orders
(2) Requests
(3) Suggestion or implication
(4) Volunteering

16. *CONTROLS*

A typical listing of the overall areas in which the supervisor should establish controls might be:

(1) Manpower	(3) Quality of work	(5) Time	(7) Money
(2) Materials	(4) Quantity of work	(6) Space	(8) Methods

17. *ORIENTING THE NEW EMPLOYEE*

(1) Prepare for him
(2) Welcome the new employee
(3) Orientation for the job
(4) Follow-up

18. *CHECKLIST FOR ORIENTING NEW EMPLOYEES*

	Yes	No
(1) Do your appreciate the feelings of new employees when they first report for work?	____	____
(2) Are you aware of the fact that the new employee must make a big adjustment to his job?	____	____
(3) Have you given him good reasons for liking the job and the organization?	____	____
(4) Have you prepared for his first day on the job?		
(5) Did you welcome him cordially and make him feel needed?		
(6) Did you establish rapport with him so that he feels free to talk and discuss matters with you?	____	____
(7) Did you explain his job to him and his relationship to you?	____	____
(8) Does he know that his work will be evaluated periodically on a basis that is fair and objective?	____	____
(9) Did you introduce him to his fellow workers in such a way that they are likely to accept him?	____	____
(10) Does he know what employee benefits he will receive?		
(11) Does he understand the importance of being on the job and what to do if he must leave his duty station?	____	____
(12) Has he been impressed with the importance of accident prevention and safe practice?	____	____
(13) Does he generally know his way around the department?	____	____
(14) Is he under the guidance of a sponsor who will teach the right ways of doing things?	____	____
(15) Do you plan to follow-up so that he will continue to adjust successfully to his job?	____	____

19. *PRINCIPLES OF LEARNING*
    (1) Motivation (2) Demonstration or explanation (3) Practice

20. *CAUSES OF POOR PERFORMANCE*
    (1) Improper training for job
    (2) Wrong tools
    (3) Inadequate directions
    (4) Lack of supervisory follow-up
    (5) Poor communications
    (6) Lack of standards of performance
    (7) Wrong work habits
    (8) Low morale
    (9) Other

21. *FOUR MAJOR STEPS IN ON-THE-JOB INSTRUCTION*
    (1) Prepare the worker
    (2) Present the operation
    (3) Tryout performance
    (4) Follow-up

22. *EMPLOYEES WANT FIVE THINGS*
    (1) Security (2) Opportunity (3) Recognition (4) Inclusion (5) Expression

23. *SOME DON'TS IN REGARD TO PRAISE*
    (1) Don't praise a person for something he hasn't done
    (2) Don't praise a person unless you can be sincere
    (3) Don't be sparing in praise just because your superior withholds it from you
    (4) Don't let too much time elapse between good performance and recognition of it

24. *HOW TO GAIN YOUR WORKERS' CONFIDENCE*
    Methods of developing confidence include such things as:
    (1) Knowing the interests, habits, hobbies of employees
    (2) Admitting your own inadequacies
    (3) Sharing and telling of confidence in others
    (4) Supporting people when they are in trouble
    (5) Delegating matters that can be well handled
    (6) Being frank and straightforward about problems and working conditions
    (7) Encouraging others to bring their problems to you
    (8) Taking action on problems which impede worker progress

25. *SOURCES OF EMPLOYEE PROBLEMS*
    On-the-job causes might be such things as:
    (1) A feeling that favoritism is exercised in assignments
    (2) Assignment of overtime
    (3) An undue amount of supervision
    (4) Changing methods or systems
    (5) Stealing of ideas or trade secrets
    (6) Lack of interest in job
    (7) Threat of reduction in force
    (8) Ignorance or lack of communications
    (9) Poor equipment
    (10) Lack of knowing how supervisor feels toward employee
    (11) Shift assignments

    Off-the-job problems might have to do with:
    (1) Health (2) Finances (3) Housing (4) Family

26. *THE SUPERVISOR'S KEY TO DISCIPLINE*

There are several key points about discipline which the supervisor should keep in mind:

(1) Job discipline is one of the disciplines of life and is directed by the supervisor.
(2) It is more important to correct an employee fault than to fix blame for it.
(3) Employee performance is affected by problems both on the job and off.
(4) Sudden or abrupt changes in behavior can be indications of important employee problems.
(5) Problems should be dealt with as soon as possible after they are identified.
(6) The attitude of the supervisor may have more to do with solving problems than the techniques of problem solving.
(7) Correction of employee behavior should be resorted to only after the supervisor is sure that training or counseling will not be helpful.
(8) Be sure to document your disciplinary actions.
(9) Make sure that you are disciplining on the basis of facts rather than personal feelings.
(10) Take each disciplinary step in order, being careful not to make snap judgments, or decisions based on impatience.

27. *FIVE IMPORTANT PROCESSES OF MANAGEMENT*

(1) Planning
(2) Organizing
(3) Scheduling
(4) Controlling
(5) Motivating

28. *WHEN THE SUPERVISOR FAILS TO PLAN*

(1) Supervisor creates impression of not knowing his job
(2) May lead to excessive overtime
(3) Job runs itself -- supervisor lacks control
(4) Deadlines and appointments missed
(5) Parts of the work go undone
(6) Work interrupted by emergencies
(7) Sets a bad example
(8) Uneven workload creates peaks and valleys
(9) Too much time on minor details at expense of more important tasks

29. *FOURTEEN GENERAL PRINCIPLES OF MANAGEMENT*

(1) Division of work
(2) Authority and responsibility
(3) Discipline
(4) Unity of command
(5) Unity of direction
(6) Subordination of individual interest to general interest
(7) Remuneration of personnel
(8) Centralization
(9) Scalar chain
(10) Order
(11) Equity
(12) Stability of tenure of personnel
(13) Initiative
(14) Esprit de corps

30. *CHANGE*

Bringing about change is perhaps attempted more often, and yet less well understood, than anything else the supervisor does. How do people generally react to change? (People tend to resist change that is imposed upon them by other individuals or circumstances.

Change is characteristic of every situation. It is a part of every real endeavor where the efforts of people are concerned.

A. Why do people resist change?

People may resist change because of:

(1) Fear of the unknown
(2) Implied criticism
(3) Unpleasant experiences in the past
(4) Fear of loss of status
(5) Threat to the ego
(6) Fear of loss of economic stability

B. How can we best overcome the resistance to change?

In initiating change, take these steps:

(1) Get ready to sell
(2) Identify sources of help
(3) Anticipate objections
(4) Sell benefits
(5) Listen in depth
(6) Follow up

B. BRIEF TOPICAL SUMMARIES

I. WHO/WHAT IS THE SUPERVISOR?

1. The supervisor is often called the "highest level employee and the lowest level manager."
2. A supervisor is a member of both management and the work group. He acts as a bridge between the two.
3. Most problems in supervision are in the area of human relations, or people problems.
4. Employees expect: Respect, opportunity to learn and to advance, and a sense of belonging, and so forth.
5. Supervisors are responsible for directing people and organizing work. Planning is of paramount importance.
6. A position description is a set of duties and responsibilities inherent to a given position.
7. It is important to keep the position description up-to-date and to provide each employee with his own copy.

II. THE SOCIOLOGY OF WORK

1. People are alike in many ways; however, each individual is unique.
2. The supervisor is challenged in getting to know employee differences. Acquiring skills in evaluating individuals is an asset.
3. Maintaining meaningful working relationships in the organization is of great importance.
4. The supervisor has an obligation to help individuals to develop to their fullest potential.
5. Job rotation on a planned basis helps to build versatility and to maintain interest and enthusiasm in work groups.
6. Cross training (job rotation) provides backup skills.
7. The supervisor can help reduce tension by maintaining a sense of humor, providing guidance to employees, and by making reasonable and timely decisions. Employees respond favorably to working under reasonably predictable circumstances.
8. Change is characteristic of all managerial behavior. The supervisor must adjust to changes in procedures, new methods, technological changes, and to a number of new and sometimes challenging situations.
9. To overcome the natural tendency for people to resist change, the supervisor should become more skillful in initiating change.

III. PRINCIPLES AND PRACTICES OF SUPERVISION

1. Employees should be required to answer to only one superior.
2. A supervisor can effectively direct only a limited number of employees, depending upon the complexity, variety, and proximity of the jobs involved.
3. The organizational chart presents the organization in graphic form. It reflects lines of authority and responsibility as well as interrelationships of units within the organization.
4. Distribution of work can be improved through an analysis using the "Work Distribution Chart."
5. The "Work Distribution Chart" reflects the division of work within a unit in understandable form.
6. When related tasks are given to an employee, he has a better chance of increasing his skills through training.
7. The individual who is given the responsibility for tasks must also be given the appropriate authority to insure adequate results.
8. The supervisor should delegate repetitive, routine work. Preparation of recurring reports, maintaining leave and attendance records are some examples.
9. Good discipline is essential to good task performance. Discipline is reflected in the actions of employees on the job in the absence of supervision.
10. Disciplinary action may have to be taken when the positive aspects of discipline have failed. Reprimand, warning, and suspension are examples of disciplinary action.
11. If a situation calls for a reprimand, be sure it is deserved and remember it is to be done in private.

IV. DYNAMIC LEADERSHIP

1. A style is a personal method or manner of exerting influence.
2. Authoritarian leaders often see themselves as the source of power and authority.
3. The democratic leader often perceives the group as the source of authority and power.
4. Supervisors tend to do better when using the pattern of leadership that is most natural for them.
5. Social scientists suggest that the effective supervisor use the leadership style that best fits the problem or circumstances involved.
6. All four styles -- telling, selling, consulting, joining -- have their place. Using one does not preclude using the other at another time.
7. The theory X point of view assumes that the average person dislikes work, will avoid it whenever possible, and must be coerced to achieve organizational objectives.
8. The theory Y point of view assumes that the average person considers work to be as natural as play, and, when the individual is committed, he requires little supervision or direction to accomplish desired objectives.
9. The leader's basic assumptions concerning human behavior and human nature affect his actions, decisions, and other managerial practices.
10. Dissatisfaction among employees is often present, but difficult to isolate. The supervisor should seek to weaken dissatisfaction by keeping promises, being sincere and considerate, keeping employees informed, and so forth.
11. Constructive suggestions should be encouraged during the natural progress of the work.

V. PROCESSES FOR SOLVING PROBLEMS

1. People find their daily tasks more meaningful and satisfying when they can improve them.
2. The causes of problems, or the key factors, are often hidden in the background. Ability to solve problems often involves the ability to isolate them from their backgrounds. There is some substance to the cliché that some persons "can't see the forest for the trees."
3. New procedures are often developed from old ones. Problems should be broken down into manageable parts. New ideas can be adapted from old ones.

4. People think differently in problem-solving situations. Using a logical, patterned approach is often useful. One approach found to be useful includes these steps:
   (a) Define the problem
   (b) Establish objectives
   (c) Get the facts
   (d) Weigh and decide
   (e) Take action
   (f) Evaluate action

VI. TRAINING FOR RESULTS

1. Participants respond best when they feel training is important to them.
2. The supervisor has responsibility for the training and development of those who report to him.
3. When training is delegated to others, great care must be exercised to insure the trainer has knowledge, aptitude, and interest for his work as a trainer.
4. Training (learning) of some type goes on continually. The most successful supervisor makes certain the learning contributes in a productive manner to operational goals.
5. New employees are particularly susceptible to training. Older employees facing new job situations require specific training, as well as having need for development and growth opportunities.
6. Training needs require continuous monitoring.
7. The training officer of an agency is a professional with a responsibility to assist supervisors in solving training problems.
8. Many of the self-development steps important to the supervisor's own growth are equally important to the development of peers and subordinates. Knowledge of these is important when the supervisor consults with others on development and growth opportunities.

VII. HEALTH, SAFETY, AND ACCIDENT PREVENTION

1. Management-minded supervisors take appropriate measures to assist employees in maintaining health and in assuring safe practices in the work environment.
2. Effective safety training and practices help to avoid injury and accidents.
3. Safety should be a management goal. All infractions of safety which are observed should be corrected without exception.
4. Employees' safety attitude, training and instruction, provision of safe tools and equipment, supervision, and leadership are considered highly important factors which contribute to safety and which can be influenced directly by supervisors.
5. When accidents do occur they should be investigated promptly for very important reasons, including the fact that information which is gained can be used to prevent accidents in the future.

VIII. EQUAL EMPLOYMENT OPPORTUNITY

1. The supervisor should endeavor to treat all employees fairly, without regard to religion, race, sex, or national origin.
2. Groups tend to reflect the attitude of the leader. Prejudice can be detected even in very subtle form. Supervisors must strive to create a feeling of mutual respect and confidence in every employee.
3. Complete utilization of all human resources is a national goal. Equitable consideration should be accorded women in the work force, minority-group members, the physically and mentally handicapped, and the older employee. The important question is: "Who can do the job?"
4. Training opportunities, recognition for performance, overtime assignments, promotional opportunities, and all other personnel actions are to be handled on an equitable basis.

IX. IMPROVING COMMUNICATIONS

1. Communications is achieving understanding between the sender and the receiver of a message. It also means sharing information -- the creation of understanding.
2. Communication is basic to all human activity. Words are means of conveying meanings; however, real meanings are in people.
3. There are very practical differences in the effectiveness of one-way, impersonal, and two-way communications. Words spoken face-to-face are better understood. Telephone conversations are effective, but lack the rapport of person-to-person exchanges. The whole person communicates.
4. Cooperation and communication in an organization go hand in hand. When there is a mutual respect between people, spelling out rules and procedures for communicating is unnecessary.
5. There are several barriers to effective communications. These include failure to listen with respect and understanding, lack of skill in feedback, and misinterpreting the meanings of words used by the speaker. It is also common practice to listen to what we want to hear, and tune out things we do not want to hear.
6. Communication is management's chief problem. The supervisor should accept the challenge to communicate more effectively and to improve interagency and intra-agency communications.
7. The supervisor may often plan for and conduct meetings. The planning phase is critical and may determine the success or the failure of a meeting.
8. Speaking before groups usually requires extra effort. Stage fright may never disappear completely, but it can be controlled.

X. SELF-DEVELOPMENT

1. Every employee is responsible for his own self-development.
2. Toastmaster and toastmistress clubs offer opportunities to improve skills in oral communications.
3. Planning for one's own self-development is of vital importance. Supervisors know their own strengths and limitations better than anyone else.
4. Many opportunities are open to aid the supervisor in his developmental efforts, including job assignments; training opportunities, both governmental and non-governmental -- to include universities and professional conferences and seminars.
5. Programmed instruction offers a means of studying at one's own rate.
6. Where difficulties may arise from a supervisor's being away from his work for training, he may participate in televised home study or correspondence courses to meet his self-develop- ment needs.

XI. TEACHING AND TRAINING

A. The Teaching Process

Teaching is encouraging and guiding the learning activities of students toward established goals. In most cases this process consists in five steps: preparation, presentation, summarization, evaluation, and application.

1. Preparation

Preparation is twofold in nature; that of the supervisor and the employee.

Preparation by the supervisor is absolutely essential to success. He must know what, when, where, how, and whom he will teach. Some of the factors that should be considered are:

(1) The objectives	(5) Employee interest
(2) The materials needed	(6) Training aids
(3) The methods to be used	(7) Evaluation
(4) Employee participation	(8) Summarization

Employee preparation consists in preparing the employee to receive the material. Probably the most important single factor in the preparation of the employee is arousing and maintaining his interest. He must know the objectives of the training, why he is there, how the material can be used, and its importance to him.

2. Presentation

In presentation, have a carefully designed plan and follow it. The plan should be accurate and complete, yet flexible enough to meet situations as they arise. The method of presentation will be determined by the particular situation and objectives.

3. Summary

A summary should be made at the end of every training unit and program. In addition, there may be internal summaries depending on the nature of the material being taught. The important thing is that the trainee must always be able to understand how each part of the new material relates to the whole.

4. Application

The supervisor must arrange work so the employee will be given a chance to apply new knowledge or skills while the material is still clear in his mind and interest is high. The trainee does not really know whether he has learned the material until he has been given a chance to apply it. If the material is not applied, it loses most of its value.

5. Evaluation

The purpose of all training is to promote learning. To determine whether the training has been a success or failure, the supervisor must evaluate this learning.

In the broadest sense evaluation includes all the devices, methods, skills, and techniques used by the supervisor to keep him self and the employees informed as to their progress toward the objectives they are pursuing. The extent to which the employee has mastered the knowledge, skills, and abilities, or changed his attitudes, as determined by the program objectives, is the extent to which instruction has succeeded or failed.

Evaluation should not be confined to the end of the lesson, day, or program but should be used continuously. We shall note later the way this relates to the rest of the teaching process.

B. Teaching Methods

A teaching method is a pattern of identifiable student and instructor activity used in presenting training material.

All supervisors are faced with the problem of deciding which method should be used at a given time.

As with all methods, there are certain advantages and disadvantages to each method.

1. Lecture

The lecture is direct oral presentation of material by the supervisor. The present trend is to place less emphasis on the trainer's activity and more on that of the trainee.

2. Discussion

Teaching by discussion or conference involves using questions and other techniques to arouse interest and focus attention upon certain areas, and by doing so creating a learning situation. This can be one of the most valuable methods because it gives the employees 'an opportunity to express their ideas and pool their knowledge.

3. Demonstration

The demonstration is used to teach how something works or how to do something. It can be used to show a principle or what the results of a series of actions will be. A well-staged demonstration is particularly effective because it shows proper methods of performance in a realistic manner.

4. Performance

Performance is one of the most fundamental of all learning techniques or teaching methods. The trainee may be able to tell how a specific operation should be performed but he cannot be sure he knows how to perform the operation until he has done so.

5. Which Method to Use

Moreover, there are other methods and techniques of teaching. It is difficult to use any method without other methods entering into it. In any learning situation a combination of methods is usually more effective than anyone method alone.

Finally, evaluation must be integrated into the other aspects of the teaching-learning process.

It must be used in the motivation of the trainees; it must be used to assist in developing understanding during the training; and it must be related to employee application of the results of training.

This is distinctly the role of the supervisor.

Made in the USA
Middletown, DE
22 January 2020

83567707R00117